The New Phrenology

The New Phrenology

The Limits of Localizing Cognitive Processes in the Brain

William R. Uttal

A Bradford Book
The MIT Press
Cambridge, Massachusetts
London, England

This book was set in Sabon by Wellington Graphics, Westwood, MA, and was printed and bound in the United States of America.

Library of Congress Cataloging-in-Publication Data

Uttal, William R.
The new phrenology : the limits of localizing cognitive processes in the brain / William R. Uttal.
    p. cm.—(Life and mind : philosophical issues in biology and psychology)
"A Bradford book."
Includes bibliographical references and index.
ISBN 0-262-21017-7 (hc. : alk. paper)
1. Brain—Localization of functions. 2. Cognitive neuroscience. 3. Brain—Imaging. I. Title. II. Life and mind.

QP385 .U86   2001
612.8'2—dc21

                                                        00-052534

For Mitchan

Contents

Preface

It has long been my concern that, in our efforts to exorcise speculative and philosophical considerations from what we all want to be an "objective" empirical science, psychologists may have overlooked an important methodological tool—critical analysis of the fundamental concepts, axioms, assumptions, and premises that underlie our day-to-day empirical research.

Progress in our science, using whatever criterion of progress one chooses, has been based on largely unarticulated premises and goals. Although our goals are instantiated in a series of questions that should guide and direct our experimental programs, to the degree that we have overemphasized experimental methodology and technique, we may have smothered essential consideration of the root motives and assumptions of our science.

It is for this reason that I set out to write a series of monographs that deal with the fundamental issues of psychological science. (Although I am sure all psychologists have their special lists, I have included my own as appendix A.) Two monographs served as precursors of this project. The first (Uttal, 1998) analyzed a question fundamental to psychological research—Can psychologists reduce their observations to neural, cognitive, or computational components? The second monograph (Uttal, 2000a) considered a closely related but distinct question—Are mental processes accessible, that is, can they be measured or inferred from psychological experiments?

The present book takes aim at a third, fundamental question in psychology—Can psychological processes be localized, that is, can they be adequately defined and isolated in a way that permits them to be associated with particular brain regions? I have been interested in the question of localization for many years. In Uttal, 1978, I extensively explored what the empirical findings obtained with techniques such as direct electrical recording and extirpative surgery had to say about the localization of psychological processes in the brain.

In recent years, noninvasive tomographic techniques using radioactivity, X rays, or magnetic fields, and even more exotic methods have allowed us to peer into the human brain while it is actively engaged in mental activities. As computational procedures have improved our ability to extract three-dimensional images of brain anatomy and, some have argued, perhaps even of mental functions, more and more psychologists have applied these powerful procedures to the localization question. It has become increasingly clear that the preliminary skeptical concerns I expressed in 1978 needed to be reconsidered in the light of findings made with these extraordinary technical innovations.

As in the first two books of this series, my approach is intended to be critical, but not, I hope, iconoclastic. I still choose to be a constructive gadfly and have attempted to be evenhanded in addressing the localization problem in this new era. Clearly, the studies based on the tomographic analysis of brain localization represent a work in progress. Just as clearly, we are only on the shore of a vast sea of the unknown as we attempt to deal with arguably the most complex organ that has ever existed. My prediction is that we are not likely in the near term to answer completely any of the questions raised in this series. Indeed, in many cases, it is entirely possible there may be insurmountable practical and "in principle" barriers to achieving complete understanding of the relations between brain, mind, and behavior. Nevertheless, as we strive to understand these relations, we must make every effort to find out what can and cannot be accomplished so that we do not misdirect our attention away from plausible and achievable scientific goals in our pursuit of fantastic and unachievable ones.

The recent development of the computerized tools that permit noninvasive studies of the physiology and anatomy of the central nervous system has stimulated an enormous amount of interest and laboratory research in what has come to be called "cognitive neuroscience." Much of this work on the localization of psychological functions in the brain seems to have plunged off the rock of scientific certainty into a lake of unknowns with an exuberance typical of a science suddenly provided a powerful new tool—or, perhaps, of a child given a new toy. Unfortunately, all too often inadequate attention has been paid to the conceptual, logical, and technical considerations that should accompany any scientific undertaking. It therefore falls to at least a few of us to make an extra effort to examine the situation before another exciting new technology prompts others of us to take yet another such plunge.

Indeed, so abundant, provocative, and perplexing have the findings of the new technologies and procedures been that it is time to step back and ask fundamental questions. What does it all mean? What can be accomplished? What are the capabilities of this particular device or procedure? What are its limitations? What doors has it opened to us in our quest for understanding the relationships among mind, behavior, and the brain? Where has it misled us? Which doors may never be opened? Most important of all, however, is the question I raised earlier—What are the fundamental assumptions underlying the application of these new devices and procedures to the localization hypothesis?

To understand the impact of the new tomographic procedures, we must examine the history of previous procedural developments (e.g., studies of the gross anatomy of the brain and skull, the electroencephalograph, and the stimulus-evoked cortical response) and consider where they led reductively oriented physiological psychologists as they have metamorphosized into cognitive neuroscientists. We must also consider what our definitions of psychological functions and processes themselves signify. It is here that the greatest impediments to understanding the relation between psychological constructs and brain mechanisms actually lie.

We must critically examine the new technologies and procedures themselves. So complex and sophisticated are the tomographic devices used to look at the central nervous system that what first seems obvious may, on closer examination, turn out to be far from obvious. Users unfamiliar with the technical details of these devices are susceptible to subtle, and sometimes not so subtle, misinterpretations of what they see. It is therefore only appropriate that we consider the technical strengths and weaknesses of the devices as we examine the physiology and psychology of the localization enterprise. Researchers well removed from the laboratory and the new equipment may be even more likely to overstate the implications of findings made with such equipment.

We must also examine the logic of the experimental protocols used in localization studies. We must make sure that the findings are true and valid measures of the nervous system's structure and function. It is all too easy to create "hypothetical constructs" and "just so" stories driven more by an intrinsic human urge to "explain" or stimulated by the methodology of an experiment itself than by the true psychobiology of the brain-mind.

These are the goals of this book: to examine the definitional, conceptual, methodological, technical, and logical foundations of the extensive current efforts to localize psychological functions in the central nervous system. So complex are the brain and the concepts, research paradigms, and laboratory equipment of psychology that the opportunities for misunderstanding and misinterpretation are enormous. Only by carefully analyzing all dimensions of this complex science can we arrive at even preliminary answers to the questions posed earlier.

Beyond goals, there is a deeper purpose in my writing this book. Unlike many of the "normal" or "natural" sciences, which seem to grow both vertically and laterally—to pyramid—psychology seems to grow only laterally. Scholars from the time of William James (1892) including Hammond, Hamm, and Grassia (1986), Neisser (1976), Koch (1959), and Tulving (1979) have noted this characteristic of our science.

As James (1892, p. 468) lamented:

A string of raw facts; a little gossip and wrangle about opinions; a little classification and generalization on the mere descriptive level; a strong prejudice that we *have* states of mind, and that our brain conditions them; but not a single law in the sense in which physics shows us laws, not a single proposition from which any consequence can be causally deduced. We don't even know the terms between which the elementary laws would obtain if we had them. This is no science, it is only the hope of a science.

Almost a century later, Tulving (1979, p. 3) would say of the psychology of learning: "After a 100 years of laboratory-based study of memory, we still do not seem to possess any concepts that the majority of workers would consider necessary or important." Lockhead (1992, p. 555), speaking of psychophysical scaling, came to a similar conclusion:

Any underlying, true psychophysical scale can only appear in the data as a will-o'-the-wisp with no basis to decide whether the observed scale is the true scale. Except for its esthetic appeal, which is considerable, there seems to be little reason to expect a fixed relation between behavior and the amount of energy in some attribute of a stimulus, and little reason to expect to be able to demonstrate such a function, should one exist.

The tendency for highly specific microtheories and narrowly constrained findings to proliferate in psychology is as understandable as it is pervasive and bewildering. The subject matter of this science is far more complex and multivariate than perhaps any other. Orderly taxonomies are rare; universal or even broad-ranging theories are nearly nonexistent. Indeed, those who aspire to such universality (e.g., Newell, 1990; Anderson and Lebiere, (1998) are more likely to offer programming or strategic approaches or descriptive simulations than explanatory "theories" of psychological processes.

It is not entirely clear how one can overcome this basic difficulty, given the nature of the subject matter, but it is likely that some steps toward clarifying scientific psychology can be made if we tease out the goals common to all its experimental and theoretical efforts. This means taking a metapsychological stance and seeking fundamentals and commonalities. One way to do this is to ask some basic questions. What are we doing? What do we now know? To make at least a preliminary stab at answering some of these questions is the main purpose of this series of books.

I approach this work with considerable trepidation. The scientific community at large has become so thoroughly enamored of the localization hypothesis that any single critical voice is likely to be drowned in the sea of current enthusiasm. (As I show in appendix B, the zeitgeist is particularly constraining in this research arena.)

One has only to examine the contents of one of the world's leading scientific journals—*Science*—to appreciate the impact and popularity of the current effort to use imaging techniques to locate psychological processes. Most of the articles from 1998 to mid-2000 that deal with mental processing in any way include some fMRI or imaging data. Conventional psychophysical studies based on purely behavioral observations are almost completely absent. Moreover, some of our most prestigious universities have replaced traditional cognitive (previously known as "experimental") psychology programs with cognitive neuroscience programs that completely accept both the assumptions and the findings of the search for the cerebral localization of hypothetical cognitive modules with imaging techniques. Researchers originally trained to exercise the classic psychophysical and cognitive skills are now working with devices they could not even have imagined in their graduate school days. The speed with which the imaging approach has taken over the activity of many cognitive psychologists and the number of researchers (as well as the enormous resources) committed to it suggests that any criticism of this approach is likely to encounter severe countercriticism. Indeed, even when important critical analyses have crept into the literature, they have been largely muted or ignored. Nevertheless, I have come to the point of view expressed here after a considerable amount of study, and my voice is not a solitary one. In particular, I note the important critique of cognitive neuropsychology offered by Farah (1994). Although the alternative she proposed (parallel distributed processing) is as flawed as, and perhaps explains even less than, the localization hypothesis, her criticism of the prevailing "locality" assumption was cogent and effective. Others, such as Sekuler (1994, p. 79), would seem to agree:

After all, psychology now assumes a brain that is barely recognizable as the interactive one that Farah [1994] urges us to embrace. If Farah's admonitions hold for fields outside neuropsychology, and I think they do, much of psychology plainly needs straightening out.

Clearly, we are dealing with a problem of fundamental importance to our science. My hope, therefore, is that this volume, and others like it, will lead us at least to reconsider some of psychology's fundamental issues, if not to resolve them. To proceed without inspecting our most basic assumptions is likely to prove fatal in the long run, particularly if the approach taken turns out to be misguided in some fundamental way. If this critique should eventually be deemed valid, so much the better, although I do not expect to see a counterrevolution in my time. I happily accept the fact that there is no "killer" argument that will (or even *should* until we learn just what positive advantage there is to be gained from the new tomographic approaches) lead to the immediate cessation of studies that seek to correlate brain activity imaging and what are purely psychological responses. What I hope, at a minimum, is that there will be a pause to consider some of the doubts a few of us have about this headlong plunge into a research field that is fraught, to say the least, with some serious conceptual and practical problems.

Finally, nothing in any of my books has been intended to discourage explorations and experimentation in either neuroscience or psychology. Authenticating the achievements of the former and satisfying the need for understanding in the latter should both be high-priority goals. It is only the building of fragile and ill-conceived bridges between the two fields that is problematic. In "simpler" scientific fields, reductionist approaches have worked and will continue to contribute to our understanding of the world around us. In psychology, however, the multidimensional complexity of the brain and behavior poses constraints that may never be overcome.

Acknowledgments

Much of what I have to say has been stimulated by sources other than those I can cite or recall. A student's question, a colleague's comment, a paragraph or phrase read in a context now forgotten, a deep insight expressed by a scholar far more capable than I—all have stimulated my thinking in ways that I can no longer trace. Similarly, an absurdity in another writer's presentation or even a poorly designed and interpreted experiment may have strongly influenced my point of view. To all these now invisible sources, I am grateful.

There are those, however, whom I can acknowledge and thank by name. I especially want to thank my Arizona State University colleague Peter Killeen, who has been a wise guide and sometimes moderating influence on my tendency to be hyperskeptical. Peter has introduced me to ideas I would not otherwise have encountered and has demonstrated a critical judgment I wish I could more fully emulate. Guy Van Orden, another ASU colleague, has also been a staunch supporter, advisor, and leader in the small community of those of us who want at least to raise fundamental issues. ASU's Daryl Kipke and Edward Castaneda also contributed important advice at key points in the development of this book. S. J. Klein, a dedicated student and teacher of the history of psychology, did me the courtesy of reading and commenting on chapter 3 and helped clarify some of the worst of my obfuscations.

I also want to thank Cyril "Danny" Latimer of the Department of Psychology of the University of Sydney (Australia) for making possible my stay there as visiting scholar in 1999, one of the most enjoyable and intellectually productive times in my career, and a time when much work was done on the present book. To Danny and his colleagues, especially

Rosalyn Markham and Olga Katchan, many thanks for making my visit both personally and professionally so worthwhile.

The Massachusetts Institute of Technology Press has been extremely supportive of a book that runs counter to their usual list. I am especially grateful to Katherine Almeida, who took over the production of this book late in its development. An anonymous copy editor did a marvelous job of "getting into my head" and, as a result, sharpening both my language and the conceptual structure of this work.

Finally, everything I have accomplished has depended on the support I received in so many different ways from my bride of all these many years. To Mitchan, as ever, this book is lovingly dedicated.

Thirty years ago, except for certain seemingly outdated schools of neurologists, the modular view of the cognitive system that cognitive neuropsychology offers would have seemed as implausible as that provided by Gall. The answers that have been given for a variety of phenomena discovered and documented over many aspects of perception, language, memory, and cognition might not survive. The range of conceptual problems that these phenomena pose will, however, remain. When they can be adequately answered, psychology will have become a science.

—Tim Shallice, *From Neuropsychology to Mental Structure*

Although Spinoza employed terms like "reason," "emotion," "intellect," will," he—like the modern psychologist—warned against the error of regarding such nouns as references to distinct entities or separate faculties. Instead he regarded them as convenient verbal labels for concepts or universals obtained by abstraction from the realities of individual experience. As abstractions they have no real existence, any more than whiteness apart from white objects or circularity apart from circular objects. To endow them with real existence involves the fallacy of reification, as it has to be called.

—David Ballin Klein, *A History of Scientific Psychology*

1

On Localizing Cognitive Processes: The Problem

The goal of this book is to consider relevant findings and theory and to make a tentative step or two toward answering the great question of localization theory—Can psychological processes be adequately defined and isolated in a way that permits them to be associated with particular brain locales? Embedded within this question are three subquestions:

1. Can the mind be subdivided into components, modules, or parts?
2. Does the brain operate as an equipotential mass or is it also divisible into interacting but separable functional units?
3. Can the components, modules, or parts of the mind, if they exist in some valid psychobiological sense, be assigned to localized portions of the brain?

None of these questions is new. Rather, they have been at the heart of much of scientific psychology's research throughout its history. Indeed, historically, the respective answers to subquestion 1 are the bases of many of psychology's great schisms. For example, "mentalisms" assume cognitive analyzability and "behaviorisms" typically eschew it. Given the fundamental conceptual importance of these issues, it is surprising that questions of this kind have seldom been studied in detail in recent years. In particular, modern cognitive neuropsychology bases a substantial amount of current research on the a priori assumption that affirmative answers to all three of these subquestions are justified.

This is not to assert that the ultimate answer to any of the subquestions is going to be either absolutely negative or totally affirmative. As we shall see, extreme and sometimes radical answers to questions of this magnitude and seriousness have eventually been cast aside in favor of subtle compromises or radical new reinterpretations. Nevertheless, it is worthwhile to examine the conceptual grounds on which major efforts and expenditures are being committed.

The search for understanding the relationship between the material aspects of the brain and mental functioning has always been of central importance to scientists attempting to link various aspects of behavior and cognition to particular parts or functions of the brain. It has also been important to philosophers and others interested in what the findings of psychobiological science imply about human nature.

Localization, however, is only one of what I once identified (Uttal, 1978) as the three central issues challenging psychobiology. The other two are the issue of representation at the neuronal level (how do neural networks represent, encode, or instantiate cognitive processes?) and the issue of learning (how does our brain adapt to experience, what changes occur in its neural networks as a result of experience, and how do these changes correspond to externally observed behavior?)

For several reasons, the localization issue is more amenable to experimental examination and progress than the other two. The causal factors that underlie representation and learning are likely to be found in the intricate interactions of neurons that are both minute in size and enormous in number. Indeed, as I have argued (Uttal, 1998), for fundamental reasons, representation and learning may be irreducible and intractable.

On the other hand, at first glance, localization appears to be much more tractable. It is studied at the macroscopic level and involves far fewer brain "centers" and cognitive modules than does either representation or learning.[1] It has a longer history and is more easily articulated than the other two issues. It may even be argued that progress has been the greatest, and conceptual ambiguities and technical difficulties most completely overcome, in the arena of localization, although this is not to suggest in any sense that a complete solution is either apparent or within easy reach. (Indeed, as we shall see, the study of localization encounters

---

1. We cannot, however, automatically determine the organization of even this modest number of interacting centers. Indeed, Hilgetag, O'Neill, and Young (1996) have shown that the hierarchical structure of the approximately forty visual brain centers cannot be determined from *any* amount of data. I discuss their argument in greater detail in chapter 4.

complexities and constraints in some ways no less formidable than those encountered in the study of representation and learning.) But even though we are arguably closer to some answers in the arena of localization than in that of representation or of learning, many technical and conceptual pitfalls remain that make a renewed survey of our progress toward those answers worthwhile.

Both by tradition and by law, cognitive neuroscientists have not been able to invade the human body to make the direct physiological measurements needed for correlative or linking studies.[2] They have, therefore, always been attracted to any new noninvasive technical development that might allow them to correlate human nervous activity with psychological findings. In particular, psychologists seeking to localize cognitive functions in the brain have been and are quickly drawn to any noninvasive device promising to measure and record any neural or physiological indicator, correlate, sign, or code of those functions. Even distant measures such as electrical conductivity of the skin, respiration rate, or pupil diameter were and are used as physiological correlates of mental activity. The invention of high-gain electrical amplifying devices permitted development of the electroencephalograph (EEG) and of evoked brain potential (EBP) methods for recording tiny signals from the human brain by Berger (1929) and Dawson (1950, 1954), respectively. Rapidly assimilated into the psychologist's technical arsenal, these techniques provided entirely new approaches to the study of the microvolt signals generated by aggregate brain activity in intact subjects.

More recently, cognitive neuroscientists have been drawn to even more powerful technologies such as computerized axial tomography (CAT), positron-emission tomography (PET), and magnetic resonance imaging (MRI) in their attempts to localize cognitive functions in the brain. Whatever the nature of the technology, the opportunity to noninvasively observe the brain's activity has held an abiding and almost universal appeal for cognitive neuroscientists. Whether a particular researcher presumed brain signals to be the equivalent or simply an indicator of a mental function seemed almost not to matter. The enchantment of

2. There are other reasons why psychologists have not been able to "open the black." For one, the complexity of the brain may make such an "opening" more apparent than real.

"looking into" the brain—the incontestable organ of mind—has been irresistible.

Indeed, so seductive and exciting have the new technologies been, and so important the promise of understanding at last how the brain is related to the mind, that the bedrock issues of the accessibility and analyzability of cognitive processes and brain loci have largely been ignored. By addressing those issues, I hope to shed light not only on what we know but also on what we can and cannot know about the relation between the brain and cognitive processes.

1.1   The Nature of the Problem

However scientifically challenging the search for answers to the brain-mind problem (how are brain and cognitive functions related?), it is neither meaningful nor prominent in the thinking of most of the world's inhabitants. The very posing of the problem presumes a monistic ontology and a nonmystical, realistic, materialistic, and naturalistic philosophy antithetical to the personal philosophies of most people. Regardless of how compartmentalized the personal religious beliefs of neuroscientists may be, the mere asking of the question by them presupposes an implicit acceptance of a monistic ontology and a naturalistic philosophical approach. It implies acceptance of the idea that mind is a function, process, or manifestation[3] of the information-processing mechanisms of the brain. If mind and brain represent two separate domains of reality, any attempt to correlate them becomes meaningless. Simply put, every study of the localization issue and every theory about it is premised on the idea that variations in the psychological domain are in some very direct way related to variations in the neurological domain. Make no mistake, such directness is tantamount to identity. To believe otherwise is to deny a tight enough correlation between brain activity and measures of mind to permit drawing any conclusions about the ways in which one influences the other. Thus, whatever political, humanistic, theological, or

3. My redundancy here is intentional. Perhaps, by using three words instead of one, I may convey my meaning better than with any single word, loaded as it might be with its own connotations. In any event, it is very difficult to discuss these ideas without using a mentalist vocabulary. Perhaps redundancy may substitute for definitional precision.

personal motives there may be to say otherwise, psychobiology is not only an important natural science but also the modern expression of an extreme monistic ontology.

The point of the preceding paragraph is to emphasize that the localization of cognitive functions in the brain is not just an esoteric or arcane exercise; it expresses a profound and deeply important point of view. It should be understood, however, that by championing psychobiology or cognitive neuroscience in this manner, I am in no way reneging on my promise to provide a critical analysis of its findings and conclusions, as well as of its strengths and weaknesses. The practical concerns revolving around neuroscientific research make it essential that we understand its limitations and misdirections as well as its progress and successes. Localization studies, for example, have significant bearing on both neurosurgical procedures and popular notions about child development and rearing. Inferences drawn from these studies all too easily go far beyond the legitimate implications of what has been discovered in the laboratory. How many of us have heard about the putative differences between the "left" and "right" brain and the pedagogic techniques that have "followed" from the work on split-brain patients? On the other hand, how few of us are familiar with critiques challenging the entire concept of hemispheric specialization? Efron (1990, p. 25), for example, suggests that the "thriving 'low tech' cottage industry" of psychological research purportedly into the specialized functions of the cerebral hemispheres is based on "performance asymmetries" that are, in fact, incapable of distinguishing between the separate functions of the hemispheres. Thus, left ear–right ear behavioral differences and left hemiretina–right hemiretina phenomenal differences, uncritically interpreted as differences between left and right cerebral hemisphere functions, cannot be scientifically correlated. To assume that they can leads to erroneous scientific theories and practical applications. In the classroom, similar and perhaps even more dangerously silly notions of "training a particular part of the brain" reflect a profound ignorance of the way in which most parts of the brain interact to produce unified mental outcomes.

The treatment of childhood hyperactivity with drugs of unknown mechanism and questionable efficacy (see Valenstein, 1998) also suggests that we should step back and examine contemporary views of brain-mind relationships. Whereas the dangers of incorrectly localizing a cognitive function on the neurosurgeon's operating table are self-evident, the dangers in the classroom are not so obvious.

There is thus an enormous chasm between what can and cannot be done to solve the localization problem, on the one hand, and what has actually been concluded from well-intentioned, but inadequately reasoned research, on the other. Whatever specialization and localization may occur in the brain, and however isolated the dimensions of a sensory code may be in the peripheral transmission pathways, it seems far more likely that the mind, consciousness, or self-awareness represent the merging or binding of many different underlying processes and mechanisms into an integrated singular experience. It should be understood that the unity of subjective experience therefore contradicts the hypothesis of cognitive localization in a fundamental way. Whereas the unity hypothesis emphasizes how the brain puts together mental events, the localization hypothesis emphasizes how it takes them apart. There is thus a tension between our subjective experience—the most direct evidence of our own mental activity—and the analytic assumption on which all of the work in the field of localization is premised. The attempt to marshal arguments for mental modules and cerebral region associations must assume something that does not seem, at least to a first approximation, to be so—that mental activity can be analyzed into separable components. Indeed, we shall be exploring the scientific basis of separable mental components.

1.2 A Brief History of Brain Localization

The earliest associations between various aspects of mental activity (including the elusive "consciousness") and parts of the body were most likely premised on blood rather than brain.[4] To early humans, the most immediate correlate of life was blood, whose loss typically led to the cessation of behavior, consciousness, and ultimately, life itself. Although some scholars have suggested that the less tangible process of movement itself was first thought to be the essential vital ingredient, massive hemor-

---

4. For a much more complete history of the older aspects of localization theory, see Uttal 1978.

rhaging and death were closely associated, whereas the absence of movement during sleep was (almost always) reversed on waking. Certainly, the hydraulic theories of later times associated bodily fluids, including blood, with the "mind."

By about 520 B.C.E., however, a historical record appears, one that not too surprisingly emphasizes encephalization and an almost modern appreciation of the role of the brain in controlling mental activity. The Greek philosopher Alcmaeon of Croton (550?–500? B.C.E.) is said to have been the first to propose, on the basis of his own dissections, that the brain was the organ responsible for sensation and thought. Notwithstanding later associations of thought, emotions, and feelings with the heart, it is clear that at least a few early scholars and protoscientists linked mental processes with brain activity. As our popular Valentine's Day "heart"–based language strongly attests, however, even the most fundamental and uncontroversial aspects of our science may take what seems like an eternity to overcome superstition and ignorance.

The much better known classical Greek philosopher-physician Hippocrates (460–377 B.C.E.) reverted to more primitive hydraulic theories. To "explain" the relation between the body and the mind, he introduced the concept of the "pneuma"—the "essence" of life—a mysterious substance that was supposed to be carried by the blood. On the other hand, the first atomist, Democritus (460–362 B.C.E.), argued that life was based on "soul atoms" and that those responsible for intellect and emotion resided in the head. Though not explicitly a brain theory, this point of view further supported the essential idea of encephalization, a necessary conceptual precursor to cerebralization, and therefore also to the modern localization theories.

Surprisingly, by the time of Aristotle (384–322 B.C.E.), the idea that the brain was the seat of cognition had been temporarily set aside. This great philosopher-naturalist, (whom many credit with some of the earliest "scientific" ideas and place among the greatest polymaths of all time) thought that the brain was actually only an organ to cool the blood and that the nerves were just other tendonlike supporting structures holding the body together.

The basic idea that the brain or head was the seat of our minds nevertheless persisted in Greco-Roman thought, although there was considerable confusion beyond that vague generalization. The anatomy of the brain was not well understood until the beginning of the common era, when different scholars and philosophers attributed the key role of mental representation to different parts of the brain.

The Greek scholar Galen (129–199), one of the most important physicians, biologists, and philosophers of the Roman epoch, placed the locus of mental activity in the cerebral ventricles. By concentrating, however, on the fluids that filled the ventricles rather than on the tissues that surrounded them, he reasserted the fundamentally hydraulic concept that permeated much of the thinking of the time. Describing the nerves as hollow channels through which these fluids passed, Galen speculated that the fluids conveyed information throughout the body. Whereas he attributed thinking to the ebb and flow of the fluids, he associated the solid portions of the brain with sensory and motor functions, even though the gross neuroanatomic research methods available to him could provide only the rawest kind of data to support such a conclusion. Galen's genius can be also credited with the next great conceptual leap in localizing the mechanisms of mind in the head. As far as we know, he was the first natural philosopher to separate the major mental functions into three distinct categories—the sensory-thought-motor trichotomy. This input-association-output trichotomy is still the most generally accepted and fundamental part of our thinking about brain localization as well as the organization of cognitive processes.

Other parts of Galen's theory persisted until the Renaissance. When Andreas Vesalius (1514–1564), the great sixteenth-century anatomist and artist whose diagrams of the human body still attract so much admiration, dissected peripheral nerves, he was unable to find any channels for the Galenic fluids. His dissections therefore directed attention away from the ventricles and fluids to the solid portions of the brain. Not until twentieth-century neurochemists unraveled the importance of the ionic distributions of intracellular and extracellular fluids in neural communication and integration was the importance of fluids with regard to the functioning of the nervous system once again appreciated. Over the years, the emphasis has thus shifted from the macroscopic extracellular "juices" championed by Galen to the microscopic intracellular ones identified by modern biochemists.

Once the solid portions of the brain were accepted as representing the true loci of mental activity, one of the most persistent controversies about the nature of brain tissue arose. The debate over whether brain tissue was homogeneous or heterogeneous—whether it was simply the amount of brain tissue or the particular part of the brain that accounted for the varieties of human experience and behavior—continued until modern times. As evidence of the brain's anatomical specialization accumulated, however, the debate finally came to an end: the heterogeneity of brain tissue is no longer in doubt.

That direct evidence of brain anatomy was central to developing theories of how the brain related to the mind posed a serious problem for scientists and physicians. The human body was considered to be inviolate by many religions. During the Middle Ages, the Roman Catholic Church at times firmly opposed dissection. Nevertheless, with the emergence of the first true universities in Italy around 1200, teacher-physicians such as Taddeo Alderotti (1223–1303) could once again directly study human anatomy and contribute to the accumulating knowledge of the structure of the nervous system. This trend culminated in the wonderful drawings of Leonardo da Vinci (1473–1506) and Vesalius, during whose careers human dissection was tolerated if not officially approved. It is startling to recall that these two extraordinary Renaissance men carried out what were virtually the first direct anatomical studies of the nervous system since Galen's work in the second century. Possible exceptions were the ophthalmological studies of Arabic scientists such as Yuhanna ibn Masawaih (d. 857), Hunain ibn Ishaq (d. 877), Avicenna (980–1037), and perhaps most notably, Alhazen (b. 965). Although it is not certain that they actually performed dissections, their writings and drawings added immeasurably to modern thought about the visual system.

The seventeenth and eighteenth centuries abounded with anatomic discoveries about the nervous system. Thomas Willis (1622–1675), for example, classified the cranial nerves; of greatest relevance to the issue of localization, Antonio Maria Valsalva (1666–1723) discovered that an injury to one side of the head caused paralysis on the contralateral side of the body.

Not until the nineteenth century, however, did the data necessary to substantiate neural specialization begin to coalesce. Bell (1811) and

Magendie (1822) both correctly determined the sensory role of the dorsal spinal roots and the motor role of the ventral ones. War wounds, accidents, and other fortuitous opportunities led a number of anatomists and physiologists to the conclusion that the brain was structurally differentiated, at least to some degree.

By applying electrical currents to the brain and observing which areas produced which motor movements when stimulated, Fritsch and Hitzig (1870) discovered the motor regions of the brain of a dog. This pioneering work was shortly followed by studies on the cortex of human beings. Taking advantage of a particularly gruesome skull infection that exposed the brain of a patient, Bartholow (1874) applied electrical signals from an induction coil to one side of the postcentral brain region. He observed that this stimulation produced uncontrolled, convulsion-like, movements in the leg and arm of the opposite side of the patient's body. Sciamanna (1882), in similar experiments, observed that the general region was divided into subregions. By carefully locating his stimulating electrodes (and by greatly lowering the current from the drastically high levels used by Bartholow), he was able to selectively activate muscles in the mouth and hand, among other places. Ferrier (1875), in similar studies on the monkey brain, had mapped out which regions of the motor area were linked to specific muscular activation in this animal.

A major breakthrough in the understanding of the brain came when the logic of process was reversed. Up to this point, all experiments had dealt with the sensitivity of the brain to electrical stimuli. The discovery that the brain actually produced electrical currents when activated through the natural sensory pathways was an exceedingly important development in progress toward the conclusion that the brain was not a homogeneous mass but composed of specialized regions. It would lead to some of the deepest understanding about the nature of the brain, as well as to therapeutic procedures that could not have been imagined in the first half of the nineteenth century.

The discovery of the electrical activity of the brain is attributed to an English physician, Richard Caton (1842–1926). Caton had been excited by the news from Du Bois-Reymond (1848) that a nerve produced an electrical current—what Du Bois-Reymond called a "negative variation." It was Caton's insightful extrapolation of this idea that led him to determine that the brain also produced an electrical current. In his definitive paper (Caton, 1877), he describes how he explored the regions of the brain and discovered which were the receiving areas for the several sensory modalities. Although not usually given credit for it, he found the visual receiving area in three separate species—rabbits, cats, and monkeys.[5]

At about the same time, Munk (1881) also identified the occipital area of the brain as the primary visual cortex. Other specific brain locales had previously been associated with speech by Broca (1861) and by Wernicke (1874) on the basis of brain injuries and the resulting speech impediments that resulted from these trauma. Thus, by 1900, the idea of functional brain localization—namely, that the brain had specialized functional areas—was fully ingrained in the protopsychobiology of the time. As more and more data accumulated, it became clear that different portions of the brain did have different functions.

Neuroanatomical studies in the twentieth century resulted in a very large number of findings that supported the idea that regions of specialized function were a major characteristic of the brain. Woolsey (1952, 1961) mapped the extent of the somatosensory regions and demarcated what are now thought to be the auditory regions of the brain; Tunturi's pioneering studies (1952) led to a detailed map of the auditory areas; Van Essen (1985) and Van Essen, Anderson, and Felleman (1992) mapped many of the visual regions. Indeed, with regard to sensory and motor functions, it has become indisputable that the brain is not equipotential or homogeneous but is made up a cluster of relatively specialized regions. That it is so with regard to higher-order cognitive functions, however, remains a matter of heated contention, as we shall see.

We need to distinguish between a nonhomogeneous brain in which different regions can influence different mental or behavioral processes, on the one hand, and the hypothesized role of these regions as the unique locations of the mechanisms underlying these processes, on the other. It is the failure to make this distinction that fuels many of the more imaginative theories of cognitive localization in the brain.

---

5. The complete story of Caton's important work is told in eloquent detail by Brazier (1961).

It became clear in the twentieth century that large regions of the brain, called "association" or "intrinsic areas," seemed not to be associated with any particular sensory or motor function. The immediate speculation was that these were the areas where cognitive activities such as thinking, perceiving, decision making, problem solving took place—where the raw sensory information was evaluated, transformed, and linked to the motor regions. It is here that much of the crucial and most controversial work on brain localization is being done. It is also here that proving localization of mental functions becomes most difficult. For one of many reasons, the anchors to the outside world are least defined or measurable in these areas. By contrast, the sensory regions are well anchored to the physical energies used as stimuli; the motor regions are equally well anchored to the physical mechanics of motor responses or even measurable glandular secretions. The mysterious association areas, however, are associated with constructs, metaphors, mental events, and perceptual phenomena that are much less defined or measurable. Nevertheless, much has been suggested about the role of these areas. Indeed, evaluating those suggestions is the central focus of this book.

The idea that the brain consisted of a very large number of modules with distinguishable functions and influences has not always been uncritically accepted. The major opponent to the idea of localized modules in the brain in recent times was Lashley (1942, 1950), whose studies of learning in rats led him to conclude there was no specific brain locus for the neural changes (the "engram") that must have occurred during behavioral changes produced by experience. Rather, Lashley championed a "mass action" or "equipotentiality" theory: it was simply the gross amount of cortical tissue remaining after an ablation that correlated with the presence or absence of the learned behavior. It is now believed that it was the complexity of the process Lashley used to study the learning behavior of his rats and the recruitment by that process of so many areas of the rat's brain that made the brain's activity with regard to such behavior seems equipotential.[6]

6. Lashley's a priori theory that there was no learning area, his complicated experimental design, and the actual complexity of his data all figured into his erroneous conclusions. Similar erroneous conclusions typically arise from setting arbitrary thresholds in neurophysiological recording at both the micro- and macroscopic level. See also chapter 4.

Although many psychobiologists no longer subscribe to Lashley's idea of mass action, the notion of widely distributed representation of complex cognitive processes still has significant support. For example, the definitive and now classic study reported by Olds, Disterhoft, Segal, Kornblith, and Hirsch (1972) argued strongly for the idea that even such an apparently simple learning paradigm as classical conditioning is capable of activating widely distributed regions of the brain.

The controversy between mass action and localized function is not an active arena of debate these days. There is little current opinion or theory arguing that the brain is homogeneous or equipotential or that it operates with any semblance of mass action. Rather, contemporary theory and research is generally characterized by the assumption of discrete and specialized functions in various regions. It is, furthermore, generally agreed that mass action, to the degree that anyone might report finding it, is actually the result of many brain areas and regions being involved in mental and behavioral responses that may be more complicated than originally supposed.

There is thus no question that specialized sensory and motor regions exist and that other regions are involved in, if not dedicated to, particular cognitive processes in some yet-to-be-discovered ways. On the other hand, however, it seems clear that the more complex the psychological process, the less likely it is that a narrowly circumscribed region uniquely associated with that process will be found. Much of the rest of this book is aimed at providing support for this assertion.

Once again, we see that historic controversy between extreme dichotomous positions has given way to an intermediate position under the weight of new evidence. Thus, however precisely regions can be localized for the primary sensory and motor processes, the case is not so clear when dealing with the complex transformations that occur between the sensory inputs and the motor outputs. The integrative and complex mental processes encoded in the association areas are likely to involve increasingly large numbers of identifiable brain nuclei and centers as the task complexity increases, making the brain behave in a way that superficially may be difficult to distinguish from mass action.

That more complex mental processes involve large amounts of brain tissue has been repeatedly demonstrated by many different techniques examining the localization of psychological processes. For example, in functional magnetic resonance imaging (fMRI) studies, when subjects read, the primary visual regions are most active; when they listen to speech, the primary auditory regions are most active; when they speak, the classic Broca and Wernicke areas become active. However, when subjects are required to "just think," many other regions, widely distributed throughout the association areas of the brain, become active. This oft-replicated result is independent of the technique used to measure the brain's activity—it occurs generally regardless of the method. Indeed, the spread of activity into these association areas with increasing cognitive complexity tends often to overlap with regions that were initially thought to be dedicated to purely sensory or motor functions.

To conclude, it is universally agreed that the brain is not homogeneous but made up of regions that are differentiated by function, and by gross anatomy, by cytoarchitectonics (i.e., by microscopic cell types). Controversy over this issue is virtually nil. Why, then, should the localization problem still be fraught with argument and contention? The answer to this question is evident—it is far easier to identify specialized regions in the brain than it is to define the psychological processes we wish to localize—the topic of section 1.3.

1.3   A Brief History of Cognitive Faculties and Processes

As we have seen, that the brain can be divided into regions of specialized anatomy and function is supported by a plethora of findings from research studies using a wide variety of different techniques. Biophysical measurements may be carried out to determine, for example, that electrical stimulation of a certain "motor" region of the brain will produce mechanical actions in particular parts of the body. Similarly, direct electrical recordings from the surface of the brain clearly show that there are different "sensory" areas that respond maximally when one or another of the sense organs is stimulated. Other direct electrical recordings indicate that some regions are activated during (and thus must be involved in) various behaviorally or verbally reported cognitive functions. Chapter 2 discusses a number of classical as well as recently developed techniques that make it possible to assert confidently that the brain is not homogeneous and does not function in a mass-action or equipotential manner. On the contrary, it comprises a large number of more or less isolatable regions that have specialized functions. This much is certain. Much less certain is the degree to which these regions interact or are collectively activated during even the simplest cognitive process.

Nor, as we have noted, is there an easy or direct way to define psychological or cognitive components. It is even more difficult to justify the assumption that complex mental processes are analyzable into cognitive components. Although psychologists and their predecessors have invoked a myriad of thought processes (perceptions, emotions, feelings, attitudes, and memories, among many others), defining such processes logically and empirically is in no way as simple or direct as determining specialized brain regions. The latter are anchored to a system of physical dimensions that makes them tangible and palpable. Not so for thoughts and percepts! Indeed, as I have argued (Uttal, 2000a), the accessibility of cognitive processes to researchers or therapists is probably very much more limited than is usually appreciated. At best, they can be assayed only indirectly with behavioral measures. At worst, behavior is totally neutral with regard to the mechanisms and processes that actually underlie cognitive activity. Linking behavior to real cognitive components or modules is therefore treacherous. Indeed, should the barriers to accessing cognitive processes prove insurmountable, it may be impossible.

The nature of the problem becomes evident whenever attempts are made to define psychological terms. Most definitions turn out to be either circular or operational. Many mental entities turn out on close inspection to be hypothetical constructs (MacCorquodale & Meehl, 1948) whose reality is impossible to validate because of the intrinsic inaccessibility of mental processes. Some distinguished neurophysiologists have also noted the difficulties encountered when we attempt to access mental entities. As Kandel and Kupfermann, (1995, p. 323) have pointed out:

Once psychologists acknowledged that internal representations are important for understanding behavior, they had to come to grips with the stern reality that most of what we now conceive of as mental processes are still largely inaccessible to experimental analysis.

Suffice it to say that, however unresolved the problem of accessibility is at the present time, the issue itself is intimately related to the companion problem of the definability and reality of the mental processes we seek to associate with particular brain regions. In large part, it can be argued that the behaviors we measure in psychological laboratories are only dim shadows of very complex mental and neural processes we barely understand. The further we move from the sensory aspects of cognition (which are well anchored to the dimensions of space, quality, intensity, and time) the more difficult it becomes to find particular brain regions exclusively and uniquely associated with a particular cognitive process. Without such exclusivity and uniqueness, localizing complex cognitive processes in particular areas of the brain becomes a much less tractable task.

Although it may seem at first that this extreme difficulty arises solely from the limitations of recording techniques or from the brain's inherent complexity, I argue that, on the contrary, the preeminent problem in achieving a general solution to the localization issue lies in defining the psychological processes and mechanisms for which loci are being sought. The ease and precision of defining a spatial location of a region in the brain contrasts starkly with the difficulty of defining even the simplest of psychological constructs. Just consider for a moment what "looking at something" may mean. It involves not just the sensory encoding of visual signals but, at the least, memory, perceptions, recognition, and semantic interpretation in diverse and unknown ways. If our psychological science and technology allowed us to parse an act as complex as, say, reading into components, perhaps solving the localization problem could move ahead more rapidly than it currently does. However, defining and parsing even the simplest mental process is fraught with technical and conceptual difficulties of enormous proportions. What are the dimensions of consciousness, of imagination, or of even some of the operationally best defined and superficially simplest constructs that emerge as experimental outcomes? For example, do the processes often proposed (Donders, 1868/1969; Sternberg, 1969) as the underlying components accounting for measured reaction times—stimulus identification, responses selection, and response evocation—have any independent psychobiological reality? Questions like these are not easy to answer despite the prevailing assumption that such components are real entities and not just hypothetical, post hoc constructions. As we shall see repeatedly in chapter 3 and as evidenced throughout the history of psychology, some of the putative mental or cognitive processes suggested as candidates for localization experiments are ephemeral, indeed.

In chapter 3, I shall argue that not only are psychological entities, as named and defined, highly transient; they show no signs of converging into any kind of a stable taxonomy. One longs for the precision afforded by a concrete anatomical entity anchored to the coordinates of space and time. In its place, we are confronted with phenomena such as "metacontrast" and "apparent motion" that are paradoxical in both time and space and thus elude the kind of precise dimensional measurement necessary for reliable and valid scientific analysis and explanation.[7]

There are many ways in which psychologists can be misled to construct a mental entity that has little psychobiological reality. In some cases, such psychological constructs reflect more the design of an experiment than the existence of an actual psychobiological process. For example, consider the classic delayed-response experimental paradigm whose controlling brain location was sought for and originally found in the prefrontal lobes of the brain by Jacobsen (1935). Placing the experimental animal in what must be considered to be an abnormal and unusual environment, this experimental protocol tightly structures the stimuli presented and the responses allowed. Does this resemble a natural process that may have evolved in conjunction with a particular brain location? Could a specific brain locus have evolved in anticipation of this particular experimental paradigm? Of course, this question can also be asked in several different ways: (1) Do the responses observed when an animal is placed in the delayed-response apparatus assay the function of a brain mechanism or of several brain mechanisms that can be localized in particular regions of the brain? (2) Do the constrained and observed responses in this experiment adequately model some natural behavior? My contention is that the brain localization aspects of this experiment

---

7. Although many "explanatory" mathematical theories of both metacontrast and apparent motion exist, all turn out under scrutiny to be simple, nonreductive *descriptions* of these paradoxical phenomena. It is always possible to distinguish between the mathematical assumptions that describe the phenomena and the physiological assumptions on which they are based. It turns out that the latter are inconsequential in defining the former because totally different physiological assumptions can lead to the same mathematical descriptions.

should be interpreted differently from the way they usually are. The prefrontal region should be considered, not as the "locus" of the mechanisms responsible for the delayed-response behavior, but rather as one possible region among many whose manipulation may affect, control, or influence that particular behavior.

Such a restatement represents a totally different conceptualization of the localization problem, one that offers, in place of a specific function being precisely localized (i.e., instantiated, represented, or encoded) in a particular place, the idea of one center contributing to the operation of a complex system of nodes and loci that are *collectively* responsible for the behavior. This system may consist of many parts, some of which inhibit, some of which excite, and some of which control components of the overall process—all having a much closer, if less well understood, relationship to a psychobiological reality other than the operationally defined experimental paradigm we call "delayed responding."

As another example, in any experiment that explores "perceptual learning," one could just as well be studying learning as perception; it is only the particular measurement made that determines whether one should publish one's findings in *Memory and Cognition* or in *Perception and Psychophysics*. However, even when the very same mental processes are being studied—only the researcher's emphasis differs—the probability of assigning different brain regions to the different aspects of the same phenomenon remains frighteningly high.

Furthermore, the values produced by any given measurement are only one manifestation of what is obviously the outcome of a highly complex interaction of several different, but intricately interacting processes. Which is to say that, again, it may be far more difficult than often assumed to isolate putative components of mental activity from each other. The very attempt to do so may beg the question—by assuming as given what remains to be shown.

In attempting to localize any complex cognitive process, there is always a problem distinguishing whether the associated brain region is sufficient or only necessary to elicit a given behavior. For example, clearly both the delayed response and the ability to "perceptually learn" would be abolished by removing an experimental animal's eyes. Obviously, therefore, the eyes are *necessary* for the behavior to occur. Just as obviously, however, few investigators would propose that the eyes are *sufficient* for the behavior to occur—that the neural processes accounting for "perceptual learning" are located in the eyes. Yet many investigators make exactly the same kind of fallacious association when they suggest that the absence of some behavior following surgery of a brain region (which might be necessary but not sufficient) is evidence that that region is the "locus" of that behavior. Particularly in the context of much current theory, because we are dealing with such a complex, interactive, and nonlinear mechanism as the brain, we must, at the very least, consider the logical and conceptual foundations of all localization proposals.

From the earliest work to the present day, however, imprecisely defined psychological entities or components have been associated with highly localized regions of the brain in ways deemed sufficient, but which, from the data, were only necessary at best. The history of such radical mental process–brain localization theories is not encouraging to modern efforts to localize cognitive processes in particular regions of the brain. The nineteenth-century protopsychobiologists Gall and Spurzheim (1808), for example, suggested that extremely specific mental entities (or "faculties," as they were then called) were associated with very narrowly circumscribed regions of the brain. As late as 1934, Kleist published his chart of the brain in which many different psychological properties were localized. This chart differs only slightly in concept from Gall and Spurzheim's localization chart even if the details are more modern. Where we find "hope" in Gall and Spurzheim's map, we find "singing" in Kleist's. Neither the mental faculties nor the brain locations postulated by these charts are any longer accepted.

Even today, once one moves very far from the well-documented sensory and motor regions, it is difficult to find unassailable, rock-solid data associating cognitive functions with regions of the brain that were either permanently or temporarily lesioned. (The full story of many of these historical misassociations is told in chapter 3.)

Although we are long past accepting bizarre brain charts of mental faculties such as those proposed by Gall and Spurzheim and by Kleist, the premise of isolatable psychological processes still is part and parcel of contemporary psychological science. The general idea has been reborn in the form of a modern "faculty"-brain localization hypothesis. How deeply embedded this idea is in modern psychobiology is the topic of section 1.4.

1.4   On the Ubiquity of the Localization Idea in Psychobiology

The idea that psychological functions are localized in particular regions of the brain has a long history and broad-based currency. Some of the brain-mind process associations I now list are considered to be well established by contemporary psychobiologists. Others, driven by the availability of new techniques to peer into the structure and action of even the human brain, are quite novel. (See also page 133 for a more extensive tabulation of similar studies based on the modern imaging techniques.)

What factors are driving the enormous effort to place specific, but often vaguely defined cognitive processes in highly localized regions of the brain? It seems to me that one prominent factor is the ill-evaluated neuroreductionism that dominates so much thinking in psychobiology these days. Although a powerful and useful means of explanation in many sciences, reductionism is ill suited for the complications one encounters when one attempts to build a bridge from the cognitive to the neural.

Another factor driving the current localization effort is the propensity of our language to confuse aspects of an entity with the entity itself. Furthermore, in the theories of at least some psychologists, there are traces of specious reasoning more suggestive of phrenology than psychology. The idea of a specific locations and specific psychological "faculties" has a kind of superficial validity that can be all-too-easily overextended to unreasonable categorizations of cognitive processes.

As a final significant factor, the successful application of localization research to neurology and neurosurgery in isolating local structures and lesions of the brain may have been uncritically carried forward to much of the theoretical enterprise of today's psychology.

Whatever the factors involved, the following selective list of classic and modern localization theories and ideas illustrates the widespread adoption of a localization point of view:

1. Many parts of the brain have been shown to have some visual role, an association that may have been stimulated by recording, ablation, and some of the newer imaging techniques.

a. Dresp and Bonet (1995) and Von der Heydt and Peterhans (1989) have suggested that the V2 is the locus of the illusory contour phenomenon.

b. Savoy and Gabrielli (1991) and Watanabe (1995) have suggested that V1 is the locus of the neural events that produce the famous McCullough (1965) effect.

c. Livingstone and Hubel (1988) have mapped out fine divisions of the primary visual cortex (V1) in which individual neurons in different places encode or represent attributes of a scene such as its color, form, brightness, motion, and depth.

d. Smith, Greenlee, Singh, Kraemer, and Hennig (1998), in addressing motion perception and its localization in he visual regions of the brain, distinguished between "first-order motion," which is defined by spatiotemporal changes in luminance, and "second-order motion," which is defined by more subtle dynamic measures of the stimulus. They found that the conventionally defined cortical areas respond with different degrees of sensitivity to the different types of motion.

e. Mishkin (1966) originally showed that deficits in the inferotemporal cortex inhibited visual object perception, now a well-accepted part of contemporary localization theory. (For a complete review of this topic, see Plaut & Farah, 1990).)

f. Face perception has been linked with the fusiform cortex by Ojemonn, Ojemonn, and Lettich (1992) and with the inferotemporal sulcus by Gross, Roche-Miranda, and Bender (1972), among other areas.

2. The brain structures associated with memory have been extensively studied by a number of psychobiologists.

a. Thompson (1990) has associated several nuclei of the cerebellum (the dendate and the interpositi) with the classical conditioning of the rabbit's eyelid.

b. Scoville and Milner (1957) and Iwai and Mishkin (1990) have suggested that a series of interacting brain regions is responsible for visual memory. Among many other areas that seem to be involved are the primary and secondary visual cortexes, the parietal and inferotemporal cortexes, as well as the amygdala and both sides of the hippocampus.

c. Short-term memory or working memory, on the other hand, has been associated with the prefrontal cortex by Fuster (1989) as well as by Barch, Braver, Nystrom, Forman, Noll, and Cohen (1997).

d. The hippocampus is regularly associated by Squire (1992), among others, with the storage of long-term memories. This region and others nearby seem to control the storage of long-term memory, but are not thought to store the memories themselves. It has been known since Lashley's earliest work (1929) that it took very large lesions in these regions to reduce scores in memory-dependent tasks. This and some more modern concepts (e.g., the holographic hypothesis of Pribram, Nuwer, & Baron, 1974) suggest that long-term memories may not be localized at all, but stored in a distributed fashion throughout the brain.

e. The entire limbic system has been associated with the control and regulation of memory storage by Braak (1992), among others.

3. Although speech has often been associated with both Broca's and Wernicke's areas on the cortex, "language" is a shorthand expression for highly complex processes involving the interaction of many cognitive and motor functions. Because language consists of high-level memory functions, cognitive processing of symbolic, semantic, and syntactic relationships, and the subsequent motor aspects of the articulation itself, many different regions of the brain are likely to be involved. For example, Damasio (1991) has implicated, in addition to Broca's and Wernicke's areas, the prefrontal motor area and certain regions just below it on the surface of the brain with aphasia—speechlessness.

4. The well-known motor regions of the brain originally discovered by Fritsch and Hitzig (1870) have recently been more precisely subdivided. Merians, Clark, Poizner, Macauley, Rothi, and Heilman (1997), for example, place movement programs and representations in the left parietal cortex.

5. Hunger, thirst, and ingestive behavior in general have long been associated with activity in the amygdala and in the ventromedial and lateral regions of the hypothalamus, although there is a good deal of controversy about the role of these hypothalamic nuclei in ingestive behavior.

6. In another classic study of the motivational effects of direct electrical stimulation of the brain, Olds and Milner (1954) associated the septal area of the brain with reward, pleasure, or at least some kind of repetitive behavior, although the findings of others, suggest that reward centers are scattered through widely dispersed portions of the brain.

7. Sexuality, another powerful manifestation of deeply effective motivating forces, seems to be affected by lesions or stimulation in several parts of the brain. Hypersexuality is thought to be induced by a temporal lobe lesion.

8. The reticular activating system has been associated with wakefulness since early studies by Moruzzi and Magoun (1949). Specific kinds of sleep (e.g., rapid eye movement or REM sleep) have also been associated

with specific regions of the brain such as the caudal raphe, a midline structure in the brain stem.

9. A number of regions in the midline of the brain have also been associated with emotions. The well-known and widely accepted concept of the Papez circuit includes such brain structures as the fornix, the cingulate cortex, the corpus callosum, the septum, the hypothalamus, the amygdala, and the mammilary body. Emotional processes were attributed to interactions among this system of nuclei by Papez (1937) and by MacLean (1949). Later research suggested that rage could be elicited by stimulation of the anterior and medial hypothalamus or the amygdala, and attack behavior by stimulation of some of the cerebral nuclei. (For a review of this well-studied topic, see LeDoux, 1996.)

10. Surgical or traumatic transection of the corpus callosum separates the two halves of the brain into two functionally separate units. The strange behavioral results of such a surgical or traumatic intervention have led Sperry (1968) and Gazzaniga, (1983), among others, to suggest that there exist major left-brain and right-brain functional differences, although recent work by Efron (1990) suggests that this distinction is largely mythical.

11. Thinking, consciousness, and other complex psychological processes seem to be based on widespread loci in the brain. Nevertheless, many cognitive neuroscientists ascribe such high-level cognitive functions to specific parts of the "association" or "intrinsic areas"—areas left over after the sensory and motor regions have been identified. The localization of these functions is currently on the frontier of localization research and among the most difficult—and problematic—challenges any science has ever faced.

a. One of the classic stories of cognitive neuroscience is the case of Phineas Gage, whose prefrontal cortical lobes were damaged by a explosion-driven pry bar. After the accident, Gage's personality was reported to have changed completely. He was no longer able to plan ahead or to pay prolonged attention and his behavior was described as much more "impulsive." In general, the front (or prefrontal lobes) of the brain are now associated by many different kinds of experiments with high-level thought processes, in particular such activities as planning and organizing cognitive strategies. More specialized lesions of the frontal region can produce selective deficits in behaviors such as delayed responses or alternation tasks.[8] Over the years many other "high-level" processes have

8. It should also be appreciated that even well-designed and highly controlled laboratory studies do not always lead to practical palliative therapies. The extremely tenuous association of the prefrontal lobe with erratic behavior in a

been associated with the frontal lobes of the brain: problem solving, by Luria (1966); perceptual analysis, by Milner, (1963); executive and attentional processes, by Posner and Raichle (1994, 1997); decision making, by Damasio, Damasio, and Christen (1996); and, indeed, even general intelligence, by Duncan (1995). Grafman (1994) reviews the many different conceptualizations of the frontal regions of the brain; Grafman, Partiot, and Hollnagel (1995) have tabulated a extraordinary list of functions (spanning seven and a half pages of a large-format journal) attributed to the frontal areas by large numbers of investigators. Fuster (1989) reviews this literature; his conclusions are supported in general by Robin and Holyoak (1995), who summarize the cognitive functions associated with frontal lobe under the rubric "the creation and maintenance of explicit relational representations that guide thought and action" (p. 987), further divided into "three primary functions: maintaining representations of elements in working memory to process cross temporal relationships; learning conditional contingencies; and providing resistance to interference" (p. 996).

b.   Attention has been associated with the posterior parietal region by Wurtz, Goldberg, and Robinson (1980), although Posner and Petersen (1990) and Pardo, Pardo, Janer, and Raichle (1990) place "vigilance" (a function difficult to operationally discriminate from "sustained attention") in the right frontal region as well. Laberge (1995) associates the pulvinar nucleus of the thalamus with attention. Rushworth, Nixon, Renowden, Wade, and Passingham (1997) associate the left parietal cortex with what they designate as "motor attention." As attention becomes more and more finely divided, however, more and more regions of the brain are likely to become involved. For example, visual neglect, a subtle behavioral property, is considered by Rafal and Robertson (1995) to be a composite of a number of different psychological deficiencies, each mediated by a somewhat different neural mechanism.

Clearly, the idea that specific and isolatable mental processes or functions are located in particular regions of the brain is now a fundamental assumption of modern cognitive neuroscience, born from psychobiology, itself the offspring of what was originally called "physiological psychology."

---

single experimental animal subject led some psychiatrists to one of the most disgraceful periods in neuroscience—the lobotomy craze of the thirties, forties, and fifties. For a full discussion of this pseudotherapy and the social and medical havoc it caused, see Valenstein, 1980, 1986.

1.5 Conclusion

The idea of localized regions of the brain being associated with particular cognitive functions is ubiquitous in classic physiological psychology and modern cognitive neuroscience. From the earliest records of contemplation and speculation about the relationship between mind or soul, on the one hand, and body or brain, on the other, specific regions or parts of the brain have been associated in some way with what were assumed to be distinguishable mental processes. To make such associations appears to be a normal and natural extrapolation of the realization that, on a more macroscopic level, the different organs of the body perform different functions.

It has also been repeatedly demonstrated, notwithstanding a few idiosyncratic and generally refuted theories, that the brain is not a homogeneous tissue depending solely on its total mass to carry out what are undeniably its cognitive functions. Anatomists and physiologists long ago identified the sensory and motor regions of the brain and appreciated that there were very large areas that were neither primarily sensory nor primarily motor. Because of the well-defined localization of sensory and motor functions, the idea was quickly extrapolated to an equally compartmentalized concept of complex mental processes.

For over a century, it has been assumed that the association or intrinsic areas of the brain are the loci of the mental, cognitive, or transformational processes that mediated between the sensory input and the motor output. These were the regions where decisions were made, where percepts were instantiated, and, in short, where our mental life occurred. It was an easy step from the tripartite (sensory-association-motor) brain observations to efforts to localize actions much more ephemeral, and much less well anchored, than sensory inputs or motor outputs in these association areas. This process, as we have seen, goes on with great enthusiasm today.

It is the thesis of this book that although the brain is certainly differentiated, most high-level cognitive functions cannot be justifiably associated with localized brain regions. This thesis is based, first, on the empirical evidence that high-level cognitive processes are associated with widely distributed activity in many parts of the brain; second, and perhaps even more compellingly, on doubts raised about our definitions of the cognitive processes themselves. Our lexicon of psychological processes fails us for three principal reasons:

1. Most psychological constructs are extremely difficult to define. Indeed, almost all the definitions in our psychological lexicon are circular, invoking one mentalist term to denote the meaning of another.

2. Many psychological constructs do not represent real psychobiological entities, but rather are mainly manifestations of our experimental methods and theories. Although it may be necessary to define mental processes operationally, there is no certainty that such operational definitions correlate exactly with what are, from the point of view of other criteria, real psychobiological processes, mechanisms, and events.

3. Mental action and processes are generally inaccessible and can therefore only be inferred. These inferences may not reflect processes actually going on in the brain, but may instead depend on researchers' ad hoc theories or predilections. Many mental activities, processes, or mechanisms presented as being very specifically defined are, in fact, what MacCorquodale and Meehl (1948) designated as "hypothetical constructs." Because behavior is presumed by at least a few of us to be neutral with regard to the actual underlying neural or cognitive mechanisms, we may be attempting to link these mythical, ad hoc, invented, inferred, or hypothetical constructs with specific brain regions that, at best, influence but do not uniquely instantiate or represent them.

In addition, there are some technical difficulties that call into question the validity of many theories of brain localization offered in recent years. Some of these matters are unique to the new procedures; others, however, have been with us since the first traumatic incidents and surgical or experimental lesion experiments were carried out over a century ago. Whether new or old, these difficulties should raise conceptual flags about the manner in which psychological properties are attached to particular brain regions.

Finally, we must ask a rather disturbing question. Suppose we could overcome all of the technical and conceptual issues involved in the quest for localization. Furthermore, suppose that it turned out that our brains were actually organized such that each psychological process was localized in a particular part of the brain. What exactly would that tell us about how our brain-minds actually accomplish their functions? Would it answer any of the questions posed in appendix A? As pervasive and popular as the localization quest has been and currently is, it seems that the proper level of equivalence between the components of brain and mind are to be found at another, more microscopic level, one so complex and interactive that it carries its own baggage of barriers, problems, and obstacles.

Because of these identified difficulties and other logical, technical, and methodological considerations, it is timely and appropriate to examine the entire localization issue. To do so, it is first necessary to understand the techniques used to determine the activity of specific regions of the brain. That is the goal of chapter 2.

2

The Technologies

Psychologists since the origins of the science in the nineteenth century have longed for methods to directly study the organ of mind—the brain. Some of the earliest researchers took advantage of cranial injuries; later researchers turned to controlled lesion or stimulation experiments, either on laboratory animals or, somewhat less frequently and in a much less controlled manner, on patients during surgical procedures intended to serve some other therapeutic function. For many reasons, research of this kind on both animals and humans seems to have declined in the last decade or two. The heroic earlier work of great neurosurgeons such as Wilder Penfield, Theodore Rasmussen, Lamar Roberts, and Herbert Jasper at the Montreal Neurological Institute (as reported in Penfield, 1958; Penfield & Jasper, 1954; Penfield & Rasmussen, 1950; and Penfield & Roberts, 1959), long the gold standard of knowledge in this domain, has been supplanted by newer ways of carrying out research on the kinds of problems they studied. Although others had used electricity to stimulate neural tissue, after Caton's discovery (1875, 1877) of the electrical activity of the brain the advent of electrical, electromagnetic, and then modern electronic devices in the twentieth century sparked an enormous surge of interest in the neurosciences.

This chapter will review methods, both traditional and recent, used to explore brain anatomy and function, with emphasis on those germane to evaluating the localization hypothesis. Some of the newer methods allow us to study the structure and function of the brain at a level of detail and precision that could hardly have been imagined only a few years ago.

To place the subsequent discussion in the proper spatial context, it is useful to briefly review the gross anatomy of the brain. Research methods used by brain scientists will then be presented in roughly chronological order.

2.1   The Brain and Brain Stem

To understand the localization issue, we must have at least a working knowledge of the anatomical organization of the various parts of the brain. The following paragraphs present what I believe to be the minimum needed to understand the structure of the brain and brain stem, those parts of the central nervous system relevant to the topic of localization. Few serious scholars place cognitive functions in the peripheral nerves or the spinal cord, for example, although some have attributed some perceptual functions to the sensory nerves, usually a matter of confusing the transmission properties of those input channels with localized representation of cognitive functions. (For a more complete discussion of brain anatomy, see Uttal, 1978); Carpenter & Sutin, 1983; Romero-Sierra, 1986; Fitzgerald, 1985; or any number of other modern neuroanatomy texts.)

Figure 2.1 presents a left lateral view of the major parts of the intact human brain, displaying the cerebellum, the lower brain stem, and the left hemisphere of the great cerebral mantle. This pinnacle of neuroanatomical evolution is covered with an intricate system of clefts and convolutions. Although a few major sulci (fissures or infoldings) and gyri (outward protruding portions or outfoldings between the sulci) are almost always found in the same configuration on human brains, the details of the minor sulci and gyri on the surface of the brain are thought to be more or less random in detail (Richman, Stewart, Hutchinson, & Caviness, 1975). When similar views of a variety of human brains are compared, most of the smaller divisions vary considerably from one specimen to another.

The two major landmarks common to all but a few of the most distorted human brains are the lateral sulcus, the dividing fissure between the temporal and frontal regions, and the central or Sylvian sulcus, a groove between the precentral and postcentral gyri—the anterior and posterior portions of the brain, respectively.

The visible portion of cerebral hemisphere is usually divided into several major regions or lobes, chiefly the occipital, parietal, frontal, and

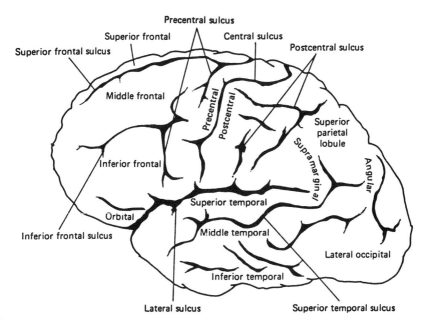

Figure 2.1
Lateral or sagittal view of the human cerebral cortex showing the major fissures and sulci. From Robinson and Uttal, 1983.

temporal lobes (see figure 2.1). Although sometimes demarcated on the basis of the two prominent and invariant sulci just mentioned, the specific boundaries of the cerebral lobes may also be determined on the basis of their physiological functions or of their cytoarchitectonics—the microscopic anatomy and arrangement of their neurons. Indeed, when defined by the anatomy of the neurons present, the boundary between separate regions of the brain becomes very sharp and distinct.

Often, however, there is no obvious dividing line between the regions defined solely by their cellular anatomy. Most cortical regions defined by alternative criteria or by the macroanatomy of the brain can be located only in general terms. Of these alternative criteria, functional (physiological) measures are by far the method of choice for determining the extent and function of particular brain regions.

It is important to keep in mind that there are indisputable regional differences in both the macroanatomy and the microanatomy of the brain, which is not, from the point of view of any technique, homogeneous:

different regions have distinctly different properties. Most notable among these are the primary sensory and motor regions to which the sense organs project. Any criticism of the functional localization of cognitive functions must acknowledge this important structural fact.

Figure 2.2 shows the standard planes of dissection commonly referred to in neuroanatomy. The most widely accepted system of defining locations on the surface of the brain, however, was devised almost a century ago by Brodmann (1909), whose map of the so-called Brodmann regions, was based purely on a cytoarchitectonic examination of the morphology and appearance of the neurons and their patterns of interconnection at various locations on the cerebral mantle (figure 2.3).

The cerebral cortex sits atop the brain stem, an enlarged region of the upper end of the spinal cord. The brain stem consists of the medulla (traditionally known as the "medulla oblongata"), the pons (referred to generically as the "midbrain"), and the diencephalon. Emerging as an

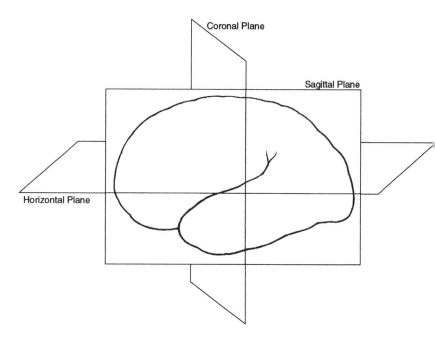

Figure 2.2
Standard planes of inspection available with tomographic methods. Drawing by Mary Zhu.

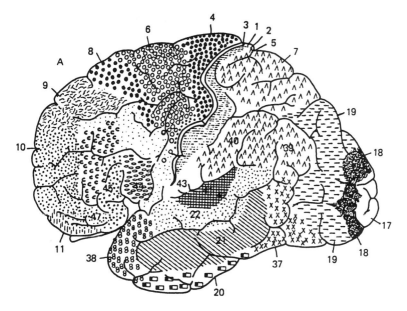

Figure 2.3
Classic and still used Brodmann classification system of brain regions based on the anatomy of the neurons (cytoarchitectonics) in each region. From Brodmann, 1909.

outgrowth from the medulla is the cerebellum, an extraordinarily intricate structure consisting of a huge number of very small neurons (perhaps a thousand times as many as in the rest of the brain). Although classically associated with the fine control and coordination of bodily movements, the cerebellum is considered by some neuroscientists (e.g., Thompson, 1990) also to be the repository for some (in particular, classical conditioning) types of motor memory. Other neuroscientists are now beginning to assign cognitive functions to the cerebellum previously assigned by virtually all physiological psychologists to some part of the cerebral cortex (for a recent review, see Schmahmann, 1997).

Embryologically, the spinal cord, the brain stem, and the cerebral hemispheres are all anterior outgrowths and expansions of the primitive neural tube that develops early in the gestation period. (The more posterior region becomes the spinal cord, the spinal roots, and the autonomic nervous system.) The human cerebral hemispheres, although quite large, are not unique nor do they possess the largest cortical surface areas of any animal. The bottlenose dolphin—a relatively small cetacean—has a brain that is as large as or larger than the human brain and much more heavily convoluted; some full-size whales have even larger brains (both blue and sperm whales are reported to have brains whose volume exceeds 7,800 cc, as compared to 1,500 cc, the "standard" volume of the human brain).

The swelling of this extraordinarily large anterior encephalized portion of the spinal cord—the cerebral cortex—is nevertheless a progressive feature as one ascends the vertebrate phylogenetic tree. Sheer size, it should be also noted, is not perfectly correlated with "intelligence," whatever this complex word may mean. For example, much of the cetacean's huge brain is dedicated to auditory information processing. On the other hand, a much larger portion of the human brain appears to be associated with high-level cognitive information processing. Of course, we humans are also distinguished by our culture, writing, and speech—properties that define our particular kind of intelligence; other animals have other kinds of "intelligence" we do not regard as highly. It is therefore sometimes difficult to make unbiased interspecies comparisons.

Our view of the brain (and our subsequent understanding of its structure) is not limited to just the surface of this remarkable organ. As discussed in chapter 1, classic Greek anatomists and Renaissance polymaths such as Leonard da Vinci were long ago able to dissect and understand the relations among some of the important internal structures of the brain. With the discovery of X rays by Roentgen in 1895, the ability to noninvasively observe the brain made a huge leap to a new level. To be sure, the usual X rays offered only a dim shadowgraph of the brain's structure, but even this clouded view was almost a miraculous development at that time. The development of fluoroscopy and injectable radiopaque dyes as adjuncts to X rays made it possible to observe active blood flow in the living brain—to form an image called a "cerebral angiogram"; in some cases, air could be injected into the cerebral ventricles to make these normally fluid-filled cavities visible—to form an image called a "pneumoencephalogram."

The shadowgraphs produced by X rays, even when they are moving, real-time images, are essentially two-dimensional images. They are produced by a beam of electromagnetic radiation passing through material differentially translucent to radiation of that particular wavelength.

X rays pass easily through tissues opaque to radiations of longer wavelengths, such as visible light. There is no way to uniquely determine from a single X-ray image the three-dimensional shape of the brain structure under study. Traditional X-ray technologies rarely, if ever, used stereographic or multi-image techniques to produce three-dimensional reconstructions of the brain. It was not until the development of modern tomographic techniques (described in detail later in this chapter) that three-dimensional reconstructive imaging burst on the scene, with its many opportunities for delving further into the anatomical structure of normal and pathological brains.

Traditional postmortem techniques also, of course, help build a preliminary understanding of the three-dimensional organization of the brain. Many organizational features not discernable in a conventional X-ray image become clear when an anatomist takes the brain apart. A cross-sectional slice through an excised brain along virtually any axis shows that the brain consists of two different kinds of tissue. The inner "white" matter is made up mainly of long, sheathed axons, which transmit information from one part of the nervous system to another. The "whiteness" comes from the composition of the myelin sheath—the lipid covering that insulates and accelerates the flow of information along axons for what may be yard-long distances in the human body. By contrast, the "gray" matter in the outer rind consists of cell bodies as well as short axons and dendrites that are not covered with myelin. Gray matter is organized into nuclei or centers that are mainly responsible for the intricate interaction of neural information arriving from many different sources. It is the complex neural computation and integration within the centers of the brain that account for the wonders of human behavioral and cognitive adaptability and complexity. In these gray regions, signals from an enormous number of cells interact to control our bodies and our behavior, as well as to produce all of the brain processes that come, in some unknown manner, to be the equivalent of the mysterious entity we refer to as "mental activity." However critical one may be of specific versions of the localization hypothesis for cognitive functions, that all mental activity occurs as a result of brain activity cannot be denied.

There are many nuclei and centers in the brain that can be distinguished by a variety of methods. Among the most useful has been the old-fashioned, but still widely used technique of staining neural tissue with various inorganic and organic dyes that selectively affect different kinds of tissues (or are affected by different kinds of interventions). The largest "nucleus" of all, of course, is the cerebral cortex itself. Figure 2.4, a cross section of the brain, gives an idea of the large number of nuclei and centers that can be visualized with general purpose stains at a more detailed level. Other techniques such as electrical recording and cytoarchitectonic methods have also been used to distinguish different structural and functional regions of the cerebrum and the brain stem.

Notwithstanding the progress made in understanding brain structure in previous centuries, the breakthrough most relevant to the localization of psychological functions is the development of tomographic imaging techniques in the past few years. These remarkable techniques and the machines and mathematics that make them possible are capable of producing extraordinary images and maps of the brain's structure; we can now determine the location and even the time course of processes that occur during brain activity. Some of the new techniques described in this chapter allow neuroscientists to see structures and activity deep within the cerebral cortex or the brain stem in a way that instantiates the wildest hopes and dreams of previous generations of psychologists and neuro-anatomists alike.

As a result of a variety of techniques, some well established and some remarkably novel, many of the brain regions, originally defined in terms of their anatomy, are now considered to have highly specialized cognitive functions. In chapter 1, I surveyed a sample of the associations now claimed between mental and brain processes. A particularly popular idea discussed there is that specific cognitive functions are controlled by or equivalent to activity in narrowly circumscribed regions, possibly by one or a few of the many centers and nuclei that have been identified in the brain by other methods.

The prototypical localization experiment attempts to show concomitant activity in one of these brain regions as a mental or behavioral process takes place. This approach is based on a number of assumptions, some conceptual and some technical, all of which must be critically evaluated if we are to understand both the true accomplishments and the possible failures of the entire localization enterprise. Only by examining the technical methods used to measure and compare brain activity and

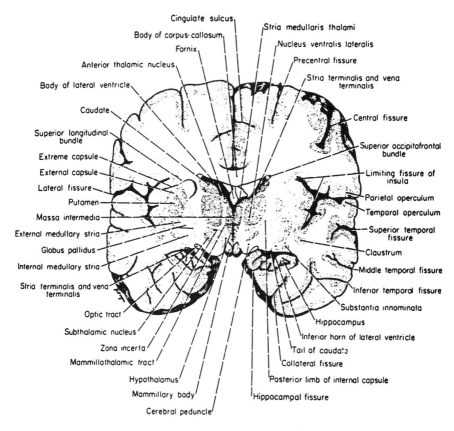

Figure 2.4
Cross section of the human brain, showing the relationship of the cortical mantle and some of the most important subcortical nuclei. From Crosby, Humphrey, and Lauer, 1962.

structure can we shed light on the potential problems encountered when these methods are used to localize cognitive functions.

2.2   Anatomical, Stimulating, Recording, and Imaging Techniques

As noted in chapter 1, the complex, but exceedingly important, scientific problem of localizing psychological functions in the brain has two components. The first component is the definition and construction of sufficiently well defined mental entities for which a locus can be sought.

(Chapter 3 presents the arguments that this is the more difficult part of the localizing enterprise.)

The second component is, at first glance, much more straightforward. It is the measurement of the particular parts of the brain region that have some definable, localizable, physiological, structural, and functional attributes that allow them to be compared with the psychological functions they are supposed to control, represent, produce, or even "be."

The initial problem faced by any researcher with such a goal, of course, is that the brain is enclosed within the skull. The first attempts to invade the skull for therapeutic (rather than religious or sacrificial) reasons occurred surprisingly long ago. There is abundant evidence that therapeutic trephination was used by the Cro-Magnons of the upper Paleolithic period (perhaps as long as 40,000 years ago). Further, many other, more recent preliterate cultures in South America, Africa, and Oceania have independently developed this drastic surgical procedure. (For an account of prehistoric neurosurgical procedures, see Mettler and Mettler, 1947—an elegant, and now classic, history of medicine.)

Notwithstanding ample evidence that some patients recovered from their trephinations, the reasons for not invading the skull to observe the brain are both several and persistent. One major reason is that it is simply too dangerous. Patients with skull injuries, whether accidentally or intentionally imposed, have a very bad habit of dying or being noticeably incapacitated. Among all of the surgical techniques developed until the middle of the twentieth century, manipulating the brain was the one that produced some of the most terrible consequences, even if the patient survived.

Closely related to the general dangers of accessing the brain are more specific ones: it is not always evident what damage is being done during brain surgery until after the procedure is over. The brain itself does not produce pain when injured. Therefore, a surgeon has to be excruciatingly careful not to do damage regions that might produce some subsequent sensory, motor, or cognitive deficit after the patient has been sewn up. Cutting the wrong area could blind, mute, paralyze, or affect the essential cognitive processes of a patient in complex and what remain mysterious ways.

Another major reason not to invasively explore brain structure and function as a scientific enterprise has been the special status given to the human body, particularly by organized religions throughout the last millennium. Chapter 1 discussed how long it took for anatomy in general, and neuroanatomy in particular, to become acceptable medical practice. The Roman Catholic Church, among others, discouraged the dissection of corpses during the Middle Ages and the early Renaissance. Indeed, autopsies are still frowned on by some contemporary religious sects, and many others in our society have secular objections to the procedure. Experimentation on living humans has had even less acceptability, for compellingly powerful ethical and social reasons, particularly in the last half of the twentieth century. The twentieth century witnessed a healthy growth in society's unwillingness to permit human experimentation except under the most stringent of conditions. Full, informed consent on the part of patient or subject, community approval and oversight, and, perhaps most important of all, a totally justified and redeeming reason are all routinely required before even behavioral studies on humans can be carried out in hospitals and universities.

New procedures to study both the structure and the function of the brain, without invading its bony vault, have therefore been continuously sought for both therapeutic and scientific reasons. Today, there are many noninvasive ways to study the brain and its functions, not the least of which is the observation and analysis of motor and verbal behavior—the tools used by psychologists. Although there are many questions about the accessibility of mental processes (Uttal, 2000a), there is no question that we can answer at least some of the knotty problems about human brain function by using appropriately constructed psychophysical and psychometric techniques to observe behavior. Although there are many barriers that prevent us from solving all brain-mind problems, there certainly are some that can be resolved by behavioral methods. For example, the sensitivity thresholds of the visual and auditory receptors are well understood; accurate inferences can be drawn about their functional nature purely on the basis of psychophysical studies. In this chapter, however, we are mainly concerned with techniques that allow us to study the anatomical structure and physiological functions of the associative areas of the brain. It is to a discussion of these techniques that we now turn.

2.2.1 Electrical and Chemical Stimulation

In some cases, researchers can determine the function of a particular region of the brain by directly manipulating it and observing the produced behavioral effects. This was one of the earliest methods used to define what came to be called the "motor regions" of the cerebral cortex. Several different methods can be used to produce brain activity including the deposition of an activating chemical directly on the exposed cortical surface. However, given the electrochemical nature of the nervous system, one of the most straightforward, easily controlled and measured ways to determine which regions mediate which muscular activities is to use electrical stimulation.

By no means a new idea, electrical stimulation of nervous tissue was carried out as early as 1660 by Jan Swammerdam (1637–1680), who unknowingly used electricity, produced by a bimetallic contact, to stimulate the muscles of a frog's heart. Swammerdam hung the heart between a silver wire and a brass contact—an excellent source of the very small electrical voltages necessary to stimulate motor units.

In 1791, Luigi Galvani (1737–1798) carried out a much more complete set of experiments in which he stimulated a frog's leg muscle with what he knew to be electricity. He observed that when electrical signals, generated by lightning rods, by dissimilar metals, or even by another frog were applied to the frogs muscle, it twitched. It is Galvani to whom credit is historically given for identifying the electrical sensitivity of the nervous system.[1]

In the latter half of the nineteenth century, both electric batteries (voltaic piles) and electromagnetic induction coils were being used by physiologists such as Claude Bernard, in 1858, to study neuroelectric phenomena and Fritsch and Hitzig (1870) in their pioneering study of the motor cortex. The real breakthrough came in the twentieth century with the sequential development of vacuum tubes and solid-state elec-

---

1. The previously known sensitivity of the brain to electrical stimulation should not be confused with Caton's subsequent discovery that the brain produced its own recordable electrical signals.

tronics. Devices then became available to produce precisely defined and controlled amounts of electrical stimuli. Researchers could not only determine the shape of the applied stimulus voltage but, even more important, they could maintain constant currents, unaffected by the varying impedance loads created by the neural tissue, over the duration of the stimulus.

Electrical stimulation, among its other advantages, is convenient and easy to use. Although initially used to determine the limits of the motor regions of the brain, with the development of surgical techniques (by neurosurgical pioneers such as Penfield) in which the patient could be kept awake during an operation, electrical stimulation could be used to define the limits of sensory regions by simply asking subjects what they felt, heard, or saw when the current was applied. It could also be used to define the critical and necessary regions for speech by observing the interference effects of locally applied electrical stimulation on articulation.

Beyond the classic input and output regions, however, the use of electrical stimulation to chart the brain becomes more problematical. Studies of regions involved with central or cognitive processing depend on introspective reports by patients or subjects who, in the surgical situation, are not always capable of producing clear-cut answers to what they "think they are thinking." Even under normal conditions, such introspective reports are fallible and problematic.

Electrical stimulation has another major technical problem associated with it. The extent to which current is leaking or short-circuiting to regions other than the one directly stimulated is not always clear. Thus there is always some doubt whether the "localized region" being activated is actually limited to where the electrodes are placed. Indeed, to apply any electrical stimulus requires two electrodes—an anode and a cathode—and the path of the current between them is, for all practical purposes, indeterminate in the wet, heterogeneously packed tissue of the central nervous system. Other procedures have therefore been sought that more definitively delimit the region being stimulated.

One such procedure used over the years is the application of chemicals. Substances such as strychnine can activate well-defined regions of cortical tissue by virtue of the specific sensitivity of neurons to these substances. Activity generated in this way can be traced to other portions of the brain or the effects observed as overt behavior.

Chemicals applied systemically to the nervous system provide another means of exploring some aspects of brain localization. A particular substance—for example, a hypothesized transmitter—may accumulate in a particular part of the brain and leave signs of the location of this region later when the tissue is examined in postmortem studies. Similarly, because many radioactive tracer substances are metabolized only in restricted regions of the brain, they (or their breakdown products) may accumulate in a particular region and leave a trace that can be seen on autoradiograms of the sectioned postmortem tissue. Other substances may fluoresce under the influence of ultraviolet light to signal where in the nervous system they have accumulated and thus where they are utilized during brain activity.

Although chemical tracers of the kind just mentioned may have very specific action on a certain transmitter system or even on behavior, whether they should be used at all is extremely controversial. We still have a very limited understanding of how they alter mental phenomena at the level of neural interactions. (For a critical assessment of the relation between drugs and mental health, see Valenstein, 1998.)

2.2.2 Surgical, Chemical, and Cryogenic Extirpation Techniques

A number of approaches to localizing a region of the brain associated with some psychological process have been taken throughout the history of neuroscience. The approach discussed in the previous subsection, "selective activation," involves stimulating selected intact tissues and observing the effects on behavior. In an effort to limit the region under study more precisely than can be done by applying electrical stimuli or even chemicals to selected intact tissues, neuroscientists have taken an opposite approach, "selective deactivation," using a variety of methods to remove, temporarily or permanently, selected brain regions, and again observing the effects on behavior.

It is important to appreciate from the outset that there are many hidden assumptions on which this approach is based. The main assumption is that the region removed or otherwise deactivated operates in functional independence from other regions that might be involved in the psychological process under study. It should be pointed out that this assumption and others considered in chapter 3 are most likely unjustified. The brain centers and nuclei do not, even to a first approximation, operate in such splendid isolation. Rather there is an enormous amount of interaction, both in an excitatory and inhibitory fashion. Thus it is always uncertain what the observed effect of removing or otherwise deactivating a particular brain region really means. Did it release some other region from inhibition? Was it the actual locus of the phenomenon under study? Did it perform some necessary antecedent process without which the phenomenon could not take place? Was it merely a remote controller or was it the actual site of the mechanisms subserving the observed phenomenon? Many of these questions are not well answered by any of the lesioning techniques because of the high degree of interconnection between so many different regions of the brain.

Indeed, the growing evidence that brain regions are *not* functionally independent may explain why the deactivation approach has fallen out of favor in recent years. It also should raise concern about some of the new technologies that are being currently substituted for the older methods.

The most common selective deactivation techniques in the mid-twentieth century have actually disconnected or removed particular regions from the rest of the brain, whether by surgery, chemicals, or cryogenics. The classic selective deactivation technique has been the surgical lesioning (extirpation, ablation, or removal) of the cortical area of interest. This procedure produces a permanent and, under ideal circumstances, a relatively well defined lesion of the cerebrum or brain stem. The reasons for selecting a particular area for surgical removal to test some specific version of the localization hypothesis vary. Previous evidence from a fortuitous accident may have suggested a relation between the area to be studied and some behavioral or cognitive process. The experimenter may simply have had an inspiration that this might be an interesting place to work. Perhaps this inspiration was stimulated by analogy to some other animal model or by a report of some accidental human neuropsychological phenomenon. Very often there was some preliminary evidence, sometimes obtained with another technique such as a microelectrode or electroencephalographic recording that suggested activity correlated with the psychological phenomenon might be found in a particular place. Finally, some exploratory surgery may have been undertaken simply to see what would happen if this or that area was deactivated.

With the exception of a few therapeutic surgical procedures on humans, carried out for other than research purposes, surgical extirpation has been applied almost exclusively to experimental animals such as rats, cats, and monkeys. Although cats and rats are convenient, cost little, and are easy to maintain, monkeys are preferred because of their closer phylogenetic similarity to humans.

The protocol for a lesion experiment is deceptively straightforward. Following the surgery and a suitable recovery time, the experimental animals are tested on some standardized behavioral test. Their test results are then compared with those of a control group—or, better, with those of animals subjected to a sham operation—to determine the effect of the lesion.[2] Learning and memory, maze running, detour behavior, emotional behavior, decision making, and visual and tactile discriminations have been among the many things tested to determine the effects of removing a given area.

Like electrical stimulation, however, surgical extirpation is subject to technical difficulties. The boundaries defined by a surgical procedure are not always quite as clearly demarcated as the experimenter would like. Even with the best procedures, the surgical lesion does not define sharply demarcated regions with precise anatomical boundaries, much less functional ones. When one is dealing with a system of such overlapping functional regions as the human brain, the sharpness of one's scalpel does not guarantee the precision of the extirpation. Furthermore, concomitant damage to fibers of passage routed beneath the removed cortical areas sometimes produces unrelated effects at distant and unexpected locations.

---

2. In a sham operation, all surgical procedures are carried out except the procedure defining the experiment. For example, if the goal was to test the effect of removing a particular area of the brain, in the sham operation control, the animal would be anesthetized, its skull opened, and the pia and dura matter cut, but the area of concern would not be removed. Because of the unpredictable effects of secondary factors such as anesthesia, sham operations are the best kind of control for experiments of this sort.

Most fundamentally, as noted earlier, the brain system's complexity is always greater than any version of the localization hypothesis suggests. A particular psychological or behavioral function almost certainly involves more than a single area. The area under study may inhibit or even disinhibit some other area (i.e., release it to perform a function it could not carry out prior to the operation). Interaction, rather than isolation, is probably far more typical of brain organization than the simplest version of the localization hypothesis suggests. Yet it is on the assumption that regions are modular and functionally independent that such a version and the interpretation of experiments used to test it are usually based.

Furthermore, the trauma of brain surgery is great. The need to allow an experimental animal sufficient time to recover from its surgery may also inadvertently allow it to recover the lost function by transferring it to some other brain locus—the ubiquitous "recovery of function" artifact that so confused some of the early pioneers in this research field.

For these reasons, and for other more mundane and practical ones (the rise of the animal rights movement, the availability of new noninvasive techniques, and the increasing expense involved in experimental brain surgery—particularly with respect to the animals most useful to the science, monkeys and apes) there is much less this type of research than in the earlier decades of the twentieth century.

Alternative methods have been developed that overcome at least some of the limits of lesion-creating surgery. Chemicals now exist that can functionally deactivate regions of the brain, either temporarily or permanently. Substances such as kainic acid, for example, can irreversibly terminate neural activity in a relatively restricted area by overstimulating the glutamate postsynaptic receptors. The topical application of haloperidol, on the other hand, produces a functional lesion that can actually be reversed after a period of time. It works by temporarily blocking dopamine receptors in the postsynaptic regions. After a time, it can be washed off and the normal function returns. Application of lidocaine locally and temporarily stops the electrical activity of neurons by blocking sodium ion channels.

Similarly, cryogenic blockade of neural function has been used with the expectation that after defrosting, the function of the treated region can return. This would provide an important self-control that would allow the behavior of the experimental animal, before, during, and after the experimental deactivation to be compared. Given the vagaries of individual differences, there could be no better anchor than using a subject as its own control.

2.2.3 Direct Electrical Recording of Cortical Responses

The stimulation techniques work especially well for determining the location of regions that are primarily motor: blocking or eliciting motor behavior can be directly observed. If, however, one is interested in studying the sensory areas or other cognitive processes, the reverse problem is encountered—although it is relatively easy to stimulate the system with natural stimuli, it is relatively difficult to observe the resulting neural response. Stimulation with the normal or adequate stimuli for a given sensory modality (as well as electrical stimulation of afferent nerves) produces subtle and complex patterns of electrical activity in the corresponding receiving or sensory areas of the brain. Determining the brain locations into and onto which these afferent signals project has been one of the most important and active areas of neuroscience research for about a half century.

In the earliest experiments on brain electrical responses carried out by Caton, primitive recording devices (e.g., string galvanometers) were used to measure induced brain activity. These devices were slow and insensitive; they deformed and distorted the time course of the signals elicited in the brain because of their own low impedances and prolonged time constants. The key to answering sensory localization questions lay in the technological development of modern high-impedance, high-gain, high-speed electronic amplifiers. Connected to appropriate contacts or electrodes, such amplifiers could produce a deflection of an oscilloscope trace or a sound on a loudspeaker each time a specific neural center or even a single neuron had been activated by a particular stimulus.

High-input impedance is an essential aspect of amplifiers in devices used to record brain signals. If the input impedance of the recording device is too low, then part of the signal is shunted (i.e., short-circuited) through the recording device, and the true form of the response distorted. If the input impedance is high, however, the electrode and amplifier have essentially no effect on the bioelectrical processes of the neural tissue, and the biologically generated signal itself is much less strongly affected.

Direct electrical recording can take place in two distinctly different ways, each of which is specialized for particular purposes. *Macroelectrodes* (relatively large electrodes) can be used to pick up the accumulated activity of a huge numbers of neurons—recordings that are variously called "compound" or "pooled responses." Macroelectrodes can be constructed from virtually anything that provides good electrical contact. Some of the original macroelectrodes were simply tufts of cotton soaked in saline solution or even the pith from a birch tree; others have been made from metals. (For an elegant discussion of early studies of the electrical activity of the brain, see Brazier, 1961.)

Alternatively, *microelectrodes* (very small electrodes) may be used to record the responses from single neurons. Microelectrode technology has improved enormously over the last few decades. The trick is to make an electrode small enough in diameter to penetrate the cell membrane into a neuron without destroying it. The membrane of a neuron is sufficiently strong and elastic so that it seals itself around a small puncture wound and maintains the integrity of the intracellular fluids even if the electrode is kept in place for a prolonged period of time—sometimes as long as a day.

The response recorded with a microelectrode depends on the type of neuron and the role that neuron plays in the complex network of the nervous system. Some neurons, such as the receptors and the bipolar cells of the retina and other short and compact information-integrating cells of the central nervous system, produce only local responses, which decline with distance and can be accumulated with other similar responses. On the other hand, cells specialized for long-distance communication by virtue of their elongated axons produce a specialized kind of nondecremental response, called the propagating spike action potential. The magnitude of this response depends only on the metabolic state of the neuron and does not decline as the signal is propagated to a distant part of the nervous system.

Microelectrodes with micron-diameter tips have been made both from metal, by electrolytic polishing, and from glass, by drawing a heated glass tube down to an equally fine point and then breaking the drawn region to yield a pair of usable electrodes. The glass tube is filled with a conducting solution to produce a conducting point (the solution), surrounded by an insulating sheath (the glass); the metal point (the conductor) is usually lacquered with some kind of an paint (the insulator) to achieve the same geometry. The effect in either case is the same—to produce a fine electrically conducting core that can be inserted into a single neuron, while at the same time maintaining electrical isolation from the intercellular fluids. Either technique can produce tips smaller than 1 micron.

The problem of the input impedance of the high-gain amplifiers used in neurophysiology is of special importance when one is using microelectrodes. The combination of a high-impedance electrode with a low-impedance amplifier would create a voltage divider that could completely hide the signal being studied. Most of the very low voltages produced by a neuron would be sensed across the high-impedance microelectrode; the amplified signals would be an inconsequential portion of the actual neuronal response.

Virtually all of these technical problems have been solved. The technology of recording electrodes and amplifiers is now well advanced and one can buy items off the shelf for the most demanding studies of the function of single neurons. Compared to other biologically generated voltages, the voltage recorded from within a neuron (more correctly, across the cell membrane of the neuron) is quite high, as high as 140 millivolts (mv) across the membrane of a receptor hair cell in the cochlea of the inner ear, although the usual transmembrane voltage is only 65–70 mv. Signals at such voltages are well above the noise levels of even ordinary-quality amplifiers. As we shall see later in this chapter, other biologically significant signals can be at much lower voltages—only a few microvolts (μv). Signals of very low voltages are obviously present and physiologically effective in the synaptic and cell hillock regions of a neuron. It is here that local potentials can summate and collectively influence neuronal responses even though they are orders of magnitude smaller than the classic spike action potential.

The newest development in the microelectrode field is the invention of multiple electrode systems that allow the activity of many cells to be recorded at the same time. Modern large-scale integration techniques, originally developed to facilitate the construction of computer chips, has been applied to meet this need. Systems with over a hundred electrodes have been reportedly used in acute preparations; even the more serious technical difficulties of chronic preparations can be met with as many as sixty-four electrodes.

Two problems, however, remain with the multielectrode approach. First, an individual high-gain preamplifier is required to record signals from each of the tiny electrodes, which makes for a cumbersome system, although one that can be constructed with conventional equipment. The output signals from the array of preamplifiers are usually multiplexed by some sort of a special-purpose switching computer so that all of the information is eventually channeled along a single line. Some preliminary processing (e.g., tagging when each neural response occurs and the number of the electrode at which the signal was recorded) can be carried out by the multiplexing computer. The pooled and preprocessed information is then sent to a more powerful host computer in which the signal processing and analysis is completed.

A second and even more formidable problem with multielectrode arrays is how to deal with the explosion of data produced by such a system; an experimenter and the host computer can quickly be swamped by the enormous amount of information generated by a cluster of 64 or 100 electrodes, which indeed would overwhelm even large-scale computer facilities. For this reason, few host computers use all of the data that may be generated by a multielectrode array. Although it was originally hoped that such an array would provide a means for analyzing the sequential dependencies and interactions of many neurons, in reality, systems of this sort are mainly applied to the computation and presentation of a topographic map of the spatial distribution of neuronal responses.

It should be further noted that even when the amount of data is not overwhelming, a complex, nonlinear system composed of only a few cells may produce results that cannot be analyzed. When one considers that chaotic and unpredictable neural interactions, for example, may be produced by as few as three neurons (Harmon, 1959), the hope that a multielectrode array will be able to untangle the complex interactions of a physiologically or psychologically significant neural network all but vanishes.

Although, in some situations, measures such as a vector defined by the properties of the original electrodes may be used to characterize the system, no one has been able to model the action of a neural system in all of its complexity for even a few neurons. Thus it may be advantageous to take advantage of the accumulating power of macroelectrodes to directly produce compound or pooled potentials as an alternative to the hurculean, but ultimately ill-advised attempts to record from so many cells simultaneously.

Although macroelectrode recording at or below the surface of the brain has, as we have seen, also been used to localize the brain regions associated with behavioral functions, neuroscientists have sought noninvasive techniques to accomplish the same thing. The first significant such technique is our next topic.

2.2.4   The Electroencephalogram

Thus far, we have discussed recording signals with electrodes at or below the exposed surface of the brain. In the first decades of the twentieth century, however, some extraordinary discoveries were made, originally in Poland and Russia, that allowed researchers to record brain signals through the intact skull. For almost forty years after Caton's experiments, the only recording instrument available had been the primitive string galvanometer—a relatively slow and insensitive measuring device. In 1913, however, working with curarized intact dogs, Pravdich-Neminsky reported recording tiny transcranial voltages, in what came to be called an "electroencephalogram" (EEG). The critical and enormously influential next step was made in 1925 by Hans Berger of the University of Jena, who published the results of a study (Berger, 1929) of signals obtained through the intact skull of a human being. Berger's first observations included the frequently confirmed observation that mental activity such as attention could inhibit these tiny EEG signals. He was also among the first to note that the human EEG signals, like those observed earlier by Pravdich-Neminsky in dogs, were spontaneous—that is, they were generated when no identifiable external stimuli were present.

One of the most important analytic features of the EEG is its frequency spectrum. EEG signals vary with time and appear to be the summation of a number of different voltage oscillations occurring within five classically identified frequency bands: the very slow delta waves (1–4 Hz), theta waves (7–9 Hz), the high-energy alpha waves (10–12 Hz), the even faster beta waves (21–23 Hz), and the very fast but low-energy gamma waves (~ 50 Hz). Combinations of these frequency components have been tentatively associated with normal and pathological conditions over the years.

The impact of the discovery of the EEG on neurology, psychiatry, and psychology was enormous. Here, it was hoped, was the magic technique that would allow behavioral scientists, in particular, to directly examine and measure the activity of the human brain and to correlate brain activity with mental functions. Alas, there are still fundamental barriers to understanding the human electroencephalogram. Indeed, just how limited the EEG is has not always been clear to many practitioners of this technique. Thus, for example, some of the earliest results from Berger's lab were ignored and their implicit warnings unappreciated. Specifically, the most energetic frequency component of the electroencephalogram— alpha waves—seemed to be associated with "idling" activity: alpha waves were "blocked" or deactivated, rather than activated, when subjects became mentally active. The correlation between the major frequency components of the EEG and mental activity was, therefore, essentially negative.

Other more imaginative applications of the EEG produce "conclusions" that usually turn out to be little more than science fiction fantasies. No one has yet been able to connect these supposed indicators of our thought processes directly to the electronic equipment for control purposes other than in the crudest, binary (on-off) manner. The typical way in which this illusion of "direct mental control" was implemented was to use signals such as the EEG (or even motor units in the muscles) that were under indirect control by higher-level neural mechanisms. Subjects could learn to control these signals in ways that are still not well understood but that could provide simple inputs to electronic controls. Such a phenomenon, however, no more demonstrates a direct connection between a subject's "thoughts" and a computer than does using a keyboard or the electromyogram from some other, uninjured part of the body to control a prosthetic arm.

No convincing proof exists, furthermore, that supports the idea that the EEG can be used as a lie detector. Even the associations between EEG frequencies and sleep cycles are more correlative than explanatory. No psychologist has yet been able to demonstrate a solid association between specific thoughts and these erratically changing scalp potentials: because the EEG is a cumulative measure of all neuronal activity in the brain, the details of the interactions within the myriad of neurons in the network are lost.

Indeed, there has even been some criticism suggesting that the EEG may not even measure neuronal activity. For example, Kennedy (1959) suggested that the EEG is actually a product of the physical motion of a charged body—the mass of the brain. He proposed that the EEG is produced by mechanical actions such as the cardiac pulse that shakes the brain in a rhythmic manner. To prove this point, Kennedy demonstrated that a crock of gelatin shaped like the human head produced signals very much like the alpha rhythm of the EEG when electrodes are attached to its side and it is repeatedly tapped at a rate approximating that of the heart beat.

Notwithstanding this possible electromechanical effect, however, the EEG has proven clinical uses. It can definitely localize a tumor or lesion, or demonstrate some other gross abnormality. It can also, in some situations, determine when a person is brain-dead, asleep, in one or another stage of anesthesia, or suffering from an epileptic attack that has no external signs or from any of a number of other brain disorders. What it has not been able to do, however, is to provide tight and reliable correlations of brain functions and localizations with psychological states. Early work sought EEG correlates of variables such as personality, attention, and emotion. Little of this work seems to have had any success. Interpretations of the EEG are still very much an art exercised by an "expert," rather than a precise quantitative exercise. The two main reasons for the continuing failure to find reliable EEG correlates are the diffuse nature of the responses and the lack of any tight linkage to definable stimuli. The next step in the development of techniques to measure brain activity, however, initially promised to overcome at least some of these problems.

2.2.5   The Evoked Brain Potential

Once it was established that electrical signals could be detected through the intact skull, attention could be paid to overcoming some of the technical problems with free-running or spontaneous EEGs. Foremost among these problems, EEG signals could only be loosely linked to psychological and behavioral measures or even to the time scale of external stimuli. For example, although an experimenter could easily direct a subject to "count from 100 to 1 without speaking," the time scale of such a behavioral sequence (and of its measured EEG) was simply too long to determine any fine correspondences between these endogenously generated "stimuli" and electrical brain responses. On the other side of the coin, one advantage that the EEG did exhibit was that the signals were fairly easy to record, typically, at voltages as high as 100 μv.

To link the electrical response of the brain to stimuli on a finer time scale, investigators in the early 1940s tried to stimulate the various sense organs with specific impulsive stimuli to evoke or generate a response that could be recorded using skull electrodes and EEG amplifiers. The result was total failure. These early experiments did not produce a detectable response—one distinguishable from the biological "noise" generated by the brain and the electronic interference produced by the electronic equipment of that era. Two possibilities existed: (1) the response signal was not there; (2) it was there, but so small as to be undetectable by virtue of low signal-to-noise ratios. The latter alternative eventually proved to be true. The problem was to extract these minute response signals—"evoked brain potentials" (EVBPs)—from the noise when they were only about 10 μv or so in amplitude and when the combined noise from the electronic equipment and the ongoing EEG might be ten or a hundred times higher.

After World War II, Dawson (1950, 1954) followed up on work that had been used to enhance the tiny return signals from transmitted radar pulses during the war. He suggested that a simple averaging or superimposition technique could also be used to accomplish this feat for the very small EVBPs. The idea was that the brain responses linked to the stimulus would be nonrandom and would therefore repeat from trial to trial, sequentially reinforcing themselves. On the other hand, the "random" noise from the amplifier and the quasi-random EEG would both sometimes be positive and sometimes negative and thus would tend to cancel themselves out as a function of the square root of the number of accumulated signals. To extract and measure a stable EVBP. the stimulus had to be presented a large number of times—typically, 50 or 100 times.

Dawson's first device (1950) was a bank of electronic storage capacitors, which stored the charges in sequential order by moving a commutator to distribute the charge corresponding to different time epochs of the EVBP onto different capacitors. In this manner, a series of voltage measurements accumulated that approximated the shape of the EVBP. Although Dawson also used photographic superimposition techniques, the real breakthrough came when digital computers were applied to the task to average, rather than simply accumulate, sequential signals. Using a statistical averaging procedure, highly accurate evaluations of the shape of an evoked potential could be made. Figure 2.5 is an example of an EVBP produced by an electrical stimulus to the wrist. Recordable signals can also be obtained from the visual (Beatty & Uttal, 1968), auditory (Teder-Sälejärvi & Hillyard, 1998), as well as from the somatosensory system.

As the accurate averaging procedure became standardized and new types of all-electronic equipment became available, the procedure was offered as a hardwired program on special-purpose digital computers. Ultimately, the arrival of the general-purpose, personal computer destroyed that special-purpose market. Currently, personal home computers using relatively simple analog-to-digital conversion input devices and equally simple programs are the devices of choice for processing EVBPs.

The evoked brain potential became a popular tool for physiological psychology researchers in the latter half of the twentieth century. Various components of the EVBP have been associated with various brain regions, from there, the leap was often made to specific cognitive processes. Positive EVBP signal components, highly localized, recorded mainly over known visual, auditory, or somatosensory areas, and occurring some 30–40 msec after a stimulus, have been interpreted as emanations from the primary sensory cortices. Slower waves, recorded over the entire brain, were later associated with the state of wakefulness (Uttal & Cook, 1964). This EVBP component was thought to be emitted as a diffuse result of activity from the reticular region of the brain stem.

Another EVBP component, recorded at the very top center of the skull at its maximum strength, was designated the "contingent negative variation" (CNV) by its discovers (Grey Walter, Cooper, Aldridge,

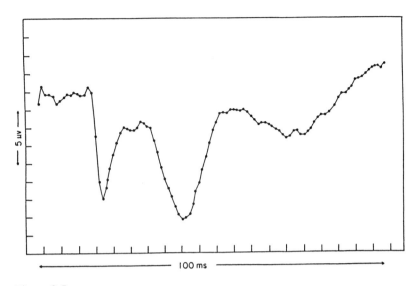

Figure 2.5
Evoked brain potential (EVBP) from the human somatosensory system showing the fast early components and the later slow wave. From Uttal and Cook, 1964.

McCallum, & Winter, 1964). The CNV has been associated with the relationship between two sequential stimuli and can be enhanced by a conditioning procedure that links the two stimuli so that one stimulus is contingent on the other.

The EVBP technique continues to hold an enormous fascination for some psychologists. The magnitude of the effort dedicated to this neuroelectric indicator is nowhere better evidenced than in the massive volume written by Regan (1989), which catalogues medical and scientific applications of the EVBP technique and, perhaps better than any other source, documents the full range of interests affected by it. Nevertheless, the technique has from its inception been beset by difficulties. The possible contamination of the brain signal with electromyographic activity, the essential nonlinearity of some of the mathematical systems (beyond averaging) commonly used to extract the EVBP, the spread of signals from one part of the brain (or part of the skull) to another, the very slight differences all too often presented as conclusive data with inadequate measures of variability, and the conceptual confusion of signs with codes

(Uttal, 1967) all contributed to the lessening of interest in this technique. Moreover, as cited by Regan (1989, pp. 53–56), there have been the following technical and statistical difficulties in interpreting the EVBP:

1. There is a considerable uncertainty about the latency between the stimulus and the triggered EVBP that can distort the signal.

2. Signal and noise in the EVBP may not be statistically independent. That is, the EVBP may be linked in some ways to the EEG cycle.

3. As a result of (1) and (2) and the vagaries of the averaging process, the system may sometimes show no response where a response is actually present.

4. Because the brain system may not be "stationary" over the time it takes to stimulate and record 50 or 100 responses, what is being measured may, in fact, be the average of a number of different stages that may differ significantly.

EVBPs can be used reliably in determining the timing relations between cortical activity and other stimulus or behavioral measures such as eye movements (Wauschkuhn et al., 1998) or in determining the integrity of specific questionable sensory pathways in apparently deaf children (Bruneau, Roux, Guirin, Barthilimy, & Lelord, 1997). To declare EVBP signals the equivalents of human mental processes, however, as opposed to simple indicators of transmission channel integrity, is a stretch of logic to the breaking point.

Be that as it may, the shift in attention away from the EVBP technique had little to do with conceptual or technical difficulties—most practitioners in pursuit of localization results seemed to ignore such difficulties. Rather, it was driven by the next important development in the correlative study of brain and mental activity—the invention of tomographic techniques. These, in turn, emerged from the much older techniques of X-ray radiography.

2.2.6 Classic X-Ray Imaging Procedures

Before considering some of the wonderful new three-dimensional techniques for examining brain structure and function, we need to understand both the power and the limitations of the classic X-ray imaging procedure. The discovery of X rays by Wilhelm Konrad von Roentgen in 1895 had an extraordinary impact on the history of modern medicine.

The importance of the new technique was immediately recognized, and medical X rays were in widespread use within months of Roentgen's original report.

The discovery of X rays is a familiar tale of scientific readiness and good luck. Roentgen was working with the Crookes vacuum discharge tube when he discovered that mysterious emanations from the tube caused some chemicals in his laboratory to luminesce, even though the chemicals and the Crookes tube were separated by a lightproof shield. Roentgen was awarded the first Nobel prize in physics in 1901, only six years after his discovery, clearly indicating the extraordinary importance of his discovery and the immediacy of medical appreciation of what it signified.

It is now known that X rays are produced by high-energy electrons thermally emitted from a negatively charged and heated filiament (the cathode). These negatively charged electrons are attracted to a positively charged metal electrode (the anode), which is also contained within the same evacuated tube as the cathode. The voltage difference between the anode and the cathode accelerates the negatively charged electrons and thus increases their kinetic energy. The magnitude of the voltage difference between the electrodes thus determines the energy with which the electrons bombard the anode. When the negative charge on the accelerated electrons interacts with the charged components of the nuclei of the atoms of the metal in the anode, the electrons change direction. This change of direction itself is the primary source of X rays. According to a basic law of electromagnetism, whenever a charged particle (such as an electron) is accelerated or decelerated (as it has to be in order to change direction), it gives up energy in the form of electromagnetic radiation. Indeed, a change in the amplitude or direction of movement of charged particles is the ultimate source of all electromagnetic radiation, regardless of wavelength. This holds true for radio waves as well as for charged particles circulating in a synchrocyclotron. "Ultrabright" X rays are produced by oscillating the position of electrons that are travelling at velocities near the speed of light (Altarelli, Schlacter, & Cross, 1998). Most conventional medical X rays, however, are considerably less energetic because they are produced in machines that operate at much lower anode-cathode accelerating voltages.

This brings us to the next important point. X rays (wavelength $\sim 10^{-11}$ m) are qualitatively no different from any other kind of electromagnetic radiation, which differs only in its wavelength, and the energy associated with wavelength—from radio waves ($\sim 10^{-1}$ m), to infrared (10^{-5} m), visible ($\sim 10^{-7}$ m), and ultraviolet ($\sim 10^{-8}$ m) light, to cosmic rays ($\sim 10^{-14}$ m).

Nevertheless, because electromagnetic radiations of different wavelengths have different energies, they also have distinguishable properties. For example, they tend to penetrate different materials to varying degrees. Thus, even though the human body is mostly opaque to visible light, X rays are selectively transmitted through tissues in a way that permits us to visualize what would otherwise be invisible. The wavelengths of X rays used in conventional medicine vary from approximately 10^{-10} to 10^{-12} m. Measures of wavelength, however, are not traditionally used in this field. Rather, this kind of radiation is usually characterized by its energy. The relationship between wavelength and energy is defined by the following equation:

$$E = hf \tag{2.1}$$

where E is energy in electron volts (eV), h is Planck's constant (6.62 $\times$ 10^{-27} erg sec), and f is the reciprocal of the wavelength of the radiation times the speed of light ($1/\lambda c$).

The wavelength range of 10^{-10} to 10^{-12} m therefore represents an approximate energy range of from 15,000 to 150,000 eV. For convenience, this measure is most commonly expressed in thousands of electron volts or kilo–electron volts (keV).

An easier way to make the conversion directly from wavelength to kilo–electron volts (keV) is to use the following equation:

$$E = \frac{1.24}{\lambda} \, \text{keV} \tag{2.2}$$

where λ is the wavelength of the X ray in nanometers (nm), one nanometer being equal to 10^{-9} meter. (Incidentally, the highest-energy X rays now being produced are measured in giga–electron volts—or billions of electron volts.)

Because the angles at which the electrons are deflected in an X-ray tube, and thus the magnitude of their acceleration, varies as a function of the spatial relationship between their trajectory and the position of the atomic nuclei of the target metal on the anode with which they interact, a given X-ray tube emits X rays across a wide spectrum of energies. Indeed, a typical medical X-ray spectrum, such as that shown in figure 2.6, is continuous from 15 to 120 keV, with a peak determined by the voltage applied between the electrodes of the X-ray tube. A few subpeaks may occur on the continuous energy spectrum; the actual energy of these subpeaks depends on the particular metal of the anode.

The technology of X-ray equipment design, now almost a century old, is well developed. Many factors contribute to the voltage level to be used and the design characteristics of the entire system. Filters and shields constrain the emissions from the tube to a narrowly collimated beam so that good focus can be achieved. The rate at which a given X-ray tube can be pulsed is extremely important because of heating limitations and the resulting physical deterioration of the anode by the impacting beam of electrons.

One of the most important factors in determining the parameters of the X-ray beam is the particular medical application. Most chest and abdominal X rays require relatively high voltage (60–85 keV), although mammograms are taken with low-voltage X rays (25–30 keV). Conventional X rays of the brain are usually taken with 70 keV systems. (For more technical details about X-ray devices and their use, see Dowsett, Kenny, and Johnston, 1998.)

The traditional means of producing X-ray radiograms is to place the patient between the X-ray emitting tube and some material that is sensitive to the emanations. To minimize X-ray exposure to the subject, special, highly sensitive photographic films have been developed for X-ray recording, and film is still the most common medium for permanent X-ray records. New X-ray detectors that provide direct data input to computers have even higher sensitivity and permit immediate reading of the radiograph. Thus, if it is necessary to take another X ray, it can be done without having to recall the patient at some later time.

Such a record, whether made on film or by a one-shot data-entry device, is only a static, two-dimensional snapshot. The process of dynamic *fluoroscopy* (real-time observation of X-ray images) requires a sensitive screen that can convert continuous X rays into a moving TV-like image.

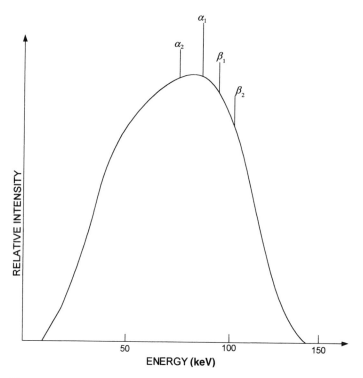

Figure 2.6
X-ray emission spectrum of tungsten. Note both the continuous spectrum and the spectral lines produced at relatively high keV levels. Drawing by Mary Zhu.

Fluoroscopes work by reversing the original process—the X rays that pass through the patient are converted back to electrons, which then activate special fluorescent screens. These screens emit visible light patterns for direct observation in exactly the same way a computer terminal or TV does. Of course, motion picture cameras can also be used to record the images over long periods of time.

Considerable research has gone into the development of improved imaging materials. Engineering laboratories have developed films and other sensitive media that require only short and low-level exposures, xeroradiographic materials that produce high-contrast images, and fluorescent screens that emit higher levels of light (for fluoroscopy). Regardless of their particular makeup, all these materials are designed to record the distribution of the residual X rays that have passed through the object or person interposed between the tube and the sensitive material. Tissues or materials that absorb X rays more strongly allow fewer X rays to pass through to the sensitive film or screen than do tissues or materials that absorb less strongly.

It is clear, therefore, that even at its best an X-ray radiogram of the kind we are describing is a dim shadowgraph of whatever is interposed between the X-ray tube and the sensitive medium. If the beam spot is well collimated (that is, if it consists of a beam of parallel rays) and the spot size is relatively small, a reasonably sharp image of the cumulative vertical absorption of the intervening tissue can be produced. Bones, bodily fluids, and other tissues absorb the X rays to different degrees. For many purposes, such as the location of a tumor, the determination of a break in a bone, or the measurement of the size of a fluid-filled cavity within the brain or in one of its blood vessels, the noninvasive nature of the X-ray procedure explains why its importance was so immediately recognized by Roentgen and those in the medical profession who followed him.

On the other hand, conventional X rays, such as the one shown in figure 2.7, do not allow us to "see" the soft tissues of the brain in the detail possible with the newer tomographic techniques: they are only two-dimensional images of a three-dimensional object; all of the components that lie along the path of a ray of the radiation contribute collectively to the final density on the exposed film plate. Although one can, of course, take another picture and locate something by triangulation or by simple stereoscopic procedures, to produce a true, full, three-dimensional image of a large portion of the body requires a more elaborate procedure. The remainder of this chapter deals with the extraordinary developments in noninvasive, three-dimensional imaging that have offered such promise to psychology, biology, and medicine in the past few years.

2.2.7 Computer-Assisted X-Ray Tomography
Conventional X rays can be used to generate three-dimensional pictures. I have already mentioned that two pictures can be taken from slightly different viewpoints and the disparity (differences) between the pictures used to produce simple stereograms. *Linear tomography,* an early version of the more powerful computer-aided techniques, is a somewhat

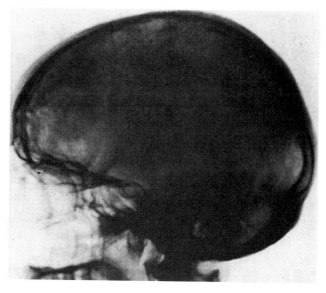

Figure 2.7
Standard X-ray image of the brain. Note that the brain is barely visible with this kind of transmission radiogram. From Robinson and Uttal, 1983, used with the permission of the Division of Neuroradiology, Department of Radiology, University of Michigan.

more intricate procedure in which both the X-ray source and the sensitive film physically move in a coordinated way around a pivot point during the exposure. This technique produces a relatively blurred image of all of tissues except those lying on the same plane as the pivot point.

Far more precise three-dimensional images, however, can be created using *computer-assisted tomography* or *computerized axial tomography*—the classic CAT scan, developed independently by physicist Allan Cormack and electrical engineer Godfrey Hounsfield, both of whom were outside the academic world. Hounsfield worked for an engineering firm and Cormack in a hospital when each individually, driven by the practical needs of their jobs, invented the tomographic reconstruction principle.

Tomography nowadays refers to a wide variety of reconstruction techniques that can be used to produce three-dimensional images or maps of objects that are differentially transparent to several different kinds of electromagnetism or radiation. The prefix *tomo-* refers generally to a volumetric (i.e., three-dimensional) measures. Tomographic images are composed of three-dimensional addressable image locations called "voxels" (volume elements), by analogy to the two-dimensional addressable image locations called "pixels." Three coordinates are required to locate a particular voxel.

All tomographic techniques, regardless of the kind of signals used to image the internal structures or hidden processes of body, work by developing images of single planes within the body. The three-dimensional or volumetric map is obtained by imaging a succession of these planes, which can then be examined or manipulated in various ways (e.g., by rotation, translation, magnification, or by pseudocoloring) to observe other planes of observation not actually measured. For example, a longitudinal slice of measurements through the body may be pooled with other such slices to reconstruct a transverse image plane. Even more striking is the ability of a tomographic system to reconstruct and visualize a three-dimensional map or model of the inside of a body—all the while without violating its physical integrity.

Tomographic techniques have also been used in geophysics to determine the structure of the earth, in nuclear physics to examine the containment pattern of the plasma in a fusion reactor, and even in engineering, to examine the material inside an oil pipeline or sewage pipe. Anthropologists have used these techniques to look at Egyptian mummies or to determine the volume of the brain of an extinct animal from its fossilized remains still encased in stone. Recently, a tomographic reconstruction of the fossilized heart of a dinosaur suggested that the heart was four-chambered and that the dinosaur might therefore be warm-blooded.

Tomography can also scan with acoustical or microwave signals as well as with X rays. The major scanning signals with which we are concerned in this book, however, are those to which the interior of the living human body, especially the brain, are at least partially transparent, and which are therefore selectively absorbed by the body, but not to a degree that would cause significant tissue damage.

The CAT scan (often abbreviated CT scan) differs from other techniques in significant ways. A major step forward from either the standard X ray or the linear tomographic technique, it makes a large number of measurements of low-level X rays emanating from a fan-shaped beam, as the X-ray tube and a partial or complete ring of radiation detectors rotate around the body. Figure 2.8 diagrams this arrangement, in which many measurements are taken through the body at a large number of different orientations.

At each orientation, each of the detectors picks up a signal that is the analogue of a shadowgraph for the single ray from the X-ray tube that intersects that particular detector. In this case, however, many such "scores" or "values" are accumulated—there are several detectors, several rays, and, most important, several positions of the apparatus at the different orientations of the tube as it rotates around the body of the patient. The collection of detector scores at one orientation is referred to as a "view." The number of views is determined by the number of rotational steps as the tomographic system rotates. The path taken through the body from the X-ray source to one detector is referred as a "ray." The number of rays is determined by the number of detectors activated at each viewing position.

Data collected in this manner provide the necessary clues to image a single transverse slice of the body. The third dimension (the longitudinal axis) is acquired by shifting either the equipment or the patient a small distance along the longitudinal axis after each rotation has been completed. The resulting set of slice images thus produced collectively constitutes the full three-dimensional reconstruction of the examined part of the subject's body. After all of the slice images have been reconstructed, using straightforward image-processing algorithms, a computer can generate slice images along other axes and planes from the collected voxel information; it can do so for rotations along any axis, not just along the three cardinal axes defined by the orientation of the body.

The thickness and number of the transverse slice images gathered along the body depend, respectively, on the thickness of the fan-shaped beam and on how far the equipment is shifted along the longitudinal axis of the body between each set of rotations. More important, this technique lets us reconstruct a full, three-dimensional map of the body or object being examined by taking an appropriately large number of measurements.

To understand how this three-dimensional image is reconstructed, we have to understand how a single transverse slice image is produced. The

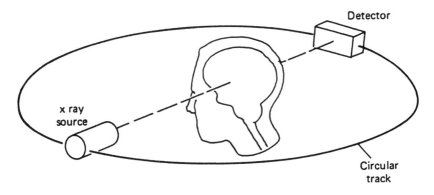

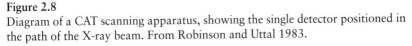

Figure 2.8
Diagram of a CAT scanning apparatus, showing the single detector positioned in the path of the X-ray beam. From Robinson and Uttal 1983.

amount of data to define one transverse slice image gathered in one rotation around the body can be very large.

The trick is to go from this very large database to an viewable two-dimensional image for each transverse slice by means of a process called "reconstruction." Consider what happens when X rays pass through an enclosed high- and low-density object, respectively. X rays passing through the high-density object are much reduced in amplitude, producing lower-values measurements in the detectors, whereas X rays passing through the low-density object are less reduced in amplitude, producing higher-value measurements. This phenomenon allows the CAT scan device to reconstruct an image. As just noted, the goal is to go from this mélange of overlapping readings to a spatially accurate map of the transverse slice. This process produces a picture exemplified in a much-reduced form in figure 2.9. The first step in tomographic reconstruction is to organize the data into a two-dimensional matrix, with the detector values for each ray forming one axis and the number of each view forming the other. This matrix is represented in a digital computer as a very large database of pixels, although the data remain in a raw form and must be processed to produce a usable image.

One way to accomplish this is simply to apply what is called "backprojection" algorithm: all values of the rays for all the views are simply added together, and this sum used for all the pixels along that

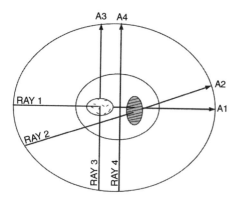

Figure 2.9
Diagram of CAT and PET tomographic techniques. The amount of radiation detected at each detector (A1–A4) depends on the combined density of the tissue in the pathway of the various rays to the detector. For example, ray 1 will be most heavily attenuated and ray 4 will be least heavily attenuated. These differences can be analyzed to produce the striking three-dimensional maps of the brain. Drawing by Mary Zhu.

particular ray. In the simplest implementation of such an algorithm, the values of all the rays passing through a particular point in the two-dimensional array mapped by the tomographic process would be added together. Where a dense object was located, a lighter band would appear, indicating that less radiation had made its way through to the detector. Where a less dense object was located, a darker region would appear indicating that more radiation had made it through to the detector. In this manner, dark and light spots would appear in the reconstructed image corresponding to the denser and less dense regions of the image. (The third dimension, as I have already noted, is obtained by physically shifting the entire apparatus with respect to the imaged part of the body.)

The problem with this simple backprojection technique is that it produces a seriously blurred image, one contaminated with streaks and starlike patterns of false images caused by the overlap of the various rays and the rotational geometry of the typical tomographic system. Backprojection images can, however, be cleaned up to a substantial degree by preprocessing the data with Fourier transforms and high-pass spatial frequency filtering, or by convolving the original data with what is essentially an edge-enhancing kernel.

Another classic technique for processing data of this kind is to use a transformation invented by Radon (1917) that was originally designed to detect straight lines in much the same way as the more familiar Hough transform. A reverse form of the Radon transform can be used to convert lines (such as the cumulative values constructed along the rays in the backprojection procedure) into regions of varying density in a domain defined by ρ and θ, where ρ is the distance to the origin and θ is the angle of ρ with respect to a perpendicular of the original line. The cumulative values along a ray are thus transformed into points in the Radon space; by accumulating a set of these points, an image of the slice of the object can be formed.

Although the mathematics of tomographic reconstruction are sometimes arcane, this qualitative discussion should give readers at least a sense of what is being accomplished in a CAT scan (see figure 2.10 for an actual CAT scan of a brain).

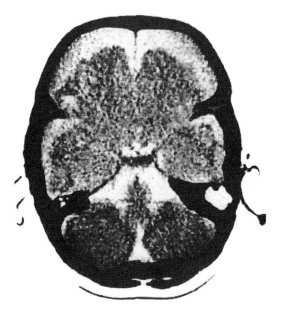

Figure 2.10
Image of the human brain produced by a CAT scanning procedure. The black regions are bone. Used with the permission of J. E. Faulkner, Medical Imaging, Good Samaritan Hospital, Phoenix, Arizona.

We need to appreciate three drawbacks of this procedure, however. First, like a conventional X ray, the CAT scan produces only anatomical information. That is, it tells us nothing about the functions of the system, only something about its physical structure. Like the conventional X ray, it may be extremely useful in detecting or studying structural abnormalities such as tumors or broken bones. It may even be useful to guide the course of surgery, but for several reasons it cannot tell us what the system is doing. For one, however complex, a CAT scan simply detects relative X-ray opacity; for another, it takes a considerable amount of time to carry out even one scan.

Second, a relatively powerful computer is needed to process the huge mass of data forthcoming from a CAT scan apparatus to produce reasonably high-resolution pictures such as those shown in figure 2.10. And third, the procedure exposes the body to high levels of radiation, although lower than some other X-ray procedures because of the high sensitivity of the CAT scan detectors.

Having noted the CAT scan procedure's drawbacks, we should remember that all of the X-ray and tomographic techniques discussed in this chapter have one enormous advantage—they are all noninvasive: no surgery is required to peer into the insides of a living human body. For examining anatomical structure, whether normal or abnormal, these techniques represent a breakthrough of epochal consequence. Only recently have psychologists been able to take advantage of these impressive engineering developments, as analogous techniques to explore the function as well as the structure of the nervous system have emerged. We turn now to one of the first of these functional techniques.

2.2.8   Positron Emission Tomography

Another means of providing the penetrating signals necessary for tomography is to introduce a radioactive substance into the body and to use the energy emitted during radioactive decay as the means of generating a similar three-dimensional image of the interior of the body. This is the basic idea behind *positron emission tomography* (PET).

The PET scanning technique has one enormous advantage over the conventional X-ray and CAT techniques. Whereas those two older techniques depend on the selective absorption of the X rays by the anatomical *structures* of the body, the PET scan technique allows us to examine the *functions* carried out by various parts of the body (including—and most germane for this book—the brain) by injecting specially selected radioactive substances into the body for the study of specific metabolic activities. The basic assumption on which the psychological applications of the PET scan technique is based is that, with a radioactive tracer, the amounts of a substance metabolized by the brain can be indirectly measured to show which regions are actively metabolizing that substance and which are not. Alternatively, again with a radioactive tracer, the amount of blood flowing to a particular region may also be correlated with activity in the region. The use of the fluctuating blood supply as an indicator of localized brain activity is based on the additional assumption that blood flow is directly correlated with the amount of oxygen-consuming neural metabolic activity taking place. This assumption is, in turn, based on the observation that metabolites are oxidized in greater amounts by active cells than by inactive ones. Thus the oxygen flow to active areas must be greater where there is more activity—and, thanks to selective uptake of the radioactive tracer, more radioactivity as well, than where there is less. This chain of assumptions holds not just for neurons but for all cells in the body. The next link in this chain is to assume that the site of a particular cognitive activity is where neural activity is greatest. This assumption, however, is nowhere as clear-cut as the metabolic ones that preceded it.

If detectors sensitive to the energy emitted during enhanced metabolic activity or blood flow are appropriately placed, and tomographic techniques similar to the ones described are appropriately applied, then images of both structure and function can be obtained from the PET technique. The following paragraphs flesh out this bare-bones description of the process.

To understand how PET scan images, which are the product of several different sciences acting together, can be used to localize cognitive processes in the brain, we must, first, know something about the biochemistry of metabolism in the area of interest—for us, the brain. Second, we must know something about radioactive decay and the detection of the particles emitted when nuclei break down. Third, we must integrate this knowledge with the mathematics and computer data processing of tomography, already briefly introduced. Finally, we must know something about the localization problem and the enormous advantages and disadvantages of the extensive technology and physics being applied to it.

First, let us briefly consider the biochemistry of the brain. Neuronal activity is, for the most part, is thought to be energized by the oxidation of glucose. The relevant part of this metabolic activity takes place mainly at neural synapses, where the transmitter substances are presynaptically created, diffused, and then captured by postsynaptic receptor sites. If a region of the brain is neurologically active, the consumption of glucose by and the blood flow to that region are both higher than normal, the latter being functionally dependent on the former. If, however, the region is neurologically inactive, both indicators are low. It has now been established (Roland, 1993) that the two measures are closely related and either or both can be used to determine the amount of activity in a particular region of the brain. In current practice, blood flow, which can measured faster and easier than the metabolic rate per se, is the preferred indicator of brain activity in a PET scan.

It is important to remember that, because the PET scan is primarily a measure of localized metabolic activity, it is particularly weak at discriminating between regions that may have substantially different tissue structures and functions if they are metabolizing at the same rate. More important, it cannot distinguish between different cognitive processes if they are encoded in the same place but by very different neural network arrangements. A PET scan can tell us only where something is happening, not what is happening there. Indeed, to distinguish between different functions, other, more problematic logical and methodological assumptions must be accepted.

The initial task in a PET scan is to pick a radioactive tracer that can be used to measure blood flow. Currently, blood flow tracers include gases, such as krypton or carbon dioxide, and liquids, as strange as O-Butanol or as familiar as water, that either are or contain radioactive isotopes. Roland, Kawashima, Gulyas, and O'Sullivan (1995) give a concise and lucid discussion of the various metabolic tracer substances that have been used in PET scanning in recent years. According to them, the currently preferred tracer substance for the study of blood flow in the brain is the radioactive form of water H_2O^{15}.

A normal, nonradioactive isotope of oxygen (O^{16}) has sixteen nuclear particles (i.e., its mass number is 16) and is quite stable. A highly unstable radioactive isotope of oxygen (O^{15}) with only fifteen nuclear particles (mass number 15) can be produced by bombarding nitrogen with a beam of protons from a particle accelerator, usually a small cyclotron. When this O^{15} is combined with hydrogen it produces radioactive water (H_2O^{15}).

The unstable and radioactive isotope O^{15} tends to decay spontaneously and quickly back to the stable isotope N^{15} having fifteen protons and neutrons. The half-life of O^{15} is 2.04 minutes; that is to say, half of the remaining unstable atoms decay every two minutes. This is the reason that hospitals must now have their own particle accelerators situated near the PET scan lab. The unstable H_2O^{15} must be quickly injected into the subject before it decays. This disadvantage is overcome by two advantages. The radiation level is sufficiently high and the decay rate sufficiently fast for measurements to be made and for any residual radiation to quickly clear the body of the patient or subject.

The critical feature that makes the PET scan work is that the spontaneous decay of an O^{15} atom is accompanied by the emission of a positron—the positively charged antiparticle of the more familiar electron. The positron cannot exist for long among the negatively charged and much more numerous electrons in the environment; indeed, as soon as it encounters a stray electron, the two annihilate each other. A "typical" positron travels only a few millimeters in brain tissue before being annihilated. Nevertheless, this relatively short distance is sufficient to degrade the PET image. The resulting blurring of the image occurs in part because the critical events—the decay of the oxygen atom and the annihilation of the positron as it combines with an electron do not occur at exactly the same place.

All is not lost however. The mutual annihilation of the positron from the decaying O^{15} atom and a fortuitously available electron gives rise to a pair of gamma rays that must, in accord with the laws of conservation of momentum and energy, travel off in exactly opposite directions.

Furthermore, the two gamma rays must together have exactly the same amount of energy that was present in the positron and electron pair prior to their mutual annihilation. The key to understanding how the PET scan technique works is appreciating that simultaneity and diametrical opposition are both necessary to determine than an O^{15} atom has actually decayed, namely, that a gamma ray detected is a consequence of that decay and not just some random, unpaired event. To summarize the discussion thus far, the number of O^{15} atoms that decay is taken to indicate the amount of blood flow at a particular location, and the amount of blood flow is taken to indicate the amount of brain activity at that location—which is what we set out to measure in the first place.

To determine that an O^{15} atom has really decayed and that a detected gamma ray is not random requires (1) that two gamma rays be detected; (2) that the two gamma rays be detected simultaneously; and (3) that they be detected traveling in opposite directions on the same line. If all three conditions are met, the information obtained can be used to generate the basic data for the PET scanning operation—the *line of response*.

Task 1, detection, is accomplished by the hardware. Typically cylindrical and circular in cross section, a PET scan device is set up so that the subject can be inserted into its center. Figure 2.11 diagrams the various components of such a device, including a ring of crystal detectors (made up of photosensitive substances such as bismuth germanate or sodium iodide). For each gamma ray detected, the crystal detectors generate another photon with a lower energy than either one of the photons created by the positron-electron annihilation. The flash of light produced by the secondary photon generated is amplified by a photomultiplier tube to produce an electronic signal.

Tasks 2 and 3 are accomplished by special coincidence circuitry, which determines that detectors exactly opposite each other have been activated at exactly the same time. As noted, the temporal and spatial coincidence of the signals establishes the line of response—the basic data for subsequent computer processing. It is from a database built up of all of the measured lines of response that the three-dimensional reconstruction of the tissue image depends. This database is computer-processed using algorithms and procedures that, for all practical purposes, are the same

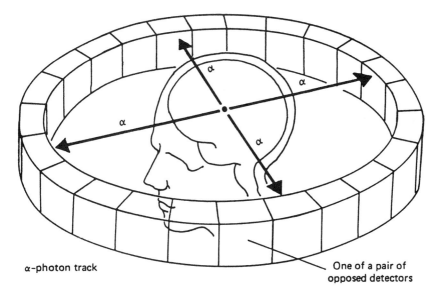

α-photon track

One of a pair of
opposed detectors

Figure 2.11
Diagram of PET apparatus, showing the diametrically opposed coincidence detectors that must be simultaneously activated to detect a pair of photons marking the annihilation of a positron from a radioactive tracer in the subject's body. From Robinson and Uttal, 1983.

as those described for the CAT scan. The images may also be sharpened by Fourier filtering or some other edge-enhancing or sharpening algorithm to produce the classic PET scan display. Figure 2.12 shows a typical PET image reconstructed from processing all of the lines of response obtained during a PET scanning procedure.

PET scan images must be clearly distinguished from CAT scan images. The PET scan measures differences in metabolism, whereas the CAT scan measures differences in anatomy. The PET scan is thus particularly useful for the study of neural activity, just as the CAT scan is excellent for the study of neural structure. However, the two techniques have one major similarity—their final images represent a transverse slices across the longitudinal axis of the body and, as such, can be pooled and processed to produce images along other axes and planes.

For a long time, the PET scan's ability to produce a functional image of metabolic activity was unique. The development of functional magnetic

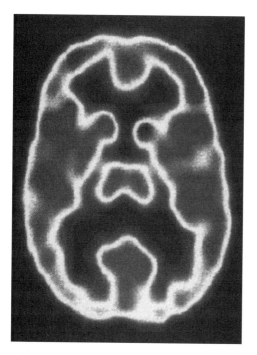

Figure 2.12
Image produced by a PET scanning procedure. Used with the permission of E. M. Reiman, J. T. Frost, and J. Cong, PET Center, Good Samaritan Hospital, Phoenix, Arizona.

resonance imaging (fMRI) provided an alternative and sometimes more precise means of producing the same kind of functional image. Although, along with the conventional X ray, the PET scan will likely have specialized uses for some time to come, fMRI has become the procedure of choice for cognitive neuroscientists. Let us now consider the extraordinary predecessor of fMRI.

2.2.9   Magnetic Resonance Imaging
Conventional X-ray, CAT, and PET scanning procedures all require that external energy pass through or be introduced into the body. Although ionizing radiation (such as X rays) and radioactive materials (such as H_2O^{15}) post ever smaller risks as detection equipment becomes more sensitive and therefore able to produce useful images with much smaller

doses than before, there is still some concern that even very low doses of ionizing radiation (whether X rays or positrons) may have a cumulative effect on the body of the patient or subject. Early in the history of tomography, it would have been almost too much to hope for that a superior technique would come along that would pose no such risks and that would use the very constituents of the human body to noninvasively produce a three-dimensional tomographic image of structure, function, or both.

Amazingly, this is exactly what happened with the development of magnetic resonance imaging, which certainly ranks among the most important medical and technological developments ever. MRI equipment now provides extraordinarily detailed pictures of the body with neither the invasiveness of surgery nor the dangers of ionizing radiation and with a clarity that makes many of the older technologies virtually obsolete. How the MRI technique came to be developed is a remarkable story in itself.

Magnetic resonance imaging can be traced to discoveries made in the mid-twentieth century by three groups of physicists: Rabi, Zacharias, Millman, and Kusch (1937, 1939), Purcell, Torrey, and Pound (1946), and Bloch, Hansen, and Packard (1946). Unlike Roentgen's discovery of X rays, the early discoveries of these scientists were neither totally unexpected nor unprecedented. Nevertheless, although based on the remarkable quantum theories of the 1920s and 1930s, these discoveries led to a practical application—MRI imaging—that no one initially expected.

Rabi et al. (1937, 1939) originally discovered the phenomenon of nuclear magnetic resonance (NMR) and developed a method for measuring the magnetic moment of the atomic nucleus—the basis of the modern MRI device. To do so, they used a beam of ions, accelerated in the same manner in which electrons were accelerated in a Crookes tube, an X-ray tube, or, for that matter, even in a modern TV. Later, Purcell et al. (1946) and Bloch et al. (1946) almost simultaneously developed a similar technique for measuring the same magnetic moment phenomenon in "condensed"—solid—matter.

To understand how these esoteric physical phenomena were manipulated to create an output signal to produce the same structural and functional information provided by CAT and PET scanning procedures, we need to examine the terms that make up *nuclear magnetic resonance.* The first term, *nuclear,* refers to phenomena involving the nuclei of atoms. Which leads us directly to the second term, *magnetic.* Whereas the color of light emitted by an agitated atom, for example, a thermally excited tungsten atom, is determined by the properties of that atom's orbital electrons, NMR is dependent on the *magnetic* properties of protons, which along with neutrons are the main components of an atomic nucleus. Individual protons, in addition to their electrical properties (a proton has a positive charge equal in magnitude to the negative charge of an electron), also have a tiny magnetic field with a north and south pole and lines of force passing from one of these poles to the other, just like a small bar magnet. If the nucleus of an atom has an odd number of protons (e.g., hydrogen with 1 proton, nitrogen with 7 protons, or phosphorous with 15 protons), then that species of atom becomes a candidate for the NMR process. The odd number means that there will be a net magnetic orientation or polarization in one direction when the tiny magnetic fields of all of the protons are aligned. Which particular atomic species is selected for examination is determined by the frequency of the applied radio frequency signals, to be described later. The critical consideration in NMR, the compatibility of the natural frequency of the atom with the frequency of the applied radio signals, leads us to the third term in NMR—the term used to describe that compatibility— *resonance.*

Because the nucleus of a hydrogen atom consists of only one proton, both the analysis and the implementation of the MRI system based on NMR concepts are greatly simplified. Because hydrogen is also one of the two constituents of a water molecule and the body is made mainly of water, the MRI process is mainly an examination of the properties of water in our system. This is not to say that the protons of atoms other than those in water molecules do not contribute to the imaging process, but merely to emphasize that this generally innocuous and certainly ubiquitous constituent of the body (normal, nonradioactive water) provides the main physical foundation of the MRI technique. Indeed, there has never been any evidence of tissue damage from the strong applied magnetic fields, and evidence of only minimum tissue heating from the applied radio frequency signals, used in MRI (although, of course, the procedure could produce unpleasant results in patients with pacemakers or artificial metal hips).

To return to the details of nuclear magnetic resonance, the magnetic poles of the body's protons are randomly oriented in their normal situation. If, however, a strong magnetic field is applied to the body, after a short, but measurable period of time, the magnetic fields of many of the protons become aligned to produce a much stronger cumulative magnetic field along a common axis. The direction of this axis is determined by the strong applied magnetic field, generally produced by a large magnet coil that completely encloses the subject's body, although newer (open-magnet) systems are becoming available.

Each of the tiny proton "magnets" has another measurable property in addition to its magnetic field orientation—it is also spinning around the axis of its magnetic field, in a plane perpendicular to that axis, as shown in figure 2.13. The pattern of the spin is not perfect: the proton not only spins but also wobbles or *precesses* about the axis of its magnetic field. The degree to which this precession or wobble occurs depends on the strength of the large magnetic field originally applied. Indeed, the frequency (F) of precession is precisely defined by the Larmor equation:

$$F = \alpha B, \tag{2.3}$$

where α is a property of the individual type of nucleus defined as the ratio of two physical properties of the proton—its magnetic moment and the angular momentum of its spin—and B is the strength of the applied magnetic field. Thus each species of atom has a particular Larmor frequency at which it best absorbs energy, in other words, at which it *resonates*.

The precession of the magnetic moment of all of the protons acts as an radiating antenna in exactly the same way as the change in the direction of an electron's trajectory was the source of the radiation we called "X rays." The radiation in this case, however, is of a much lower frequency, falling into the range of low-frequency radio waves (approximately 50 MHz).

This brings us to the next critical step in the evolution of nuclear magnetic resonance into magnetic resonance imaging. In addition to a

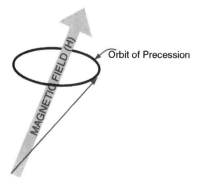

Orbit of Precession

MAGNETIC FIELD (H)

Figure 2.13
Diagram of the precession of the axis of a proton in a strong magnetic field. This precession radiates radio signals at the frequency specified by the Larmor equation. Drawing by Mary Zhu.

magnetic field, radio frequency signals are now brought into play—created by passing electrical signals of the proper frequency thorough a small antenna (i.e., another coil of wire) positioned close to the previously magnetized tissue. These radio frequency signals produce a second, although smaller, magnetic field that slightly changes the direction of the cumulative magnetic field of the protons aligned by the large magnetic field—and thus also the precession of their magnetic moment. The change in precession in turn causes a change in the radio frequency signals radiated by the cumulative magnetic field.

In the procedure of choice, as the smaller magnetic field produced by the small coil is pulsed—turned on and off—the cumulative magnetic field of the tissue is first changed from, then allowed to relax back to the original state induced by the large magnet. The critical effect here is that, as the precession of the aligned protons in the cumulative magnetic field relaxes back to the original state determined by the large magnetic field, the radio frequency signals emitted by the cumulative magnetic field also change.

The radio frequency signals radiated from the precessing cumulative magnetic moment of the tissue under study can be picked up by the same small coil antenna that transmitted the pulsed radio frequency signals. The strength of these radiated signals depends chiefly on

1. the resonant (i.e., same-frequency) relationship between the processing magnetic moment of the aligned protons and the pulsed radio frequency signals;
2. the number and density of moving or mobile protons; and
3. tissue motion.

The key to understanding this complex process is the nature of the changing magnetic moment as it relaxes back to its normal state at the end of the radio frequency pulse. Two measures can be made of what happens during this relaxation time: the longitudinal time constant (T1) and the transverse time constant (T2).

T1 refers to changes that occur in the direction of (i.e., parallel to) the large magnetic field. Thus, after the application of the small radio frequency pulse, the spontaneous return of the magnetic moment to the direction specified by the large magnetic field is measured. T1 varies substantially with tissue type—the essential property permitting the construction of the MRI map of inaccessible parts of the body. T1 is a number representing how fast the magnetic moment "relaxes" back to the original precessional state determined by the initial large magnetic field. This relaxation process is precisely defined by the properties of its constituents. Like other time constant measures, T1 is determined as the time it takes for the relaxation to recover all but 37 percent of its original orientation (the usual way of dealing with an asymptotic curve.)

T2, although a similar measure of the time constant of a relaxation process, is a function of the relaxation along the plane perpendicular to the applied large magnetic field, rather than along it. T2 is also dependent on tissue types and their constituent molecules. For both T1 and T2, the relaxation process involves the transfer of energy to the surrounding tissues, and this transfer depends on the molecular structure of these tissues. T2 is considerably more complicated than T1 because the perpendicular or transverse relaxation occurs at different speeds for protons of the different atoms and thus also molecules of different tissues. Protons in tissues with long T2 time constants ultimately produce bright regions in the final images; those in tissues with short T2 time constants produce darker regions.

Thus far, we have concentrated on how signals may be obtained from the body to produce a tomographic image by manipulating the magnetic and radio frequency energies applied to it. A brief summary may be helpful.

1. The tissues under study (for us, the brain) are placed in a strong magnetic field to align the protons of the constituent atomic nuclei along a single magnetic axis or direction. This is necessary because the magnetic moment of many randomly oriented protons would simply cancel each other out and produce no measurable magnetic field or effect.

2. The protons precess about the magnetic axis defined by this strong magnetic field at a frequency determined by the Larmor equation.

3. After the protons are aligned by the large magnetic field, a pulse of radio frequency signals is applied from a small coil antenna, creating its own smaller magnetic field. This smaller field, by temporarily misaligning the magnetic moments of the protons from the uniform direction induced by the large magnetic field, changes their precessional state.

4. When the radio frequency pulse terminates, the protons tend to relax back to the direction of the strong magnetic field, again changing their precessional state, which causes them to emit radio waves with particular frequencies (radio frequency signals) and time-constant decay properties.[3]

5. These radio frequency signals can be measured to determine two time constant values (T1 and T2) for the tissues being scanned and thus provide the raw data necessary to produce a three-dimensional image.

6. Depending on the particular application of the MRI procedure, either the T1 or the T2 scores can be used to image the tissues.

It was the monumental development of an idea by Raymond Damadian (1971) that gave rise to the currently ubiquitous MRI device. The essential details of this remarkable leap from pure physics to clinical device can be briefly related (for the exciting story in considerably more detail than is appropriate here, see Mattson & Simon, 1996).

---

3. In practice, two kinds of radio frequency pulses are applied—one that produces a 90-degree deviation and one that produces a 180-degree deviation in the angle of precession. By varying the interval between the radio frequency pulses and by combining the 90-degree and 180-degree pulses at appropriate intervals, one can map out the image of a transverse slice of the human body, with different tissues represented by different image intensities.

Damadian's hope was that certain tissue, particularly cancerous tissue, might produce T1 and T2 relaxation values that differed from those of normal tissue. Using a newly developed type of NMR device (earlier versions had been around for over a decade), Damadian (1971) showed that test tube portions of tumors from a cancerous rat produced much higher T1 measurements than did normal rat tissue. In this same paper, he also reported that a variety of normal tissues each produced different relaxation times. From these different T1 and T2 values came the insight that different tissue types would produce different image intensities.

Damadian went to on to suggest the next important logical step—extending what were previously only "test tube" experiments to experiments on the intact human body. To take that step, he and his colleagues would develop and patent a practical MRI device in 1972.

The first whole-body MRI images produced by Damadian and his colleagues required an enormous amount of ingenious practical engineering. Because none of the magnets and many of the other devices required for a working MRI system were available off the shelf, they had to be hand built by Damadian and his group. It was not until 1977 that they were able to make the measurements that allowed them for the first time to produce a primitive map of the inside of a living human body without any kind of invasive surgery or ionizing radiation.

From that point on, the advantages of magnetic resonance imaging over other techniques were so obvious that a number of commercial corporations immediately entered the fray, committing huge engineering teams and enormous capital to the development a marketable MRI device, although it should be noted that many other engineers and scientists also helped develop modern MRI scanning equipment.

The recitation of Damadian's contribution, however, is not the end of the story. There is one question yet to be answered. How are the measurements of the T1 and T2 relaxation time constants converted into a spatial map of a slice of the body? In other words, with all of the relaxation radio frequency signals being emitted at the same time from many places, how do you tell which signal comes from which place?

Damadian's original device did it the hard way. The device was arranged so that the measurements were made a particular point in the body—the so-called sweet spot. The resolution of this image was not very good—about the size of a pea. Then, to measure the NMR response at some other point, the subject was physically moved to translate the sweet spot to another place in the subject's body. In this manner, by repeatedly moving the subject about inside the magnet in all three dimensions and taking measurements each time, an anatomical map could be laboriously produced.

Modern techniques of creating an image from T1, T2, or both measurements are based on a quite different idea, originally formulated by Paul C. Lauterbur, who suggested that a gradient magnetic field be imposed on the strong, aligning magnetic field. (A gradient MRI field is one that systematically changes across the subject.) This idea, combined with the back-projection method we have already discussed and other subsequently developed mathematical tools, made the radio frequency signals (radiated by the protons as they relaxed back from the perturbed state to the orientations defined by the large magnetic field) dependent on their spatial location. Lauterbur began work on this important development about the same time that Damadian was doing his pioneering work in 1971, but did not publish his technique until two years later (Lauterbur, 1973).

Lauterbur's technique (1973) depended on the fact that, whereas all the radio frequency signals emitted by all the protons would be the same if all were in the same strength magnetic field, their frequencies would differ if the magnetic field was not the same everywhere. Thus, by using a nonhomogeneous field with gradients of magnetic strength, one could interpret the emitted frequency differences in terms of different positions inside the body. In this manner, both the subject and the magnet used in an NMR whole-body scan could remain in the same position and the scanning necessary to make one slice image done entirely electromagnetically.

If the magnetic field is kept constant over the body, however, then the emitted signals depend on the substances present in the body. In this manner, the anatomical structure of the system can be examined to produce information like that obtained from an X-ray CAT scan.

As easy as it is to express these ideas, the problem of extracting the image from the measurements was far from simple. It took a number of further developments to arrive at a complete system capable of full, three-dimensional imaging. Imposing a controlled gradient of field strength on the main magnetic field (as opposed to keeping it uniform) was ultimately accomplished with three additional small coils at right angles to each other, each adding a linear gradient (positive on one side, negative on the other, and zero in the middle) to the main magnetic field. Although, typically, these gradients are only one thousandth as strong as the main magnetic field, this is enough for the emitted radio frequency signals to provide the necessary spatial localization information. By controlling the order in which these additional coils are activated and how they are combined, one can produce an image of any one of the three planes along which the body is oriented.

The resultant complex patterns of radio frequency relaxation responses produced by the controlled gradients of the magnetic fields are subjected to Fourier analysis and computer-processed to produce a final MRI image, such as that shown in figure 2.14. With vastly improved color-added and three-dimensional imaging methods, the results obtained are extraordinary. MRI images have replaced exploratory surgery in what must be considered one of the most significant medical advances ever. (For the technical details of how patterns of radiated radio frequency signals are transformed into a pictorial display, see Dowsett et al., 1998.)

One major psychological problem remains. A modern MRI device involves a family of five different concentric coils; the engineering is so demanding and the design so restricted by the physical principles involved that, for a full-body MRI scan, the subject must be placed in a narrow, coffinlike tube. Anyone who has been in such a device knows how uncomfortable this may be, given the prolonged time (often more than an hour) required to accumulate all of the necessary information to reconstruct an image. This seemingly irrelevant detail has made the device very inhospitable for many people. Although newer, open devices have been designed and constructed, they do not yet provide the same precise resolution available from traditional MRI systems.

The spatial resolution of a modern MRI scanning device is now finer than a cubic millimeter. Because of its high precision and sharp contrast, and because it involves no ionizing radiation or radioactive materials, MRI has become a centerpiece of modern medicine in less than a decade.

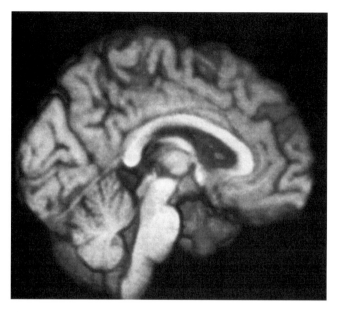

Figure 2.14
Image produced by the MRI scanning procedure. Used with the permission of E. Reiman, J. T. Frost, and J. Cong, PET Center, Good Samaritan Hospital, Phoenix, Arizona.

Magnetic resonance imaging is without question among the crown jewels of medical science, ranking with anesthesia, germ theory, and antibiotics. The original motivation of Damadian and Lauterbur was to develop a means of detecting abnormal (cancerous) tissue. This very practical goal was achieved beyond even their most extreme expectations—MRI devices are now used routinely to scan for metastatic cancers—but it is the applications of MRI to other fields of medicine and to the neurosciences that have produced some of the biggest surprises. Again, it must not be overlooked that this profoundly humane medical development was based on the purest kinds of basic physical research—research that had no inkling that so obscure a phenomenon as the magnetic resonance of protons could play such an important role in improving the quality of human life.

Thus far, we have spoken of MRI as a tool for studying the structure of the brain. Amazingly, and of greatest relevance to the main goal of this book, it can also be used to study the function of various regions; it is to this topic we now turn.

2.2.10 Functional Magnetic Resonance Imaging

When the PET scanning technique was discussed earlier in this chapter, it was pointed out that the radioactive decay of a particular type of elemental material—O^{15}—could be used to indicate its concentration at various locations in the brain. Because the concentration of oxygen was correlated with the blood flow to the region under study, the blood flow with glucose metabolism, and glucose metabolism with neural activity in that particular region, the PET scan could be used to measure that activity.

With a slightly different chain of correlations, MRI can also be used to observe which regions of the brain are active. When used to determine the function, as opposed to the anatomical structure, of the brain or any other portion of the body, MRI is referred to as "functional magnetic resonance imaging" (fMRI).

Unlike the PET scan, however, fMRI measures, not the radioactivity of O^{15}, but the difference in relaxation time constants of two different kinds of hemoglobin: oxygenated hemoglobin (in blood carrying oxygen to the cells of the body) and deoxygenated hemoglobin (in blood returning from those cells to the lungs). A molecule of oxygenated hemoglobin, for obscure reasons, responds only weakly to an applied magnetic field, whereas a molecule of deoxygenated hemoglobin responds quite strongly. The key to using fMRI to determine the relative amounts of oxygenated blood is thus to distinguish the strong magnetic susceptibility of deoxygenated hemoglobin from the weaker susceptibility of oxygenated hemoglobin. To accomplish this task, another measure often used to evaluate the effect of a radio frequency pulse, $T2^*$, the time constant of the relaxation that occurs in a nonhomogenous magnetic field, is the indicator of choice. With all other properties and procedures of remaining the same as in MRI, fMRI is simply tuned to measure $T2^*$ and to provide radio frequency pulses that can perturb the precessional frequencies of protons within hemoglobin.

The specific effect of increased neural activity is thus to increase the amount of deoxygenated hemoglobin, which is reflected in a greater value for $T2^*$, and thus stronger radio frequency signals from the active region compared to inactive regions. Because the absolute value of the differences measured, and ultimately converted to image intensities, is rather small, most fMRI data have to be processed by subtracting a set of "rest" data from those obtained when the subject was carrying out the task of interest. (We shall consider the key role played by this subtractive method later when we examine attempts to correlate mental states and activity in particular parts of the brain.)

To summarize, like the PET scan, fMRI provides a means of indirectly estimating the amount of neural activity in regions of the brain, working from a logical chain of correlations. Additional brain activity leads to higher glucose metabolism, which leads to high oxygen demand, which leads to higher blood flow. As the oxygen in the newly arrived blood is used up, the hemoglobin changes from a form that is not magnetically susceptible to one that is. The change in $T2^*$ values as oxygenated hemoglobin becomes deoxygenated can be measured and the data converted to an image showing the functional, as opposed to the anatomical, properties of the human brain.

The technology of fMRI scanning is changing very rapidly. Recent discussions of current progress in both the technology and its applications can be found in Yuasa, Prichard, and Ogawa's review (1998) and at Hornak's web site (1999). Reiman, Lane, Van Patten, and Bandetti (2000) provide another lucid discussion of the PET and fMRI technologies. Of particular interest is event-related fMRI (see page 194). Furthermore, new techniques are appearing on the scene that use both magnetic and optical sensors. For example, a number of novel optical techniques using near infrared light or visible light have been developed recently. Gratton and Fabiani (1998) review the advantages and disadvantages of these techniques; Koizumi, Yamashita, Mai, Ito, and Watanabe (1998) describe their method for looking at blood flow with optical methods.

The fMRI technique, which has attracted much attention in recent years among psychologists and neuroscientists, provides the basis for a surprisingly large portion of the corpus of modern psychobiological work. It is particularly important, therefore, that anyone attempting to exploit fMRI be aware of the technical details underlying its application.

With this information in hand, and with an appreciation of the power of these extraordinary imaging systems, we can now turn to the other side of the problem. If one is to localize cognitive processes in the brain, one must have not only a powerful imaging system (which we clearly have) and a nonhomogeneous brain (which no one disputes), but also a very clear definition of the cognitive processes being localized. Although it may not seem so to most people, psychologists and lay persons alike, defining and understanding the psychological aspect of the localization task are not as easy as understanding how the sophisticated imaging devices it uses work. In the next chapter, I review the history of faculties, mental components, and other ideas about modular cognitive processes.

3

Is a Taxonomy or Even a Lexicon of Cognitive Processes Possible?

Plurality is not to be assumed without necessity. . . . What can be done with fewer [assumptions] is done in vain with more.

—William of Ockham

Entities are not to be multiplied without necessity.

—Anonymous

The great interpreter and historian of experimental psychological thought E. G. Boring is reputed to have said, "Intelligence is what intelligence tests measure." Herein lies the kernel of the greatest problem faced by psychology in general and the essence of the difficulty one faces when one attempts to localize mental processes or components in particular parts of the brain. The difficulty is that, beyond the physically anchored sensory and motor processes, it is has always been extremely difficult to define exactly what is meant by a psychological, cognitive, or mental term. Yet, in the search for the brain loci responsible for psychological processes, we glibly go about trying to locate some such nebulously defined entity in the three-dimensional space inhabited by the brain. Clearly, if what one seeks to localize is itself nebulous and ill defined, finding a particular brain locus in which it is uniquely or even partially represented is going to pose a considerable challenge—a challenge fraught with its own conceptual, technical, and logical difficulties. This criticism holds true no matter how precisely the coordinates of the brain regions themselves may be defined.

How do we deal with this formidable obstacle—ill-defined mental modules, faculties, traits, or components? One way is to examine the various psychological processes and mechanisms that have been proposed over the years to see if there is any convergence toward a consensus on what these mental components might be. In other words, is there any scientific basis for a reductive classification of mental components that permits us to develop an orderly taxonomy based on sound cladistic logic? Knowing either that there is a basis for a taxonomy or that no such basis exists because of the unavoidable hypothetical and speculative nature of mental components would be extremely helpful in evaluating the prospect of localizing mental functions in the brain. Indeed, asking this question should have been an essential part of the formative stages of the program of brain localization research.

In pursuing such a question, the difficulty of defining mental processes has arisen repeatedly. There is probably nothing that divides psychologists of all stripes more than the inadequacies and ambiguities of our efforts to define mind, consciousness, and the enormous variety of mental events and phenomena. All of us have been involved in disputes that are ultimately seen to founder on the definition of mentalist terminologies. There is probably no greater source of psychological gobbledygook than our disagreements over the meaning of some mental term or, even worse, our efforts to show how the brain "produces" (or any other of a host of relational terms) "mind." The question we must answer is whether this state of affairs is a fundamental epistemological condition or one we have reason to hope can eventually be overcome. Determining taxonomic plausibility to the satisfaction of a reasonably large number of my colleagues is thus not going to be easy.

Unlike lepidopterists, who have the relatively simple task of gathering and classifying butterflies, psychologists have few such convenient physical anchors. Organizing the myriad proposed psychological components—"butterflies"—of our minds has been and is one of the great unfulfilled challenges of our science. Indeed, it is not only unfulfilled; it has not, in my opinion, been adequately engaged. Rather, hypothetical psychological constructs are invented ad lib and ad hoc without adequate consideration of the fundamental issue of the very plausibility of precise definition.

Where entomologists have objective measures such as the number of legs or wings and the physical types of antennae (as well as the new measures offered by DNA analyses), psychologists have far less objective metrics on which to base our definitions. Indeed, the hugely disorganized body of processes, ideas, phenomena, and other ephemeral entities that psychology confronts is probably far more bewildering than the 1.5 million species of insects currently thought to exist. Psychology does not even have simple dimensions such as "number of" or "shape of" along which to classify and organize our specimens.

Boring's astute comment about "intelligence" (the social consequence of "who owns intelligence" is well discussed in Gardner, 1999) holds for virtually every other psychological or cognitive entity ever discovered, described, or hypothesized by any student of the mind. Boring's few words point up both the nebulousness of our ideas about what makes up mental life and the impossibility of anchoring such nebulous ideas to independent measurements generally. At best, he is saying that it is only by operationalizing our "butterflies" can we begin to approach definitions and categories of psychological function. Nevertheless, this is exactly what psychology does not, in general, do. Indeed, such an objective, operational approach to psychology has largely been rejected in recent decades.

There may be no more compelling nutshell argument for the necessity of an operational and positivist (and thus, by implication, behaviorist) approach to psychological concepts than the one implicit in Boring's comment. Although I have dealt with this issue in previous works (Uttal, 1998, 2000a) and do not wish to belabor the point here, if their efforts are ever to bear fruit, mental taxonomists must appreciate that *how* we measure in large part determines *what* we measure—or, perhaps more precisely, what we *think* we are measuring. For psychology, more than any other science, this is a profound problem and one that must be resolved before we attempt to identify the behavioral outcomes of experimental protocols with what may only be murky shadows or even illusions of real mental processes and mechanisms.

The tendency to concretize and reify the ephemeral is endemic in psychology. No matter how often or eloquently we are warned about the significance of "hypothetical constructs" (e.g., MacCorquodale & Meehl, 1948) the tendency to treat as real that which is, at best ad hoc or invented, is pervasive. How often we forget their admonition that hypothetical constructs are inferences, interpretations, subjective judgments, descriptive (as opposed to explanatory) theories, and sometimes no more than convenient labels. To avoid the all-too-seductive trap of letting our inferences become our facts, we must keep in mind that the behavioral data on which these inferences are based are actually neutral with regard to the actual mechanisms: an infinite number of behaviorally indiscriminable alternative inferences and potential mechanisms are possible, many, perhaps even most, of which are plausible. (For a more complete exposition of this point of view, see Uttal 1998, and the formal automata theorems in Moore, 1956.)

Of course, there are many pragmatic or humanistic arguments that what is "real" is what is convenient or useful or what "dignifies" some aspect of human existence for reasons above and beyond the strictly scientific. However, the confusion of speculations about what are clearly nonunique hypothetical constructs concerning the organization and nature of human cognition with entities that have actually evolved over the millions of years of organic evolution almost certainly leads to missteps in the development of a valid understanding of the nature of the human brain-mind.

There is no better evidence that identifying hypothetical constructs with psychobiological realities is a fragile strategy than that reflected in psychology's historical concern with cognitive components. The names for these cognitive components have come and gone along with the fashions of the times. The centerpiece of a point of view about the nature of the human mind in one generation is forgotten or ridiculed in the next. Where today, indeed, would one find even the most enthusiastic fMRI researcher searching for Freud's "Id" or Gall's "acquisitiveness?" Nevertheless, psychologists are seeking to localize some equally tentative and perhaps equally transitory new hypothetical constructs among the many centers and nuclei of the brain. Indeed, vaguely defined concepts such as language, emotion, or consciousness, and other mental processes of uncertain specificity and existence are all too easily deemed both specific and "real" enough to be localized in a particular portion of the brain.

As I suggested earlier, the inadequate and nebulous definition of psychological constructs poses the principal problem for localization research. Let us now review earlier taxonomies to determine whether psychology is converging toward a generally acceptable taxonomy of mental processes and mechanisms.

3.1   Previous Taxonomies

The effort to organize mental processes into some kind of classificatory order is not new. Each generation's psychologists or protopsychologists seems to have suggested one based on their own contemporary worldview. Certainly, from the dawn of language, and perhaps from even earlier methods of interpersonal communication, a rich vocabulary or set of nonverbal symbols of mental events existed that described experiences, feelings, memories, intents, desires, emotions, and other kinds of thought. In prescientific times, when the problems of the mind mainly resided in the domain of philosophy and religion, the concept of mind was for the most part dealt with interchangeably with that of the soul; in modern times, mind, held to be a function of a physical, mortal brain, has been distinguished from soul, held to be immortal and independent of the physical body. The Greek philosophers, for example, Plato (d. 347 B.C.E.) had their own systems of thinking about thinking.[1] Augustine (354–430) perpetuated what was essentially the Platonic view that the soul had certain faculties, such as memory, imagination, reasoning, and will, that were responsible for human actions.

The first formal prototaxonomies of mental processes of the kind I wish to consider here, however, arose much later. In what is still one of the best histories of scientific psychology, Klein (1970) points out that Maimonides (1135–1204) had developed a surprisingly complete and modern-sounding list of mental faculties. Although there were other, less well defined, mental properties about which Maimonides was not as specific, the following gives the flavor of his taxonomy:

1. The nutritive faculty, which consisted of
a. the power of attracting food;
b. the retention of food;

---

1. I am indebted to my colleague Professor Sherwin J. Klein for calling my attention to some of these early faculty psychologies and for commenting on later portions of this chapter.

c. the digestion of food;

d. the repulsion of superfluities;

e. growth; and

f. procreation.

2. The appetitive faculty (attributed primarily to animals and to the primitive aspects of human thought), which consisted of

a. desire;

b. love;

c. hate;

d. anger; and

e. fear.

3. The rational or reasoning faculty (exclusively limited to human thought), which consisted of

a. practical reasoning; and

b. theoretical reasoning.

Later, Thomas Hobbes (1588–1679) and René Descartes (1596–1650) offered their mechanistic theories of the nature of humanity and its relation to other parts of our world. In particular, it is often overlooked that the father of the reductive method, Descartes, championed the idea that the mind was more or less indivisible.

From these early ideas emerged the early associationist theories of the British empiricists including John Locke (1632–1704), David Hartley (1705–1757), Thomas Brown (1778–1820), James Mill (1773–1836), and his son, John Mill (1806–1873), among many others. Not all of the proto- and fully developed associationists were convinced of the existence of separable faculties—Locke, for one, agreed with Descartes about the unified nature of mental processes. However, even Locke contributed to the evolution of what came to be called "faculty psychology"—the idea of mind as a collection of quasi-independent components.

By the time of the introspective structuralists—Wilhelm Wundt (1832–1920), Edward Titchener (1867–1927) and the philosopher James Ward (1843–1925)—and for much of this century, the prevailing taxonomy included a long list of basic sensations that had to be combined by associationist processes to produce more complex perceptions, thoughts, feelings, and emotions. Even Watson, the great behaviorist (who, as a behaviorist, should have been more committed to a holistic point of view) adhered to the idea that the higher levels of cognition were constructed in some way from the components of stimulus and response.

An avalanche of new vocabulary and ideas championing the separateness of the components of mental activity, however, occurred with the emergence of modern "cognitive" psychology, the newest version of traditional mentalism. The main difference between behaviorism and cognitive mentalism is their respective attitudes toward the question of the *accessibility* of mental processes. The behaviorists asserted that mind is not directly accessible, whereas the cognitivists asserted that it is.

A second issue distinguishing these two great schools of thought revolves around the *analyzability* of mental processes. Behaviorists argue that mental process are unitary and that externally measured responses do not therefore allow us to analyze mind into its components, even if they do exist (an issue on which behaviorists of different stripes continue to disagree.) The core of much cognitive thinking in recent years is just the opposite—cognitivists very strongly argue that mind is made up of a system of more or less isolatable and independently assayable components. Unlike behaviorists, therefore, cognitivists accept that it is plausible—indeed, sensible—to search for the internal structure and architecture of the mind as well as that of the brain.

Many cognitivists assert that they are studying the information-processing characteristics of the human mind. This technique, they argue, gives them the opportunity to consider things such as mental maps or mental rotation (to name only two). Unfortunately, this information-processing approach is fraught with the same problems as any other mentalism. It assumes that the internal structure can be accessed and analyzed and, as such, is subject to the same criticism as any other reductive approach. (For a complete analysis of the distinction between the two schools of thought on these issues, see Uttal, 2000a.)

The mentalist theory that mind is made up of separable and identifiable components is clearly stated in a recent book by Pinker (1997, p. 21):

The mind is a system of organs of computation, designed by natural selection to solve the kinds of problems our ancestors faced in their foraging way of life, in particular, understanding and outmaneuvering objects, animals, plants, and other people. . . . The mind is organized into modules or mental organs, each with a specialized design that makes it an expert in one arena of interaction with the world. The modules' basic logic is specified by our genetic program. Their operation was shaped by naturals election to solve the problems of the hunting and gathering life led by our ancestors in most of our evolutionary history. . . . On this view, psychology is engineering in reverse. In forward-engineering, one designs a machine to do something; in reverse-engineering, one figures out what a machine was designed to do.

Pinker is crystal clear here on his commitment to the "modularity and separability of mental processes" even if he does not provide us with the empirical justification for his version of contemporary cognitive psychology. On the basis of that commitment, he vigorously supports the analytical approach of modern cognitivism—and presumably also the localization effort. In so doing, however, he also inadvertently highlights the great difficulty faced by localization theorists—the still unsatisfied need to sharply demarcate that which is to be localized.

What we see exemplified in Pinker, 1997, is the a priori assumption that mental modules and "organs" exist and can therefore provide a conceptual basis for the entire localization enterprise. This is done in the face of a surprisingly large amount of empirical evidence to the contrary. I argue here that, by accepting this a priori assumption, psychology abdicates its responsibility as a profession to evaluate the logic of its primary fundamental premises—the accessibility and the analyzability of mental activity. This is not to say that no one has ever undertaken such an evaluation. Indeed, a few psychologists and scholars who identify themselves as philosophers, but who deal with psychological questions, have done so.

One of the most eloquent analyses of the possible existence of mental modules was provided by Fodor (1983), who in his brief, but intellectually formidable monograph considered many of the target topics of this chapter. Among the most important contributions that Fodor made was to provide a taxonomy of taxonomies; he proposed (Fodor, 1983) four classes of taxonomies—ways mental processes have been or may be categorized:

1. *Neo-Cartesian taxonomies. These* are based on the assumption that psychological faculties, like the organs of the body, are innate and

thus virtually fixed from the moment of conception.[2] Fodor specifically highlights Chomsky's view (1980) of language as innate and predetermined, although Fodor argues that Chomsky is actually speaking about innate knowledge rather than a material structure and that pieces of "knowledge," rather than specific organs, characterize the psychological faculties.

2. *Horizontal functional taxonomies.*   These are based on the assumption that behavior is generated by combinations of psychological faculties rather than by the isolated and independent properties of these faculties. According to Fodor, the horizontal taxonomists hold that many categories of mental processes involve horizontal interaction between the faculties to produce the more familiar psychological entities such as attention or perception. Although the faculties themselves are not application specific and can provide inputs to many behaviors or mental processes, individually they are constant and stable from one application to another, just as the same computer algorithm or "object" may be used in many different applications.

3. *Vertical functional taxonomies.*   By contrast, these taxonomies are based on the assumption that psychological faculties exist as independent entities, individually reflecting their nature in the form of highly specific patterns of behavior. According to Fodor, the vertical taxonomists hold that horizontal interaction between these faculties is secondary if it occurs at all. He cites modern attempts to link specific behaviors with specific brain regions as good examples of a vertical taxonomic approach.

4. *Associationist taxonomies.*   These are based on the assumption that psychological faculties really do not exist in any general form, but rather consist of much smaller elements (Fodor suggests that many associationists still concentrate on reflexes as these elements) associated by an overriding set of common rules or laws. It is these rules or laws which must be classified and organized if we are to build a useful taxonomy of mental events.

Although with his taxonomy of mental taxonomies Fodor helps us organize our own thinking about the fundamental premises of psychologies that attempt to modularize mind, this is by no means to suggest that, in

2. Given Descartes' holistic view of the mind, it is not clear why Fodor chose to call this class "Neo-Cartesian." Perhaps, he was emphasizing Descartes' concern with the innateness of knowledge and its relation to rationalism, rather than his antielementalism.

doing so, he has somehow solved the huge problem faced by psychologists. As Fodor himself concluded (Fodor, 1983, pp. 104, 38): "There is practically no direct evidence, pro or con, on the question whether central systems are modular"; indeed, that "our cognitive science has in fact made approximately no progress in studying these processes . . . may well be *because* of their non-modularity."

If this is so, Fodor went on to say, and if our research methodology is necessarily based on a modular strategy, then there may well be profound limits to what we can expect from cognitive psychology.

So as not to leave us without an epistemological toehold, Fodor invoked the more holistic and initially undifferentiated approach of, among others, the Gestalt psychologists and the Watsonian and Skinnerian behaviorists. This approach denies the innate, traditionally rationalist argument of all generations of Cartesians in favor of an empiricist philosophy that asserted that everything had to be learned and that the mind was initially blank. There are no categories or modules of mind, at least at first, and those which may develop later are defined by experience rather than by our genetic heritage. Although the controversy over the innate versus the learned aspects of this argument has commanded the attention of many psychologists, the most significant current controversy is between proponents of psychobiological modularity, on the one hand, and proponents of a holistic and empiricist approach, on the other.

It seems to me that Fodor has made a strong (even if unintended) case for a kind of revitalized behaviorism, in which the search for the architecture of mental processes and mechanisms is recognized as hopeless. It also seems to me that Fodor would support the position that attempts to localize mental modules in particular brain regions are misdirected and that much of cognitive neuroscience research is due for careful reconsideration. I do not agree, however, with his assertion that "convincing arguments for non-modularity should be received with considerable gloom." Quite to the contrary, I believe that a full appreciation of what can and what cannot be done in psychology would represent one of psychology's crowning achievements.

It is also somewhat disconcerting to see Fodor's ideas presented as supporting modularity in general, when he is careful to limit modularity to a narrow part of the mental domain—sensory and perceptual processes, defined by the differential sensitivity of the various receptor organs. (I shall consider his contributions in this regard in greater detail later in this chapter.)

The following subsections present a more extensive discussion of the specific maps, taxonomies, lists, and lexicons of discrete mental processes that have been proposed.

3.1.1 John Locke's "Ideas"

The roots of our current theories that thinking is organized as a collection of quasi-independent modules or faculties can be traced back to the writings of the classic Greek philosophers, as I have noted. The trail toward wide acceptance of the concept of components of mind can also be discerned in the writings of Thomas Aquinas (1224–1274). Other theologian-philosophers, such as Pierre Gassendi (1592–1655) and Christian Thomasius (1655–1728), also posed their respective theologies and psychologies in terms of the mind being made up of separable components. Regardless of his role as a religionist, each was in the train of ideas that led directly to empiricism, a nontheological philosophy asserting the primacy of experience and sensation as the determinants of the contents of our mind.

The British empiricist John Locke (1632–1704) was one of the first to formulate a more or less modern taxonomy of mental processes. Using the word "idea" to characterize mental processes, Locke distinguished between simple and complex ideas, and between the primary and secondary qualities of those ideas. Simple ideas were the basic raw sensations; complex ideas were formed from combinations of those simple ideas. Locke suggested that complex ideas could be reorganized into new versions, whereas simple ideas, constrained by their physical foundations and the biology of our nervous systems, always produced the same uniform mental response.

Although Locke's distinction between primary and secondary qualities was related to the dimension of complexity, it emphasized another aspect of our experience—the ability or power of the stimulus to produce experiences. A primary quality of a stimulus, he argued, always directly and unequivocally produced a particular response; it directly defined the response, whether or not it was perceived. For example, the experience of redness was driven entirely by the primary quality of the stimulus object. The same perceptual response was always produced by a stimulus having the same physical primary quality.[3] A secondary quality, on the other hand, was a derivative of some organizational aspect of a stimulus object. For example, according to Locke, musical melodies are derived from the organization of the acoustic signal components and depended on the interpretive construction of the percept by the observer.

The concept of "ideas" was Locke's precursor of faculties and included a wide range of different mental components. His list included perception, reflection, memory, contemplation, discerning, distinguishing, naming, and abstracting. He also distinguished three types of complex ideas, namely, modes, substances, and relations.

This is but barest outline of the theory of mind that Locke (1690) proposed in his monumental *An Essay Concerning Human Understanding,* which had an enormous impact on subsequent philosophy and, as we see, equally seminal influence on psychology. As a particularly explicit attempt to develop a taxonomy of human mental processes, it clearly was the ancestor of the faculty psychologies that were soon to follow.

3.1.2   Christian Wolff's Faculty Psychology

Widely recognized as the first academic psychologist, Christian Wolff (1679–1754) holds a special place in the history of psychology. Virtually all of his predecessors has been independent scholars free of the constraints imposed by academic or administrative institutions. Wolff, who was trained as a mathematician, played a pivotal role in the debate over whether mental processes could be measured—he strongly championed the idea that they could be measured if adequately defined. Immanuel Kant (1630–1714), who championed the contrary point of view (based on his notion that the mind was always active), was such a prestigious philosopher that it was not until the nineteenth century that psychophysicists made the case for our ability to measure at least "simple" sensory properties.

---

3. It is now known that the perception of the hue of a patch of "colored" light is not determined solely by its component reflected wavelengths but also by the spatial relationships it has with other "colored" patches (Land, 1977).

Wolff is celebrated principally for his classification of mental functions, however. He argued that one had to be very specific about what one wished to measure, and this meant developing a list of the faculties of mind amenable to measurement. Wolff specifically suggested that the faculties such as attending, remembering, and perceiving existed in relative independence. Other, more complicated faculties, however, presented students of the mind with a difficulty that still bedevils modern psychologists—How do you tease apart the components of an intricately interacting system when all you can observe is their collective function? The need to justify measurement was father to Wolff's concept of independent faculties: acting on a set of preconceived notions, his felt need for an objective approach to the nature of mind overwhelmed his obligation to meet the requirements for consistency and solid empirical grounding—bad science then as now.

Wolff believed that there were many faculties, indeed as many as there are words to describe them.[4] He went on to suggest that these supposedly independent faculties interacted with each other to produce the unified experiences, perceptions, cognitions, and other mental activities of which we are all aware. Indeed, he proposed a precursor of the very modern idea of associative memory by suggesting the conceptual mechanism of "redintegration," the process by which the activation of any particular portion of a memory stimulates the evocation of the other portions of that memory. Many modern cognitive theories, especially the list-processing computer models, have incorporated similar ideas into their conceptualization of cognition.

Wolff was followed by many others who premised their psychologies on the assumption that mental faculties existed as real components of the human mind. The Scottish scholars Thomas Reid (1710–1796), Dugald Stewart (1753–1828), and William Hamilton (1788–1856) also argued for the existence of quasi-independent mental processes, although their theories were purely mental and psychological and had no physiological postulates attached to them. The question of where in the brain these

---

4. This is a harbinger of troubles to come. How can any taxonomy be accepted that simply names the faculties but does not show how they are related to each other? Yet this unlimited ability to name new psychological entities still bedevils the entire localization effort as well as psychology in general.

mental faculties were located would not arise until later. Nevertheless, the sensory modalities as well as such "higher" faculties as friendship, attention, and ambition were considered by these philosophers as independent mental modules that might someday be independently assayed.

3.1.3 The Phrenological Taxonomy: The Brain, the Skull, and the Faculties

Franz Joseph Gall (1758–1828), trained as an anatomist, lives on as one of the most notorious, proto-psychologists of the last three centuries. Joined in a peculiar relationship with another contemporary anatomist—Johann Spurzheim (1776–1832)—Gall produced what was initially one of the most influential theories of mental faculties proposed up to that time. It lasted only long enough to become one of the most thoroughly discredited theories in the history of physiological psychology. Spurzheim, in particular, championed the theory that (1) the mind was made up of a number of separable mental components; (2) these components were localized in particular regions of the brain; and (3) finally and most destructively to their proposed psychology, these brain regions were associated with particular topographic features on the surface of the skull. The theory implied that, by palpating the bumps on the skull to determine their size and position, one could work back to estimates of personality and mental ability.

Thus a radically new emphasis—craniology and brain localization—was added to the preexisting tradition of mind as a system of numerous independent (separable) component faculties. The idea of separable components of mind went back at least to Wolff and the Scottish school of thought—both Reid and Stewart had long lists of psychological faculties much like those later proposed by Gall and Spurzheim—but probably had analogs in almost any historical school of psychological thought one might choose to examine.

Although there is considerable controversy whether either Gall or Spurzheim was directly influenced by Wolff or the Scottish philosophers (see, for example, Klein, 1970, p. 671), there is no question that the same concept of distinctive mental modules runs through all these systems of psychological thinking. It is important to appreciate that, however outdated the phrenologists' list may be, it certainly was not revolutionary nor antagonistic to the ideas prevailing at Gall and Spurzheim's time. It was their emphasis on brain and, particularly, on skull localization that added a novel element to the modularity point of view. What is surprising is how wrong they could be about something as fundamental as the relation of the brain's contours to those of the skull despite their professional backgrounds (both Gall and Spurzheim were neuroanatomists). As anatomists, they certainly should have known that brain bumps simply do not transfer to skull bumps.

Most psychologists at work today laugh at the "bumps on the skull" idea that Gall and Spurzheim (1808) offered as the main tenet of phrenology or, as it was sometimes called, "craniology." This evolutionary outgrowth of the preexisting faculty psychology tradition seems, at first, a distant and antique idea that should best be classified among the charlatanisms of the nineteenth century. However, there are two things that suggest that such an offhand rejection of their teaching is not in order. First, few psychologists today appreciate the enormous popularity of the movement. At its time, phrenology was ranked with Darwin's theories, at least in the popular mind. Although many scientists of the time severely criticized it, they provided at least a modicum of scientific respectability to phrenology. We must acknowledge Gall and Spurzheim's proposal of one of the first specific theories of brain localization. Right or wrong (and they were certainly wrong with regard to almost every technical issue), they did associate particular brain (and to their eventual and ultimate ridicule, skull) regions to a very specific set of psychological properties or, as they had come to be known by that time—"faculties." Although one may challenge this fundamental assumption (as I do in this book), this idea still has a wide, if cryptic and implicit, acceptance in modern cognitive neuroscience.

What were the phrenological faculties? In the table of contents of his well-remembered, but thoroughly reviled book *Outlines of Phrenology,* Spurzheim (1832) provides a very crisp taxonomic outline of the psychological faculties that he and Gall had developed. Indeed, it is a taxonomy with categories of order and genus that reflect the great biological taxonomy of Linnaeus. I abstract it here as another example of the many different ways in which the putative modules of mind have been categorized.

Special Faculties of the Mind

Order I
Feelings or Affective Faculties

Genus I   Propensities

Desire to live
Alimentiveness
1. Destructiveness
2. Amativeness
3. Philoprogenitiveness
4. Adhesiveness
5. Inhabitiveness
6. Combativeness
7. Secretiveness
8. Acquisitiveness
9. Constructiveness

Genus II   Sentiments

10. Cautiousness
11. Approbativeness
12. Self-esteem
13. Benevolence
14. Reverence
15. Firmness
16. Conscientiousness
17. Hope
18. Marvellousness
19. Ideality
20. Mirthfulness
21. Imitation

Order II
Intellectual Faculties

Genus I   External Senses

Voluntary motion
Feeling
Taste
Smell
Hearing
Sight

Genus II   Perceptive Faculties

22. Individuality
23. Configuration
24. Size
25. Weight and resistance
26. Coloring
27. Locality
28. Order
29. Calculation
30. Eventuality
31. Time
32. Tune
33. Artificial language

Genus III   Reflective Faculties

34. Comparison
35. Casualty

True to the depth of his commitment to Gall and to the phrenology movement, Spurzheim went on to make quite explicit his feelings that this was an earthshaking enterprise. In addition to pointing out its importance to morality and religion, he went on to argue in the Table of Contents that

• phrenology is the true philosophy;
• phrenology is indispensable to the study of insanity;

- phrenology guides our judgment in social intercourse; and
- phrenology is the basis of education.

Despite this ostentatious puffery, the most persistent vestige of the phrenological theory is the diagram of the head on which these mental properties were mapped (figure 3.1). Modern systems of mental components make the phrenological terms and associated skull regions seem archaic and somewhat ridiculous. Nevertheless, one can still find replicas of this drawing in curiosity shops around the world. Unfortunately, it remains one of the most familiar icons of psychology to the general public.

Davies (1955) has written an elegant history of the phrenology movement, emphasizing its shortcomings, but also its profound impact on American thinking in particular. Davies points out that both Edgar Allan Poe (1809–1849) and Walt Whitman (1819–1892) were vigorous supporters of phrenology and their writing reflected many of the ideas about which Gall and Spurzheim had written in their technical works. There were also several publishers totally dedicated to publishing books on the topic and serials such as the *American Phrenological Journal* were widely read by many segments of society.

On the other hand, acceptance of phrenology was certainly not universal. Davies (1955) quotes an 1815 evaluation of Gall and Spurzheim's Phrenology by the *Edinburgh Review,* (p. 268), a prestigious scientific journal of the time: "Such is the trash, the despicable trumpery, which two men, calling themselves scientific enquirers, have the impudence gravely to present to the physiologists of the 19th century, as specimens of reasoning and induction."

Today no professional scientist takes either phrenology's list of faculties or its anatomical associations seriously. Indeed, it was the list and anatomical associations that led to the downfall of Gall and Spurzheim's system and the loss of what they might have offered to our current understanding of the relationship between the brain and mental processes. Nevertheless, one does not have to dig too deeply into modern cognitive psychology to find concepts that differ little from those of these two outcasts.

Other critics with distinguished scientific reputations during that time also joined the fray. French physician Pierre Flourens (1794–1867), an

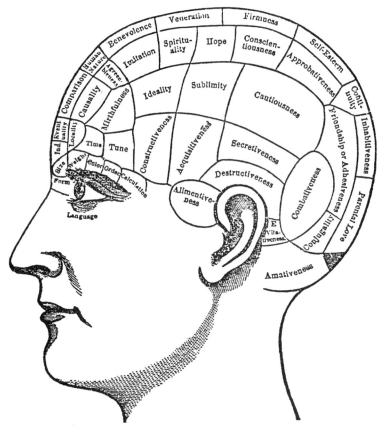

Figure 3.1
Gall and Spurzheim's "Phrenological Head" (ca. 1832). Still available in curiosity shops everywhere.

important and highly regarded experimenter whose main technique was to surgically remove portions from the brains of a number of different animals, concluded from his studies that the brain was much more integrated than the phrenologists had proposed and that psychological functions were broadly represented throughout the cerebral cortexes. The animals that Flourens operated on appeared to gradually lose their behavioral repertoire, and no location seemed to be associated with any of the mental faculties that the phrenologists had suggested. Flourens thus assumed that there was, at the very least, a close interaction between the local areas of the brain, to the extent that no area was associated exclusively with any mental process and, more, that mind was a distributed process of the brain.

Flourens was not just a scientific antagonist of phrenology; he wanted to ridicule and defame its proponents, to extirpate phrenology from the body of science as effectively as he removed a portion of the brain. For example:

Nothing is known of the intimate structure of the brain, and yet people are bold enough to trace upon it their circumscriptions, their circles, their boundaries. The external surface of the skull does not represent the brain's remarks, yet the same M. Vimont [a phrenological contemporary of Spurzheim] inscribes the following twenty-nine names on the skull of a goose! (Flourens, 1846, p. 92)

Far more important, Flourens presented what was considered to be the most effective scientific refutation of phrenology at his time. His empirical arguments had much more impact than did any speculative philosophical counterattacks. Indeed, so effective was his criticism that it inhibited thinking about brain localization for many years. Even though Flourens was correct in putting an end to the phrenological nonsense, he effectively delayed our understanding of the actual organization of the brain. It was not until the 1860s and 1870s Fritsch and Hitzig (1870), Broca (1861), Ferrier (1875), Wernicke (1874), and not until the 1950s that Penfield and his colleagues (Penfield & Jasper, 1954; Penfield & Roberts, 1959), restored the concept of a nonhomogeneous brain, and the prevailing modern view of brain organization reemerged. Nevertheless, the whole localization exercise might have been more carefully thought through and some of the nonsense might well have been avoided if cognitive neuroscience had heeded Flourens's view rather than succumbing to the forces driving the subdivision of mind into modules. Unfortunately, the localization research program was from the outset controlled by so many compellingly simple assumptions that, nonsense and all, it was very likely an inevitable step in the evolution of modern physiological psychology and its descendents. That it is now time to go on to the next step is one of the messages this book.

Thus, for all of phrenology's ridiculous correlations between mind, brain, and skull, three of its working assumptions persist to this day. If we peel off the craniology from Gall and Spurzheim's phrenology and concentrate on their notions of physiological and psychological specificity (however incorrect in detail), we can still discern the persisting influence of some of their key ideas or, perhaps, the parallel evolution of them. Specifically, the phrenologists were operating under one major and two corollary assumptions. The major assumption is one with which few scientists now disagree—the mind is a function of the brain. In a world of theological dualisms, this was a critically important, if not a completely original, assertion. In fact, Davies (1955) tells us, that the Austrian government of the time forbade Gall to lecture about phrenology just because of its theological implications.

The two persisting corollary assumptions, once again stripped of their phrenological particulars, are

1. the mind is made up of a number of independent mental processes or faculties; and
2. each of these processes is controlled or embodied in a particular region of the brain.

When examined *in abstracto,* as I have done here, phrenology seems not quite so absurd or alien to our times as when it is clothed in its specific conceptual failings, mental absurdities, and anatomical errors. Even Flourens was willing to give Gall (if not Spurzheim) credit for his other neuroanatomical accomplishments:

Gall . . . was a great anatomist. His idea of tracing the fibers of the brain is, as to the anatomy of that organ, the fundamental idea. The idea is not his own: two French anatomists, Vieussens and Pourfour du Petit, had admirably understood it long before his time; but at the period of his appearance it had been long forgotten. . . . It was a great merit in Gall to have recalled the true method of dissecting the brain. (Flourens 1846, p. 128)

(For more complete histories of phrenology, see the excellent and thoughtful analyses by Boring, 1929/1950, Klein, 1970; and Davies, 1955, among others.) For the moment, it is clear that, although the "bumps on the skull" idea is no longer with us, the idea that mental components exist and that they can be assigned to specific locations of the brain very much is. Indeed, the central problem facing cognitive neuroscience is how to deal with the unproven assumption that mental processes are as accessible, separable, and localizable as are the material aspects of the brain. Among the questions that must be asked concerning this assumption are the following:

1. Is modern cognitive neuroscience, in its search for the brain locations of mental processes, in some cryptic manner, a resurrection of some of the phrenological ideas (minus the absurd craniology) that properly were rejected long ago?
2. Do modern scientific psychological findings support the concept of isolatable mental components?
3. Do modern scientific anatomical and physiological findings support the specialization of various regions of the brain?
4. Will modern brain localization studies founder on the same intellectual reef that phrenology did—unjustified assignment of questionable psychological components or modules to particular regions of the brain?

3.1.4 Kleist's Map

In one of the modern manifestations of phrenological thinking, Kleist (1934) drew the map of brain functions shown in figure 3.2. The century of scientific knowledge that had accumulated between the work of Gall and Spurzheim and his own made the particular psychological processes listed on Kleist's chart different from those of his predecessors. Many of the locales shown in Kleist's map reflect new knowledge about the sensory and motor aspects of the brain. Nevertheless, there is still more than just a vestige of the old phrenological categories exhibited here. We see such notable faculties as "mood" and "constructive action" as well as specific locations for much more modern ideas such as "visual attention." Clearly, the idea that particular brain regions are the locales of highly specific mental processes was still at work in the 1930s and, as we shall see later in this chapter, continue to be important into the twenty-first century.

It is interesting to note, however, Kleist's map was probably well out of the mainstream of psychological thinking at the time. When this diagram was published, behaviorism was at the peak of its influence. Kleist, however, was a neurologist, and the vested financial and theoretical interests of these surgeons of the brain largely depended, then as now, on the assumption that mental processes can be localized in

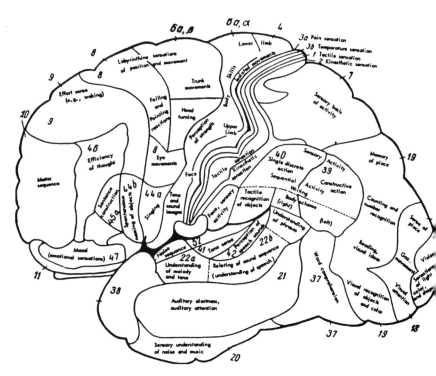

Figure 3.2
Kleist's 1934 diagram of the human brain depicting the regions in which the various cognitive modules and faculties were supposed to be located.

the brain. His map illuminates how forces extraneous to pure science (e.g., the vested interests of neurologists) can influence scientific thought.

3.1.5 Welker's Taxonomy

Many other attempts to organize mental processes into a coherent scheme have been offered from time to time by psychologists and neuroscientists. Not all have gone on to specifically associate their categories of psychological processes with particular brain regions, but almost all have adopted the second corollary assumption of phrenology mentioned earlier—that the mind is made up of a set of independent processes that can be individually identified and perhaps separately assayed.

One of the most interesting was the schema presented by Welker (1976; see table 3.1).

Welker's taxonomy is made up of a collection of processes—mental activities that overlap to a considerable degree. Each represents a naming and identification of some functional attribute of mental activity. As a neuroscientist, Welker might have been willing to associate each of these interpersonal mental states with a neural location, but this is not certain. Even so, there is in this taxonomy an implicit suggestion that the mental processes are not quite so independent and separable as was judged to be the case in many of the earlier taxonomies of mental activity.

3.1.6 Fodor's Input Processes

Fodor's thoughtful essay (1983) on modularity led him to a particular point of view concerning the categories-of-mind conundrum. Likening the mind to a computer, he suggested that any acceptable and plausible taxonomy of mental modules must be limited to what he referred to as the "input processes." Although his taxonomy of possible taxonomies of mental modules, as we saw earlier, accepts "transducers," "input systems," and "central processors" as the usually acknowledged classes of modules, only the input system modules have sufficient scientific standing from Fodor's point of view to be endowed with any measurable and verifiable form of classificatory separateness. In this regard, many of us believe he was correct, although we would add "output modules" as possible candidates for taxonomic reality.

Each input mechanism, linked as it is to the anchor of a particular physical stimulus and to the specific modality sensitive to that stimulus, is activated by a distinctly different type of physical energy or "adequate" stimulus. That we can also trace an afferent signal at least partially on its course from a receptor to the central nervous system along physically distinguishable pathways adds direct empirical evidence of modularity in the form of anatomical separateness in a way that probably never can be achieved with higher-level cognitive processes.

Furthermore, the dimensionality of each sensory modality is well defined. For example, vision is made up of channels or modules sensitive

Table 3.1
Welker's Compilation of Mental States

Conceptual category	Specific concepts
Inactive states	Sleeping, unawareness, unconsciousness, inattentiveness
Arousal processes	Activation, arousal, alerting
Awake states	Awareness, consciousness, alertness, vigilance
Attentive states	Alerting, attending, expectancy, scanning, focusing, detection, vigilance, sensitivity, orientation
Specific reactivity processes	Mobilization, threshold, set, preference, aversion, differentiation, image, expectancy, fixed action pattern, scanning, focusing, attitude, perception detection, hallucination, goal orientation, sensitivity, excitation, orientation, hallucination, goal orientation, sensitvity, excitation, orientation, discrimination, tendency, illusion, displacement, identification
Cognitive states and processes	Perception, thinking, planning, purpose, judgment, guessing, trying, will, wish, hypothesis, evaluation, imitation, cognitive content, expectancy, set, decision, insight, optimizing, competence, self actualizing, recognition, reasoning, understanding, concept formation, abstraction, symbol formation, cognitive map, cognitive model, ideation, aim, creativity, innovation, volition, plasticity, confidence, certainty, effectance, choice, purpose, assumption, conception, goal orientation, seeking
Integrative processes	Generalization, consolidation, judgment, introspection, deduction, homeostasis, programming, mediation, repression, inhibition, facilitation, insight, fixation, plasticity, closure, abstraction, assimilation, feedback, planning, ideation, learning, transaction, creativity, conditioning, symbol formation, association, integration, summation, irradiation, reafference, displacement, incubation, regulation
Experiential processes	Perception, detection, insight, confidence, introspection, perception, discrimination, surprise, confusion, competence, knowing, symbolizing, feeling, empathy, knowing

Table 3.1
(continued)

Conceptual category	Specific concepts
Motivational processes	Energy, attitude, compulsion, interest, homeostasis, optimizing, thirst, love, aspiration, hope, perseverance, craving, disposition, appetite, preference, aversion, fear, hate, joy, will, wish, drive, need, habit strength, volition, urge, curiosity, hunger, anger, anxiety, value
Affective states	Tension, boredom, sensitivity, joy, emotion, anxiety, conflict, surprise, satiation, anxiety, love, preference, aversion, impact, desire, passion, amusement, sentiment, longing
Learning processes	Discrimination, familiarization, symbolization, consolidation, incubation, learning, insight, fixation, abstraction, imprinting, conditioning, generalization, deduction
Reinforcement processes	Impact, meaning, significance, reward, reinstatement, reinforcement, inhibition, suppression, repression, trace, engram, facilitation, closure, feedback
Other change-type processes and states	Adaptation, adaptation level, satiation, suppression, feedback, forgetting, creativity, innovation, plasticity, inhibition, recovery, displacement, habituation, dishabituation, accommodation, disinhibition
Fixation states and processes	Persistence, fixation, instinct, habit, generalization, fixed action pattern, stereotypy, consistency
Memory processes	Memory (immediate, delayed), recall, habit, recognition, amnesia, forgetting, retention, trace, engram, storage, retrieval
Ability states	Discrimination, learning set, perception, achievement, adaptability, habit, acuity, capability, capacity
Maturational processes and states	Critical period, growth, differentiation, readiness, histogenesis, neurogenesis, regionalization, induction, morphogenesis, pattern formation, organization

Source: Welker, 1976, adapted with the permission of Lawrence Erlbaum Associates, Inc.

to color, brightness, edges, and so on. These attributes or dimensions are not hypothetical constructs inferred from behavior; rather, they are empirical observations measured with the units of the physical world.⁵ Both the complex integrative role and the symbolic interpretive roles played by higher-level psychological processes suggest that physical anchors (including isomorphic codes) are lost at that stage of information processing, the direct physiological evidence is elusive, and, worst of all, the anchors cannot meet the standards of an observational science. Because a thought may be triggered by a spoken word, by a visual image, or even by a very abstract symbol, we can establish neither its links to the physical representation nor its anatomical locus.

Fodor subsequently asserted that although the concept of a taxonomy of central processes or modules is deeply ingrained in psychological theory, it leaves the list open to too many other kinds of ill-defined central activities. Closure could never be achieved with such a system. This is another way of making the same point made by Skinner (1963, p. 957)—"A final objection is that the way stations [central cognitive components] are so often simply invented." It is also another expression of the conjecture offered by automata theorists (specifically, Moore, 1956) that because the number of alternative internal mechanisms is infinite, no sequence of experiments can rule them out when one is studying a "black" box such as the mind-brain system.

Fodor (1983) then offered a series of arguments that support the concept that, at the very least, input systems can be considered modular:

1. Input systems are each defined by a separate sensory modality;
2. Our awareness of sensory messages is obligatory. Although we can choose to close our eyes and not see, or not to listen, we cannot choose not to identify a visual or oral signal once we perceive it.
3. We are able to perceive only the output of input systems and have no knowledge of the codes or interpretive processes that led to a particular perception;

5. It is not generally appreciated that there is no way to go from psychophysical observations to the exact neural or chemical mechanisms that may be involved in some sensory process. Psychophysical data and molar behavior are neutral with regard to the underlying mechanisms. Nowhere is this better illustrated than in the controversy between the Young-Helmholtz trichromatic and the Hering opponent color theories of the nature of the color receptors.

4. Their speed precludes processing analyses;

5. They are relatively impermeable to cognitive (top-down) influences, that is, it is almost always impossible to override the immediate perceptual outcome of an input system—we always "see" the Poggendorf illusion no matter how well we know it is an illusion;

6. The output of an input system is "close" to the stimulus;

7. Input systems, much more closely and obviously than the central processes, are clearly associated with particular receptors, neural structures, and regions of the brain;

8. When they break down, input systems produce highly specific behavioral distortions; and finally,

9. The ontogeny of the input systems seems to be very similar from one person to another.

Fodor concluded not only that the input processes (which would be classified as "vertical" in his taxonomy of taxonomies) can and indeed must be studied from a modular point of view, but that most central processes cannot be. He wrote further, but without great detail or evidence, of the distributed and nonlocal properties of these central processes and thus of the difficulty of identifying "modules" with such a great degree of overlap and interaction.

Fodor (1983, p. 128) further supported the arguments that, for something to be considered a module, the underlying entities should "behave in isolation, in something like the way that they behave in situ." Unfortunately, the assumption that modules so behave is ubiquitous throughout cognitive psychology, even though it is probably totally incorrect (Pachella, 1974).

It is clear the Fodor saw the quasi-independent mental components or modules of many psychobiologists as being strikingly close to what others have called mental "faculties." Although these and other scientists may think that the leap from sensory input modules to modular cognitive faculties is not great, Fodor's arguments against central mental modularity speak to the contrary. And I, for one, think he is correct.

3.1.7 Chomsky's Linguistic Module

One of the most active psychological theoreticians of mind is the linguist Chomsky, whose studies led him to suggest that language development and acquisition were controlled by a particular mechanism, a module, or a component of mind separable and distinct from other components. Chomsky's ideas have been widely considered not only in linguistics but also in psychology and can be identified as another argument against the thesis that mind is holistic in nature but rather, governed by the properties of separable traits or abilities. Thus Chomsky joins others who interpret the mind to be made up of quasi-independent psychological organs or, in an older terminology, "faculties." As he puts in it an oft-quoted paragraph (Chomsky, 1980, p. 3):

We may usefully think of the language faculty, the number faculty, and other "mental organs," as analogous to the heart or the visual system or the system of motor coordination and planning. . . . In short, there seems little reason to insist that the brain is unique in the biological world, in that it is unstructured and undifferentiated, developing on the basis of uniform principles of growth or learning—say those of some learning theory, or of some yet-to-be-conceived general-purpose learning strategy that are common to all domains.

Unfortunately, to the best of my knowledge, Chomsky did not develop any taxonomy of "organs of mind" other than the one underlying speech—his particular research interest. It would have been fascinating to have seen how he transcribed these ideas to other psychological functions and domains.

Although one can easily agree with Chomsky that the brain is not homogeneous and that learning cannot be an universal explanation of the varieties of human speech, his extrapolation to the idea that all mental processes are equally modular is unsupported and remains one of the great unresolved issues in psychology.

3.1.8 The Cognitive "Faculties"

As we can see from our brief review thus far, a persistent premise of psychology, from its inception, has been that mental processes are separable components that can be assayed independently and analyzed. Psychologists such as Donders (1868/1969) and S. Sternberg (1969a) have used methods to identify such modular components as "decision time" or "response selection time" or to distinguish between serial and parallel processing. Their findings and interpretations represent one body of evidence that has been used to resolve the debate between what has been characterized as the "unity of mind versus faculty" controversy.

Even accepting the utility and convenience, if not the necessity, of having some kind of systematic dissection of the mind into components for research purposes, the issue still remains—Are these hypothetical components real or simply a convenient means of emphasizing how we are organizing our experiments? Modern cognitive psychologists usually finesse or ignore this important question. By so doing, they all too passively accept the twin assumptions of analyzability of mind and the intrinsic isolability of mental modules.

Another historical example of the ubiquity of the modular mind approach can be found in our pedagogic literature. Psychology textbooks have for some years used modularity as their main organizing theme. Whether such an implied taxonomy is psychobiological reality or just a useful teaching aid is at the crux of the issue with which this present book deals. One of the earliest modern texts of psychology, that of Bain (1859) is organized in terms of an extensive listing of putative psychological processes generally categorized as either components of emotion or volitional will.

This theme, if not the exact components, continues to this day. If we examine the contents of the first (and perhaps definitive) modern cognitive text (Neisser, 1967), we see what is clearly a modern taxonomy of psychological processes and modules. Neisser includes the following categories of cognitive processes as the topics for the chapters in his book:

- Iconic storage and verbal coding;
- Pattern recognition;
- Focal attention and figural synthesis;
- Words as visual patterns;
- Visual memory;
- Speech perception;
- Echoic memory and auditory perception;
- Active verbal memory;
- Sentences;
- Memory and thought.

Twenty-seven years later, Matlin (1994) tabulated the content matter of cognitive psychology as follows:

- Perceptual processes;
- Models of memory;
- Sensory memory and short-term memory;
- Long-term memory;
- Imagery;
- General knowledge;
- Language comprehension: listening and reading;
- Language production: speaking, writing, and bilingualism;
- Problem solving and creativity logical reasoning and decision making;
- Cognitive development.

The problem is that what may originally have been a pedagogic tool has become reified as a taxonomy of actual mental process for which a specific locus can reasonably be sought in the brain.

3.1.9 Shallice's Mental Structure
Another contemporary proponent of modularity is Shallice (1988). Arguing from the database of neuropsychology—the study of the behavioral effects of brain lesions in human patients—he suggested that there is a system of mental components that are independent of each other and, even beyond that independence, are essentially blind and deaf to each other's presence. Shallice's model of mental structure is one of the few explicit attempts in recent years to develop such a taxonomy and he is an articulate champion of the modular approach. (Later in this chapter, I will consider some of the arguments he presented for his concept of mental structure.)

For the moment, it is important to appreciate that Shallice's neuropsychology-based model is incomplete: it was based on surveys of the behavioral consequences of fortuitous damage to particular regions of the brain. Nevertheless, despite the limits and constraints under which his taxonomy was created, Shallice's work represents an important effort to create a taxonomy of mental processes or "faculties."

A sampling of the categories of mental activities identified by Shallice (1988) as a result of human neuropsychological studies includes

1. peripheral dyslexias;
2. central dyslexias;
3. agraphias;

4. phonological alexias;
5. language operations (aphasias);
6. amnesia (semantic memory);
7. amnesia (episodic memory);
8. attention disorders;
9. neglect dyslexia;
10. problem-solving disorders;
11. supervision failures;
12. sensory disorders;
13. akinesia;
14. anosognosia;
15. contention scheduling;
16. prospopagnosia.

Each of these neuropsychological deficits defines a particular psychological entity according to Shallice. Amnesia, for example, is the absence of memory of one kind or another; memory, in this case, is the mental component or faculty of "interest." Although some of the processes these deficits identify are familiar and some arcane, this list of mental capabilities represented to Shallice an ensemble of relatively separable mental modules, faculties, or components whose function can be reduced by brain injuries to specific portions of the brain.

Shallice was explicit in asserting that the sources of these defective mental processes are isolable and that this set of mental categories is based on localized lesions, but the interpretation of the significance of human neuropsychological findings is subject to some very important criticisms. Many of these criticisms were spelled out by Shallice, to his credit, as we shall see when I return to consider some of the problems he identified when mental structures are inferred from this kind of data.

3.1.10 Intelligence and the Factor Analysis Approach

The analysis of mental activity into components reached what many consider to be its apex with the development of the powerful mathematical tool called "factor analysis" by workers such as Spearman (1904), Holzinger and Harman (1941), and Thurstone (1931, 1947). Each of these psychologists had their repertoire of research tools broadened by their unusual (for psychologists) mathematical training. The main idea behind the factor analysis approach is to carry out a series of "ability" tests and then to develop a matrix of the correlations that exist between all pairwise combinations of these tests. Correlations among the various tests are supposed to indicate the presence of common mental abilities that account for their common scores. The correlation matrix is then transformed to reduce the variance among these correlations into a much smaller set of "factors" that presumably map onto the underlying mental abilities.

In other words, the complex set of relations represented in the correlation matrix is condensed into a small number of principal axes or components that represent what are assumed to be "multiple" or "primary" factors or components of the underlying mental system. This is accomplished by any one of several methods developed since Spearman's original procedure was introduced. (For technical details on how to carry out a factor analysis, see any one of extensive library of texts now available on the subject.)

Although there are many special problems associated with the application of factor analysis to intelligence testing and the study of individual differences that I do not consider in detail here, the method represents a persistent and popular theme of psychological research. Like many of the other taxonomies discussed, the factor analysis approach also seeks to uncover a set of real mental components. Perhaps better than any other, however, it represents a rigorous and formal method for suggesting what these mental components might be. Whatever mathematical peculiarities may exist that may mitigate the reality of these suggested modules or factors, such a formal approach still is to be preferred to armchair inferences in the same way that computational models are to be preferred over purely ad hoc verbal hypotheses. In making this assertion, however, it is also important to remember that, however powerful the mathematics, it is still fundamentally neutral: many plausible alternatives can, in principle, be inferred from the same set of data.

Over the years there has been considerable contention over factor analysis methods. Although I shall not consider the details of the controversy surrounding this approach to the discovery of mental components or abilities, others have pointed out some of the reasons that different data sets are factored in different ways to produce different theories of mental components. For example, R. J. Sternberg (1977, pp. 23–24) discusses some of the factors bearing on these theoretical disagreements:

1. The method of factor analysis used;
2. The model on which the method is based; specifically, the difference between a component model, which cannot distinguish between specific factors and common factors, versus factor model, which does permit distinctions between specific and common factors;
3. The criterion level at which a factor analysis is stopped;
4. The sample of mental tests included in the factor analysis;
5. The subject population sampled;
6. The interpretation of the mathematical data;
7. The criteria and methods used to determine the rotation of the data matrix (the "major source of differences among theories" according to Sternberg).

Indeed, statisticians were among the initial critics who agreed with Sternberg on the importance of factor 7. They argued that a matrix of correlations could be rotated in so many different ways that it would always be possible to find some emergent factors that supported one's preexisting assumptions. This criticism of arbitrariness has been partially countered in recent years by new methods and techniques that make the method more dependent on the actual data obtained from the ensemble of ability tests. However, many other criticisms of the factor analysis method as an entrée into the complexities of the human mind continue to be salient.

In addition to the danger of creating hypothetical constructs that do not exist, there is also the danger of ignoring components that might actually be present. Some critics have pointed out that it is not possible always to find a factor that can account for the variance in any given set of data. Thus the method has also been criticized for being insensitive to the existence of what otherwise would have to be assumed to be "real" psychological modules or components.

Mathematical and statistical esoterica aside, there is one general point we must keep in mind—the logical leap from the mathematical elicitation of the factors to the assumption that these factors actually represent biologically and psychologically significant aspects of the underlying mental activity is a theoretical and interpretive leap, not an empirical one, no matter how strong the factor seems to be nor how powerful or rigorous the mathematical method. Indeed, it is the illusion of truth that emerges from the formality of the method that may be its greatest defect.

Thus the essential question in the present context is—Are these factors prima facie evidence of actual underlying psychological components, or are they just condensed descriptions of the complex of behaviors assayed by the tests? Given the very large number of alternative taxonomies identified by the various factor analysts (a step that goes beyond the computation of the factors by the various analysis methods), it remains questionable whether there is any direct link between the output of the analytic method and the nature of the psychobiological entities that may account for the test results. The most basic issues seem not to have been resolved. For example, there is still considerable debate in the field concerning whether there is a general intelligence factor or just a collection of more or less independent intellectual skills and abilities.

Factor analysis is a tool that has been used largely by students of intelligence. It is curious how little contact there has been between this school of psychology and cognitive psychologists concerned with very much the same issues and components.[6] Although the language of the two groups may differ, both are attempting to understand the architecture of human mentation. Perhaps what most distinguishes the two is that students of intelligence are more interested in measuring the differences between individuals, whereas cognitive psychologists are more interested in the similarities and generalities that characterize human thought.

A trivial methodological difference also tends to separate the two schools of research. Intelligence testers are more likely to use paper-and-pencil tests, whereas cognitive psychologists generally prefer to use pooled statistical estimates of "reaction time" or "proportion correct" as their performance indicators. Despite their differences, however, both

---

6. A conceptually similar method, often used in cognitive studies, is multidimensional scaling (Torgenson, 1958), which defines clusters of related properties in terms of similarities. These clusters have been invoked to suggest the existence of underlying sensory or perceptual components in particular. Another method with an identical goal (and quite similar to modern cladistic methods) attempts to develop a tree structure of relationships (Jardine, Jardine, & Sibson, 1967). Still other methods exist having much the same strengths and weaknesses as factor analysis.

groups clearly are pursuing their primary goal of identifying the components of whatever it is that we call "mind."

Although the controversy about the meaning of factor analysis outcomes continues, many taxonomies of mental abilities and faculties have appeared as a result of the application of this technique. In the following subsections, I consider only a few of the many approaches to the problem of classifying intelligence traits that have been presented over the years. Some of the older approaches, although not explicitly "factor analytical" in a formal mathematical sense, were important intellectual antecedents of the technique as it ultimately evolved.

Galton's Taxonomy of Mental Abilities   Efforts to classify intelligence into a system of components predated the development of factor analysis. Testing to determine the abilities of specific individuals has developed apace with experimental psychology's general models of cognitive processing. The classic tale is that the astronomer Friedrich Wilhelm Bessel (1784–1846) noticed discrepancies between the measurements made by different assistants when they were reporting stellar transits across a reticle line on the eyepiece of a telescope. Bessel and others made extensive studies of these discrepancies and proposed that they were due, not to variability of the transit times, but rather to variations in the observers' responses—the so-called personal equation. By applying simple statistical measures such as computations of the mean value, the astronomers were able to compensate for these discrepancies and to produce the most precise measurements of stellar transit times available until modern electronic instruments became available. As Boring (1929/1950, p. 147) points out, the research underlying the personal equation corrections were, in effect, reaction time experiments. Psychologists such as Wundt and Donders almost immediately followed up on this insight with extensive studies using this still-popular measure of human mental processing.

Individual differences were also the main interest of the remarkable Francis Galton (1822–1911), one of the first to emphasize the importance of statistical measures of correlation and distributions as useful tools for comparing individuals and summarizing data. Indeed, long before the days of computer image processing, Galton suggested a surprisingly modern superimposition technique for averaging pictures of faces that he applied to the reconstruction of the face of Alexander the Great. His idea—to average the common features of a set of images depicted on coins to develop the real face of Alexander—is a precursor of modern techniques that have been used, for example, to discover that the most attractive faces are the most average (Langlois & Roggman, 1990).

Galton was an avid observer of human nature, but from the point of view of a naturalist. Rather than restricting his data collection to the laboratory, he sought out a sample of people to whom to apply various tests and measurements—not all of which were cognitive or intelligence-related. He was also interested in color blindness and what we would now call ergonomic measurements.

Although Galton (1883) did not develop an explicit list or taxonomy of mental abilities in his best-known work on the "Human Faculty," he clearly felt that human mental activity was divisible into components:

The living world does not consist of a repetition of similar elements, but an endless variety of them, that have grown, body and soul, through selective influences into close adaptation to their contemporaries, and to the physical circumstances of the localities they inhabit. . . .

I do not, however, offer a list of them, but shall confine myself to directing attention to a few heredity characteristics of a marked kind. (p. 2)

Galton then went on to discuss such psychological variables as "Energy," "Sensitivity," "Discriminability," and "Character" (contrasting men, who are "straightforward," and women, who are "coy and capricious" (attributions offensive to our modern tastes.) Elsewhere, he spoke of "conscience" and "instincts—gregarious and slavish" and wrote extensively on the "faculty" of imagery. He returned again and again to the express derivatives of the basic idea that there are separable components to the human character that can be examined independently by the student of human nature.

Although Galton exemplified an increasingly obsolescent way of thinking, one unacceptable in several important respects to current thought, he played an important role in the history of thinking about the mind; his role as an ingenious inventor of statistical techniques also cannot be overlooked. For our purposes, however, his work illustrates yet again the pervasiveness of the idea of separable attributes, modules, or faculties of human cognition.

Spearman and Thurstone's Factor Analysis of Mental Abilities   In considering factor analysis, the primary issue is, of course, what is being extracted when one rotates a matrix to produce a factor. Intelligence, like all other psychological parameters, dimensions, or components, is difficult to define, and many of us fall back on Boring's operational definition (or something functionally and denotatively synonymous with it). The debate over whether there is a general factor of intelligence that acts as an umbrella for all of the other individual abilities (or that indeed supplants them) continues with great vigor even today. As we have seen, authors such as Chomsky (1980) feel that the various mental abilities are very sharply demarcated and that no general intelligence factor must be invoked to explain language skills.

A pioneer in applying factor analysis, Spearman (1923) believed that, despite the apparent confusion among those who identified a host of psychological components, a kind of consistency at the most fundamental level had persisted over the centuries. He noted that the classic and persistent taxonomy included intellect, perception, memory, and imagination (p. 25). He went on to consider the "modern" additions to this brief list, such as planning, censorship, and selective thinking, and concluded that "modern psychology would appear to have added astonishingly little to the orthodox doctrinal foundation" (p. 26). Nevertheless, by the time he finished his book. Spearman had developed a taxonomy of cognitive processes of his own. Although he refers to them as "principles" in his text, it is clear that he is alluding to mental components when he says:

All of these cognitive processes, both noegentic and anoegentic, are aggregated together in immense numbers, just as are the organic cells of material organisms. Sometimes, notwithstanding, the single units remain still easily distinguishable. But at other times—often even when the whole operation superficially seems most simple—they may be crowded together so closely that to discriminate one from another demands the greatest care. (p. 347)[7]

It is fascinating to note the first suggestion of nonanalyzability by someone whose entire career had been based on the analyzability of intelligence (if not mind) into components.

---

7. "Noegentic" and "anogentic" are neologisms suggested by Spearman (1923) to avoid the connotational baggage of other terms of the time. *Noegentic* processes generate "new items in the field of cognition" (p. 61), whereas *anoegentic* processes depend on previously encountered concepts and experiences.

Spearman's analytic taxonomy was based on a distinction between qualitative (noegentic) and quantitative (anoegentic) dimensions that seem archaic to us nowadays. Nevertheless, it is clear that his taxonomy of cognitive principles is no better or worse than any other of his time, and it is even hard to denigrate it in the face of current taxonomies. He postulated the following seven basic "principles" (Spearman, 1923, p. 348):

Qualitative	*Quantitative*
Apprehensibility of experience	General energy
Educability of relations	Retentivity
Educability of correlates	Fatigue
	Connotative control
	Primordial potency

From these principles, many other "compound" operations could be constructed including such entities as "integration," "accuracy," "perseveration," and "attention."

My point here once again, is that there has been and continues to be a plethora of classification systems of cognitive processes, and that none has stood the test of time. Furthermore, there is little reason to assume any of our contemporary taxonomies is likely to do so. It is difficult indeed to localize a process or a function in a particular part of the brain when that process or function is so ephemeral that it does not outlast even a single generation. Each of the examples presented here uses its own vocabulary and invokes specific mental components that usually differ from those in the earlier or succeeding generations. The few terms that persist are mainly associated either with the sensory mechanisms suggested by Fodor (1983) or with the classic triumvirate of sensory, cognitive, and response processes.

Spearman's contributions (1904, 1923) were among the first to offer a formal method for identifying these ephemeral components—the technique of factor analysis. His interests, as noted, were mainly in the field of intelligence and, from this vantage point, he had some germane things to say about the analyzability of mental activity. One of the most prescient and curiously inconsistent (Spearman, 1923, p. 351) was that the procedure in testing is to apply a large group of tests together, never regarding the results of one separately, but throwing all into a common pool. The marks obtained by the testee from such a mixture can no more be expected to indicate his degree of success with any particular constituent than, say, the weighing of a pile of baggage is able to tell the weight of any particular portmanteau in it.

What Spearman was suggesting was essentially a corollary of the "black box" (Moore, 1956) limitation on analysis. The internal contradiction between this quotation and the other main theme of his life's work—the elicitation of the "factors" underlying intelligence—is thus as notable as it is perplexing.

Spearman (1923, p. 351) went on to assert the existence of his pet concept—a general intelligence factor: "What really is measured—and alone can ever be measured—by such a pooling of miscellaneous items is the factor (should one exist) which, amid continual diversification otherwise, persistently enters into them all." Is it possible that deep within this particular psychologist may beat the cryptic heart of an antireductionist and behaviorist?

Carroll's Concordance of Cognitive Factors Generated by Factor Analysis   In what certainly must be considered to be the definitive historical review in the field, Carroll (1993) has heroically surveyed the factor analysis movement, summarizing the enormous complexity of the system of cognitive components that has emerged from the application of this method in modern times. Table 3.2 displays the extent to which psychologists can go in creating hypothetical mental components. Carroll's taxonomy does not map onto any of the others we deal with in this chapter; it remains as idiosyncratic as any other and thus represents, by virtue of its enormous size, a divergence from, rather than a convergence toward, a consensus about the hypothesized components of human mental activity.

Sternberg's Cognitive Components   One of the most interesting and certainly most up-to-date approaches linking the intelligence and cognitive psychologists movements together is to be found in the work of R. J. Sternberg (1977, 1988). In 1977, this prolific student of intelligence and cognition reviewed a number of "componential" theories of analogical

Table 3.2
Carroll's Compilation of Cognition Components

Factor code	Factor name	French, 1951, code, name (no. of studies)	1963 ETS kit code, name	1976 ETS kit code, name	Guilford factors	Cattell universal index
GF ("fluid intelligence") factors						
I	Induction	I:Induction (9)	I:Induction	I:Induction	(Several)	T5
RL	Logical reasoning	D:Deduction (37)	Rs:Syllogistic reasoning	RL:Logical reasoning	EMR?	T4
RG	General reasoning	—	R:General reasoning	RG:General reasoning	CMS	T34
IP	Integrative process	In:Integration (1)	—	IP:Integrative process	—	—
J	Judgment	J:Judgment (5)	—	—	—	—
PL	Planning	Pl:Planning (4)	—	—	—	—
Gc (crystallized intelligence) factors:						
V	Verbal knowledge	V:Verbal comprehension (46)	V:Verbal comprehension	V:Verbal comprehension	CMU	T13
N	Numerical facility	N:Number (35)	N:Number facility	N:Number facility	NSI,MSI?	T10
Gv (general visual perception) factors:						
—	—	S:Space (44)	—	—	—	—
SO	Spatial orientation	SO:Spatial orientation (4)	S:Spatial orientation	S:Spatial orientation	CFS	T11
VZ	Spatial visualization	Vi:Visualization (16)	Vs:Visualization	VZ:Visualization	CFT	T14
CS	Speed of closure	GP:Gestalt perception (2)	Cs:Speed of closure	CS:Speed of closure	CFU	T3
CF	Flexibility of closure	GF:Gestalt flexibility	Cf:Flexibility of closure	CF:Flexibility of closure	NFT	T2
SS	Spatial scanning	—	Sa:Spatial scanning	SS:Spatial scanning	CFI	—
LE	Length estimation	LE:Length estimation (4)	Le:Length estimation	—	—	—
CV	Verbal closure	—	—	CV:Verbal closure	—	—
P	Perceptual speed	P:Perceptual speed (34)	P:Perceptual speed	P:Perceptual speed	(ESU,EFU)	T12

Gv (general visual perception) factors:

PA	Perceptual alternations	PA:Perceptual alternations (1)	—	—	—	—
IL	Figure illusions	FI:Figure illusions (1)	—	—	—	—

Ga ("general auditory perception") factors:

AUI	Auditory integration	AI:Auditory integration (1)	—	—	—	—
AUR	Auditory resistance	AR:Auditory resistance (1)	—	—	—	—
LO	Loudness	Lo:Loudness (1)	—	—	—	—
PQ	Pitch quality	PQ:Pitch quality (1)	—	—	—	—

Gm ("general memory")

MA	Associative memory	M:Associative memory (16)	Ma:Associative memory	MA:Associative memory	MSR	T7
MS	Memory span	Sm:Span memory (2)	Ms:Memory span	MS:Memory span	MSU,MSS?	—
MV	Visual memory	VM:Visual memory (4)	MV:Visual memory	—	—	—
MMU	Musical memory	MM:Musical memory (2)	—	—	—	—

Fluency and production factors:

FA	Associational fluency	—	FA:Associational fluency	FA:Associational fluency	DMR	—
FE	Expressional fluency	FE:Fluency of expression (3)	Fe:Expressional fluency	FE:Expressional fluency	DMS	—
FI	Ideational fluency	IF:Ideation fluency (4)	Fi:Ideational fluency	FI:Ideational fluency	DMU	T6
FW	Word fluency	W:Word fluency (8)	Fw:Word fluency	FW:Word fluency	DSU	T15
XU	Flexibility of use	—	Xs:Semantic spontaneous flexibility	XU:Flexibility of use	DMC	—
XF	Figural flexibility	—	Xa:Figural adaptive flexibility	XF:Figural flexibility	DFT	—
NA	Naming speed	Na:Naming (1)	—	—	—	—
FS	Speed fluency	PS:Public speaking (1)	—	—	—	—

Table 3.2
(continued)

Fluency and production factors:

FS	Speed fluency	PS:Public speaking (1)	—	—	—	—
SA	Speed of association	SA:Speed of association (2)	—	—	—	—
O	Originality	—	—	O:Originality	DMT	—
RE	Semantic redefinition	—	—	Re:Semantic redefinition	NMT	—
SEP	Sensitivity to problems	—	—	Sep:Sensitivity to problems	EMI	—
				lems		

Speed factors (not otherwise classified):

SD	Speed	Sp:Speed (3)	—	—
SDJ	Speed of judgment	SJ:Speed of judgment (1)	—	—

Selected psychomotor factors:

AIMG	Aiming	Ai:Aiming (7)	—
AMB	Ambidexterity	Am:Ambidexterity (2)	—
SDAR	Speed of articulation	Ar:Articulation (1)	—
FD	Finger dexterity	FD:Finger dexterity (11)	—
MD	Manual dexterity	MD:Manual dexterity (4)	—
PC	Psychomotor coordination	PC:Psychomotor coordination(10)	—
RT	Reaction time	RT:Reaction time (2)	—
TA	Tapping	Ta:Tapping (3)	—

Miscellaneous affective-cognitive factors:

AT	Attention	At:Attention (4)	—
CA	Carefulness	C:Carefulness (6)	—
PE	Persistence	Pe:Persistence (2)	—
PN	Perseveration	Pn:Perseveration (1)	—

reasoning, which required one to solve D for, given A, B, and C, an analogy of the form A is to B as C is to D. Although only one small facet of human mental activity, analogical reasoning represents a well-structured arena in which to seek out possible components of mind. Sternberg (1977, p. 135) suggested six cognitive processing steps.

1. Encoding: Identify the attributes of each term in the problem.
2. Inference: Discover the rule relating A to B.
3. Mapping: Discover the rule relating C to D.
4. Application: Generate the rule to form D.
5. Justification: Test the validity of the rules so generated.
6. Preparation-Response: Prepare for the solution and perform it.

Sternberg (1988, p. 269) later expanded on this theoretical base to develop the following, a more complete model of mental components:

1. Metacomponents (higher-order control processes)

a. Recognizing that a problem exists.

b. Recognizing the nature of the problem.

c. Selecting a set of performance components.

d. Selecting a strategy incorporating the performance components.

e. Selecting appropriate mental representations.

f. Allocating attentional resources.

g. Keeping place during the performance of the task.

h. Interpreting feedback about task performance.

2. Performance components (processes used to execute the steps in a task). These include the six processing component steps of Sternberg, 1977, tabulated above.

3. Knowledge acquisition components (learning and storing processes)

a. Selective encoding to distinguish relevant from irrelevant information.

b. Selective combining of relevant information to produce novel information.

c. Selective comparing of novel, combined information to previously stored information.

Sternberg (1988, p. 270) went on add a list of human mental capabilities that are more elaborate and complex expressions of the information-processing components just tabulated: "verbal ability, quantitative ability, inductive and deductive reasoning abilities, learning and memory abilities, and spatial ability."

It is interesting to note that any of Sternberg's suggested "abilities" and "components" might be considered to be potential candidates for a comprehensive taxonomy of psychological processes. Indeed, we have seen already how these terms or their near synonyms appear throughout our search for conceptual and classificatory order. Unfortunately, orderly cladistic coherence does not yet appear in this mélange of idiosyncratic attempts to define psychological concepts. The students of intelligence I have discussed thus far have developed their own terminology for the "abilities," just as the cognitive experimentalists have.

Gardner's Multiple Intelligence Hypothesis   Another contemporary psychologist who has also developed a specific taxonomy of mental process is Gardner (1983), who includes the following "kinds" of intelligences:

Object-free intelligence
Linguistic
Musical

Object-related intelligence
Logical-mathematical
Spatial
Bodily-kinesthetic
Person-related
Interpersonal
Intrapersonal

To which an eighth category has been added (Gardner, 1999):

Naturalist.

As specific as Gardner is in classifying the various kinds of intelligences, he hesitates to apply such a scheme to other aspects of human mentation. Indeed, his argument is that the categories in his taxonomy are only valuable when one is concerned with how we process objects in the world, and that to extend this classification system to mental processes such as "personality, motivation, will, attention, character, creativity, and other important and significant human capabilities" (Gardner, 1999, p. 74) may be ill advised. Again, even though it is limited to only one domain of psychological processes—"intelligences"—Gardner's taxonomy clearly provides another example of a modern "modular" system.

3.1.11 The Emerging "Modern" Imaging Taxonomy

Finally, there may be no better way to end this discussion of classic and modern taxonomies of mental components than to consider the various processes that have been the object of the localization quest by means of imaging techniques. The database of cognitive neuroscience is itself an implicit taxonomy of mental modules and components. The variety of mental activity invoked in this quest is voluminous and the following list is far from exhaustive, but it does give an idea of the enormous span of current research attention. Some of the targeted mental components are topics that have been of interest to psychology for many years. Many, on the other hand, are more recent foci of research attention. The particular brain areas in which these psychological processes are localized are not germane to the present discussion.

In providing a very limited sample of the mental processes being investigated with PET or MRI imaging techniques, my purpose is to show that a new vocabulary and thus, implicitly, a new taxonomy is emerging, one unfortunately based on ad hoc and methodological criteria rather than on the logical structure required of a solid cladistic system:

1. Kosslyn et al. (1999) have studied *visual imagery.*
2. Lumer, Friston, and Rees (1998) have studied the brain loci of *perceptual rivalry.*
3. Spitzer et al. (1996) have attacked the problem of *semantic information processing.*
4. Smith and Jonides (1999) have explored the role of frontal cortex in *short-term memory storage* and the *executive processes* that act on that stored information.
5. Buchel, Coull, and Friston (1999) have studied *associative learning.*
6. McIntosh, Rajah, and Lobaugh (1999), on the other hand, have explored *sensory learning.*
7. Kopelman, Stahope, and Kingsley (1997) have dissected *temporal and spatial context memory* into different processes represented by different regions.
8. Dehaene, Spelke, Pinel, Stanescu, and Tsivkin (1999) have studied the basis of *mathematical thinking,* implicating both *linguistic competence* and *visuospatial representations.*
9. Gulyas and Roland (1994a, 1994b) have studied *binocular disparity detection, form,* and *color.*

10. Roland and Gulyas (1992) have studied *visual pattern discrimination* and the *formation of visual memories*.

11. Kanwisher, McDermott, and Chun (1997), among others, have designated one or another locus in the brain as a *face perception* area.

12. Elfgren and Risberg (1998) have studied *verbal fluency* and *"design" fluency.*

13. Petersen, Fox, Posner, Mintum, and Raichle (1988) have studied the brain correlates of linguistic *single word processing.*

14. Blakemore, Rees, and Firth (1998) have studied the differential brain effects of *expected* and *unexpected events.*

15. Kastner, De Weerd, Desimone, and Ungerleider (1998) have studied *directed attention.*

16. Tranel, Damasio, and Damasio (1997) have sought to determine which brain regions are involved in the retrieval of *conceptual knowledge,* that is, the categories of concrete objects.

17. Barch et al. (1997) have assigned *working memory* and *task difficulty* to separate brain regions.

18. Cohen et al. (1997) have also explored *working memory.*

19. Smith, Jonides, Marshuetz, and Koeppe (1998) have studied *verbal working memory.*

20. Kapur et al. (1996) have studied *intentional learning of verbal materials.*

21. Lane et al. (1997) have assigned *pleasant* and *unpleasant emotions* to different combinations of parts of the limbic system.

22. Ploghaus et al. (1999) have used tomographic images to distinguish between *pain* and the *anticipation of pain.*

It is important to keep in mind that what we are concerned with here is the relationship between the mental or cognitive processes and brain regions. PET, MRI, and other imaging techniques have been used for many useful and valuable medical, surgical, and research purposes. It is the questionable application of these techniques to the localization of psychological functions that is the principal focus of this book's discussion.

Nevertheless, and with specific regard to the psychobiological issue at hand, this list, partial and incomplete as it is, does make one strong point. There are a large number of more or less inadequately defined mental components and activities that have been associated with particular regions of the brain by PET and MRI techniques and the list is growing rapidly. I contend that the recent wave of research using imaging techniques has led to a proliferation of hypothetical psychological, cognitive, or mental components without a proper foundation of clear-cut answers to the questions of accessibility and analyzability.

Implicit in this and all other lists and taxonomies presented in this chapter is the central assumption of analyzability. That is, it is increasingly clear that the a priori assumption that the mind can be finely divided into any number of components or modules is alive and well. The current approach has deep intellectual roots and has been at the core of thinking about mental processes since philosophers and scientists began to consider these issues.

Compartmentalization of mind into a set of components is a convenient concept to help us organize what would otherwise have to be considered a composite and integrated as well as unified "mind." Indeed, it may be that it is extremely difficult to study mentation in any other way. Yet exactly because of this pragmatic convenience and ease, it is possible that we are being led astray from a truer, more valid, and more realistic conceptualization of the unified nature of mental processes based on widely distributed brain mechanisms. If our search is for truth and an actual rather than a convenient or pragmatic understanding of mind and brain, then it may be necessary to consider what the alternative—an indivisible, composite, aggregated, and unanalyzable mind—might be like. This is the main alternative raised by those of us who argue against the uncritical acceptance of mental analyzability and the cerebral localization of high-level cognitive (i.e., nonsensory and nonmotor) processes. Indeed, though seemingly mute these days, there have always been critics who have challenged analyzability and suggested that what is being measured in different experiments are the measurable properties of a unified mind rather than separable entities. It is to these counterarguments, I now turn.

3.2 Arguments against Mental Faculties or Components: The Properties versus Entities Controversy

It is the thesis of this book that, although there is abundant evidence that the brain is not homogeneous, the corollary that our mental activity can be divided up into real (true, authentic, veridical, valid) components is not only unproven, but may not be tenable in the light of logical analysis, well-defined mathematical limits, and current empirical data.

The main alternative to the analyzability hypothesis is that the proposed "components" of mental activity are actually properties of some unified mind—rather than distinct entities. By implication, the modules or components of mind that have been invoked for centuries are simply manifestations of the procedures and methods used to measure behavioral functions, that is, any given mental module is a manifestation of just one of the infinitely many ways of measuring the complex, but unitary process traditionally called "mind." For example, the widespread acceptance of a family of different types of memory (e.g., short-term, working, and long-term memory) depends in large part on the methods used to study the retention of information. As new methods are developed, it is likely that other types of memory with different time constants are likely to emerge (see, for example, the previously unrecognized intermediate memory type postulated in Ishai & Sagai, 1995). What this all boils down to is—Are modular inferences from behavior truly localizable entities or merely properties of a more general mental activity?

I argue that, no matter how useful it may be or how entrenched in scientific psychology, the idea of separable mental components or modules is deeply flawed. At the very least, the whole question should be reconsidered as a research issue rather than simply accepted as an a priori fundamental premise of our science. For example, consider the study of attention, a familiar and well-used concept in cognitive psychology. What can we conclude is its actual nature? Is it a "stuff" that can be divided, allocated, and focused and that is available only in limited amounts, and thus can be localized in a particular part of the brain? Or, to the contrary, is it an attribute or characteristic of perception, measurable with appropriate psychophysical assay techniques, yet as inseparable as the diameter or whiteness of a golf ball is from the physical ball itself? We tend not to think of the properties of physical objects such as color or diameter as "things" unto themselves, but rather as properties of the object. It seems plausible that many of the psychological components or modules we seek to locate in a particular region of the brain should likewise be thought of as properties of a unified mental "object" rather than as analyzable and isolatable entities.

I propose that it is incorrect to think of attention, like many other mental activities, as a separable module and, therefore, also as a potentially localizable entity. Attention should be thought of, not as a "stuff" or "thing," but rather as an interpersonally observable attribute or property of what is essentially unobservable intrapersonal mentation, namely, mind. By doing so, we can begin to see in their proper light metaphors such as the spotlight or the distributed sheet that are often posed as theoretical "explanations" or "models" for attention. It may be even appropriate to consider attention only in terms of the operations we use to measure it and the behavior so measured, a line of logic that would lead us back to a behaviorist psychology.[8]

To support the idea that psychological components such as attention would be better considered as attributes or properties rather than entities, we have to delve deeper into the history of thinking about mental components, modules, or "faculties" as they have been variously referred to over the years. Once again, it is unlikely that the controversy between proponents of faculty psychology (in all of its forms—including modern cognitive mentalism) and proponents of a "unity of mind" approach can be resolved by any arguments or evidence presented by this book. Even more important to me than its resolution, however, is reconsideration of the issue, which I am convinced is a necessary prerequisite if localization research, using PET, fMRI, or any other technique is ever to arrive at scientifically valid conclusions—or be set aside if shown to have no scientific basis.

There is, somewhat surprisingly, a substantial body of knowledge and evidence that speaks to the issue of entities versus properties—of a family of isolatable mental components versus a unitary conceptualization of mind. In the following subsections, consider classic and modern arguments against mental components and faculties. Some of these arguments are, admittedly, as weak as those they seek to refute; others are

---

8. Some of my remarks on attention have been abstracted and revised from an earlier article (Uttal, 2000b)

more compelling. It is my hope that all will serve to raise the issue to a more conspicuous level of discussion.

3.2.1 Herbart

One of the first to challenge the early faculty psychologists' contention that mind was made up of separable parts was Johann Friedrich Herbart (1776–1841). Herbart was a philosopher-psychologist whose thinking was closely allied to the British empiricists. Good empiricist that he was, he denied that there were any innate ideas or mental processes of any kinds; our minds developed, he suggested, under the stimulation of the experiences we encountered over the span of our lives. Our experiences were created by our sensations—or, as he called them, "presentations"—that impinged on us from the outside world. Like the early associationists, Herbart suggested that the complex aspects of our mental activity arose from concatenations and linkages of the "presentations" into a variety of mental activities.

In summarizing Herbart's psychological perspective in this way, it is important that we keep two issues separate. The first is the issue of primary concern to us in this discussion—Are there separable and isolatable faculties, modules, or components of mental activity? The other issue that crisscrosses this discussion is the one raised by the controversy between the rationalists and empiricists—the argument between those (like Herbart) who believed that all mental components, separable or not, had to be learned by experience and those (like Descartes and Kant) who felt that the most fundamental ideas were innate. This controversy, the "nature-nurture" issue in current parlance, although interesting and quite important in its own right, is not germane to the issue of primary concern in this chapter. A corollary of that primary issue, of course, is—Do separable mental components have any reality beyond the convenience they offer to our experimental designs and protocols and the simplicity they offer to our theories?

Herbart (1809/1891) argued strongly against the entire concept of separable mental faculties. To the contrary, he asserted, mental faculties were the illusory expressions of a unified and fundamental mental activity. Mind only appeared to be composed of different components when examined from different points of view. Herbart was not immune to some kind of division of mental experiences. He accepted the idea that the perceptual experiences we call "sounds" differed from those we call "sights" in some fundamental ways, but not the idea that cognitive functions could be so analyzed or categorized.[9]

For example, when speaking of "classifications" (which he and his contemporaries used as a synonym for the word "faculties"), Herbart (1809/1891, pp. 39, 40, 41) said:

These classifications are mere empirical groupings without any indication of completeness, without any fixed, definite, and authorized division; hence, it will be no matter for wonder if on a closer investigation of the facts, subjects are discovered which either belong in more than one of the departments already made, or which cannot be classified in any one of them whatever. . . . The classifications made can be used only in the preliminary examination, but in no way can they be used as an exact description of that which takes place in man, for they separate that which in reality is constantly united. . . . That the classified mental faculties exist not only side by side with one another, but in relation to one another, empirical psychology acknowledges, in the fact that it employs them throughout in the elaboration of one and the same material.

Clearly, Herbart came down solidly on the side of the "unity of mind" contingent. He abhorred the reification of different psychological components for research purposes. He very likely would have been distressed by current attempts to locate these hypothetical properties or attributes in particular parts of the brain. One might also suspect that his evolving philosophy would ultimately have led him to the behaviorist camp.

3.2.2 Thorndike

The metaphor of mind as a system of separable and analyzable components of mind is a compelling and convenient one. However, as we are seeing in these subsections, it is neither a universally accepted nor a necessarily valid one. Thorndike (1923), for example, has repeatedly been cited by a number of historians for his remarks against faculty thinking:

9. Once again we can see that the input or afferent processes may be made up of components even though the central processes do not seem to have this property. Fodor (see page 96) is not alone in championing this idea.

The mental sciences should at once rid themselves of the conception of the mind as a sort of machine, different parts of which sense, perceive, discriminate, imagine, remember, conceive, associate, reason about, desire, choose, form habits, attend to. Such a conception was adapted to the uses of writers of books on general method and arguments for formal discipline and barren descriptive psychologies, but such a mind nowhere exists. (p. 366)

He went on to give his own, more positive characterization of mind: "The mind is really but the sum total of an individual's feelings and acts, of the connections between outside events and his responses thereto, and of all of the possibilities of having such feelings, acts and connections" (p. 366).

The unfortunate fact is that, despite the many historical counterarguments made by scholars such as Thorndike, the mental modularity issue still has not been adequately confronted as an issue itself, especially by those whose entire intellectual edifice depends so much on its resolution. Psychologists, regardless of what side of the argument they might be on, pontificate about the matter but do not typically confront it in the way the physical sciences deal with their important conceptual foundations. Perhaps, it is not possible to answer this question (mental processes may be truly inaccessible), but if that is the case, what credibility can be given to any of the complex theories that are based on an assumption of the existence of such hidden mental modules or components?

To his everlasting credit, Thorndike (1923) suggested why psychological "traits" appear so often—a suggestion that rings true over the decades. He conjectured that it is a result of the logic of the situation, not of the reality of mental organization. His point was that it is far easier to show how the components are *not* related (and thus independent) than to show how they are related (and thus a part of some unified entity). In other words, it is easier to develop barriers and boundaries between hypothetical modules, even when they do not exist, than to show that they are related or, even more profoundly, attributes of the same thing. He went further, to propose three reasons for this "logical" pressure toward compartmentalization:

1. The items sampled were too few. Thus two items in a test might show a low correlation, but if a more comprehensive test were carried out, the correlation would be much higher.

2. The population sampled was too diverse. Thus correlations may be spuriously lower than if the studied population had been more homogeneous.

3. The psychological traits, modules, or components proposed were actually so complex that there was no possibility of developing a simple and easy representation or analysis of them.

Thus Thorndike, in a reasoned way and using the language of statistics, revisits the "slippery slope" metaphor, suggesting that it is all too easy to slide downhill intellectually under the pressures of what may seem to be needed to support a particular point of view.

In sum, Thorndike supported a unified concept of mental activity sharply rather than the faculty or module concept that permeates so much of classic and modern psychology. It would be well for today's researchers to at least consider some of Thorndike's caveats before publishing papers based on experiments linking vaguely defined hypothetical psychological modules with brain locales, no matter how well circumscribed those brain regions might be. Whatever happens, it takes no gift of prophecy to predict with confidence that the relationship of psychological components to brain loci will turn out to be much more complicated than today's imaging explorations suggest.

3.2.3 Shallice

As a neuropsychologist, Shallice was also highly aware of criticisms traditionally made against the modularity hypothesis. In Shallice, 1988, he considered arguments both for and against modularity.[10] Shallice noted that there was great variability in the behavioral effects from one patient to another with very similar lesions. He also pointed out that the behavioral deficits observed by the neuropsychologists did not map very well onto the modules emerging from the laboratories of the experimental psychologists. Indeed, he went on to note (p. 10) that many of the observed deficits in patients reflected psychological properties that arose

---

10. For a balanced and thoughtful discussion of the problems facing those who seek to build bridges between abnormal behavior and brain lesions, there may be no better source than Shallice's fine book (1988). I draw on his analysis again in chapter 4.

not from the data, but rather from the theories of the investigator. Speaking of Lichtheim (1885) as the "doyen" of the "diagram makers" (i.e., proponents of psychological faculties or modules), Shallice (1988, p. 11) pointed out that

his theoretical system was based on a priori notions of how children learned to speak. He then deduced that certain types of patients should exist, and either described a patient of his own or referred to one in the literature. The process was theory driven, not data driven.

Given our frail ability to introspect into the logic underlying our cognitive processes, those researching localization would do well to give his remarks serious consideration.

Nevertheless, true to his own commitment to psychological components, Shallice went on to present a lucid discussion of what he believed were the four most compelling modern arguments for mental modularity, based, respectively, on (1) computational modeling; (2) linguistic theory; (3) neurophysiology and neuroanatomy; and (4) cognitive psychology. True, also, to his already well demonstrated evenhandedness, Shallice provided us with a critique of even these four arguments, pointing out that "they do not demonstrate that modularity is a general property of the system underlying human cognition. However, they do make it a reasonable assumption to use as a first pass in the interpretation of neuropsychological findings" (p. 20).

From my point of view, all of these four arguments raised for modularity by Shallice are flawed to a greater or lesser degree. First, computational models are neutral with respect to the underlying neural or psychological mechanisms (Uttal, 1998): they reflect the constraints of the programming system they are using to build their description of the behavioral responses rather than the constraints imposed by the psychobiology of the brain-mind system.

Second, linguistic theory is also neutral with respect to the actual mechanisms underlying of the behavior it seeks to explain. Drawing mainly on the strong modularity hypothesis proposed by Chomsky, it works from theoretical inferences that do little to define the true nature of mental components.

Third, even Shallice (1988, p. 21) agrees that "neuropsychological evidence does not speak definitively to the question of modularity." I would add further that the complexity of the neural system is so great and we know (and can know) so little about it that no inference drawn from brain injury data can be used to constrain theories of mental organization.

Fourth, and finally, although cognitive psychology represents the current zeitgeist, much of its quest for the modules of mind is based on assumptions of rigidity and seriality that became implausible when examined closely (Pachella, 1974).

3.3 Conclusion

In this chapter, I have reviewed many of the different components, modules, faculties, and traits that have been proposed as the elements of mental activity. There are five important conclusions that can be drawn from this review:

1. There never has been any agreement on what the components of mental activity are.
2. There seems to be no trend toward such an agreement.
3. New components are added ad hoc as new methods are introduced or new psychological theories are developed.
4. The creation of many new components is driven more by preexisting theory, ad hoc "hunches," and experimental protocols than by empirical findings.
5. The one exception to conclusions 1 through 4 concerns the sensory and motor domains. In those domains alone, there are sufficient anchors to the physical world to permit researchers to make inferences that can be substantiated.

Notwithstanding these conclusions, it is unarguable that the concept of modular faculties or components of mental activity has played and continues to play a central role in psychological thinking. There are powerful forces that drive us in this direction. First, the universe of mind, both in terms of the neural mechanics that underlie it and the interconnections among its attributes or properties, remains a Gordian knot of what may be unassailable complexity.

Second, as a result of this complexity, it may be, in theory and in practice, impossible to do any research using conventional scientific methods on mental activity without invoking the artifice of classifying and decomposing it into subdivisions.[11] The modern scientific method, as we know it, is based on Francis Bacon's naturalistic approach to science and Descartes' rigorously logical analysis—both of which strongly favored breaking down systems into their constituent parts and examining these parts in detail. Psychological instantiations of the scientific method have also emphasized the components—for example, microelectrode studies, computer models using algorithms, and traditional behavior-based psychological experiments. But, what if these instantiations are flawed in some fundamental way? What if the postulated psychological components are only hypothetical constructs created to "elementalize" what is actually a unified entity? Suppose the arguments against accessibility and analyzability are correct—what then? What if we have made a major conceptual error by misidentifying properties or attributes of integrated mental activity as isolatable entities? How would such a conclusion bear on what is being done in the imaging laboratories these days?

The problem faced by psychologists is that the anchors for independent resolution of these questions about high-level cognitive components may not be available as they are for the physical units of chemistry or physics, for example. For one thing, the proposed components or modules of mind do not have the same independent measurability that atoms or protons or even quarks do. Rather, they are largely inferences that have little in the way of independently measurable properties outside the highly structured and constrained experimental designs psychologists typically use.

Although it may be that it is far easier just to assume faculties and components than it is to search for a conclusive answer to the question of their existence there is one body of evidence that suggests an indirect answer to this question. As I look over the studies reviewed in this chapter,

---

11. Wimsatt (1974) reminds us of Simon's comment (1969, p. 86): "In the face of complexity, an in-principle reductionist may be at the same time a pragmatic holist." My agreement with this comment should be obvious, but I would go even further to suggest that the word "may" should be changed to "must." If this is done, Simon's concise words sum up the kind of ontological monism and epistemological dualism that I feel must control thinking about mental and neural modularity as well as the relationship between the brain and the mind.

one thing becomes completely clear. There is no historical trend, no evolutionary sequence, no convergence toward a taxonomy of mental components. We seem to have no community memory; the components suggested in one generation are largely forgotten in the next. In virtually every case the response to this challenge has been strictly constrained by the Zeitgeist of the moment. The putative components are based on idiosyncratic and pragmatic concerns rather than on the empirical and theoretical criteria scientists should cherish. From the time of the Greek philosophers to the most modern Factor Analytical and cognitive neuroscientific schemes, it has been all too easy to succumb to the pressure to dissect that which may not, in psychobiological fact, be separable. Statistics, convenience, and admittedly, a certain amount of utility in the naming and description of mental activities for the purposes of experimental design make modularity an easy way out of the problems generated by the enormous complexity of our mental life.

In researching this chapter, I was not able to unearth any agreement nor any sign of impending agreement, on the specific nature of the many hypothetical mental faculties, components, or modules that have been proposed. The only exception to this has been the centuries old trichotomy of sensory-transformational-response mechanisms—the classic notion of S-O-R.

Therefore, returning to the title question of this chapter,

• if psychology's goal is to develop a valid psychobiological taxonomy of mental processes, and
• if that taxonomy is to transcend the simple utilitarian level of describing the kinds of experiments we execute,
• then the answer to "Is a taxonomy or even a lexicon of cognitive processes possible?" has to be no.

The five principal reasons for this negative conclusion, already alluded to in this and my earlier books, are

1. the neutrality of formal models;
2. the neutrality of behavioral data and findings;
3. the inaccessibility of mental activity;
4. the unanalyzability of mental activity;
5. the complexity of both mental activity and its relevant neural underpinnings.

If there is no impending—indeed, no possible—agreement on what mental components are being measured or what a valid taxonomy of mental components should look like, what credence can be given to the quest to localize such phantoms? If mental components are only a semantic convenience, but have neither scientific validity nor the promise of being scientifically validated, what can be made of the ultraprecise maps showing sharply demarcated "hot spots" of neural activity when "pure" forms of these mental components are supposedly activated? Obviously, much needs to be done to answer these questions and to properly interpret the often fascinating findings from the imaging laboratories. It is likely that what these findings will turn out to mean will be far different from what we now believe they mean.

That mental modules or components are still so vaguely defined, indeed, that their very existence is problematical, is the major reason that much of the imaging work of the last decade must be reinterpreted. But there are other reasons to reconsider the findings of these studies. Some of the reasons are rooted in the technology itself, some in the mathematical tools used to analyze the data, and some in the kind of conceptual misunderstandings that led to diminished interest in other noninvasive techniques (e.g., the EEG or EVBP) that seemed so promising in previous decades. Chapter 4 pursues these additional reasons for reconsidering what it is that we are doing when we attempt to localize mental activity in different parts of the brain.

Technical and Conceptual Problems

As discussed in chapter 3, beyond agreement that cognitive processes can be grouped into three classes—input, output, and central transformation—there has been no convergence on a more detailed taxonomy of these processes. Rather, a more or less expedient and highly transitory system of definitions has been developed in each generation as new phenomena are observed or hypothetical entities created. This process of listing an ever-increasing number of what may well be temporary and convenient, but what are certainly unsubstantiated, cognitive processes is currently driven by the methods, theories, and approaches of a wide range of scientists, most notably cognitive neuroscientists. All too many invoke ad hoc and hypothetical mental processes, particularize the needs of a given experiment, or simply give a name to some observed behavior. For reasons already expressed, however, it remains extremely difficult to establish any one of these cognitive processes as a true and valid component underlying observed behavior. Any attempt to precisely define mental events or cognitive processes quickly leads to an appreciation of how elusive these events or processes are—and how circular the resultant "definitions."

Weaving throughout all of the difficulties of defining mental components are two fundamental questions. The first is whether psychological processes can be accessed, a matter dealt with more fully in Uttal, 2000a, where I argued that, whatever the underlying mental entities are, there is no valid way to access them. Neither introspective reports nor behavioral or neurophysiological measures can, in point of basic principle, provide a solid scientific means of specifying internal processes or mechanisms.

The second fundamental question is whether the mind (which may be unitary and irretrievably integrated) can be decomposed into components, modules, or faculties. As I argued in chapter 3 and in Uttal, 1998, such a decomposition is at best a methodological convenience and at worst a seriously misleading intellectual artifice. We may be driven to accepting this pseudoanalyzability by the misapplication of traditional methods of scientific analysis to what may be in reality a psychobiological unity.

The ultimate nature of mind—whether it can be decomposed or must be dealt with as a unit—remains one of the most important, yet all-too-rarely considered, conceptual conundrums in contemporary scientific psychology. This is particularly evident in modern cognitive mentalism, where the resolution of the conundrum in favor of an already assumed analyzability is taken for granted. However it may in fact be resolved, even if mind is ultimately deemed to be decomposable into components, there is at present still no agreement concerning what these components are.

There may be no more rigorous proof of the contention that we do not have good definitions of mental activity than the difficulty injected into any conversation when the ambiguously defined term *consciousness* is introduced. There is still disagreement whether this term denotes a thing or a property—an entity that could be localized or a general attribute describing some aspect of an otherwise unanalyzable process. Some workers (e.g., Tononi & Edelman, 1998, p. 1847) strongly believe that consciousness must be the result of activity distributed throughout the whole brain. Others (e.g., Posner & Raichle, 1994/1997, pp. 178–179) strongly believe that representation of consciousness cum awareness cum "executive attention system" is localized in a specific brain region—the cingulate gyrus. These directly contrary opinions are held with equal conviction despite the absence of agreement over what exactly is to be localized—or *not* localized.

In point of historical fact, the problem of consciousness has bedeviled not only contemporary experimental psychologists but also their intellectual predecessors. Indeed, a recurrent theme in the papers collected by Warner and Dzubka (1994) is that our theoretical knowledge of consciousness is virtually nonexistent. For example, Nagel (1994, p. 63) says:

We know that conscious mental processes occur as a part of animal life, and that they are intimately connected with behavior and with the physical activity of our nervous systems and those of other animals. But at the more general, one might say cosmological, level, we know essentially nothing for we do not understand why these particular connections exist. Our knowledge is entirely empirical and *ad hoc,* not theoretical.

Nagel goes on to argue that one of the results of the application of the objective physical sciences to the study of the nature of man is that it becomes necessary to eschew the study of *subjectivity*—another term that has come to be used by philosophers in the place of *consciousness.* This does not mean that we cannot study and measure human behavior (in fact, Nagel supports some psychological approaches), but it does suggest that the special features of self-awareness that characterize "subjectivity" and "consciousness" are substantial barriers to solving the mind-body problem. Indeed, Nagel further notes: "We at present lack the conception of a complete analysis of subjective, phenomenological features of mental reality in terms of an objective, physical basis and there is no reason to believe that such a thing is possible" (p. 67).

McGinn (1994, p. 114) expresses a similar point of view:

The mind-body problem, construed as a problem about the emergence of consciousness from matter, presents deep and intractable problems of understanding, manifested in the miraculous-seeming character of the psychophysical link. We do not possess the theoretical tools with which to make headway with the problem. . . . That there should exist problems that systematically escape our best theoretical efforts is antecedently highly probable, and the problem of consciousness looks like an instance of just such a problem.

As one reads through other papers in Warner & Szubka, 1994, the impression emerges that some psychologists invoke consciousness as a sine qua non for any legitimate study of mental information processing. In doing so, they often drive a dualistic wedge between the physical and the mental that violates what is to me the basic scientific assumption that all of the information-processing activities we collectively call "mind" are of the same level of reality as the biophysical mechanisms that instantiate them. Down that dualistic road lies theoretical disaster. The much more desirable alternative is to exclude the intractable such as intrapersonal consciousness from our studies and to concentrate on the interpersonally measurable aspects of our science such as behavior and physiology. To continuously evoke the indefinable can only impede and delay acquiring whatever knowledge of ourselves that is available through scientific methods.

Choosing the proper strategy, of course, requires that we distinguish between the intractable and the merely difficult. At this junction, there is obviously going to be much disagreement as to where a given problem should be placed on the spectrum from tractable to intractable. Some will judge the problem of consciousness intractable, others will deem it tractable but difficult, while still others, who consider introspective reports to be valid data, will assume that it is fully tractable, at least in the long run. My personal feeling is that the general inaccessibility of mental processes and the continued failure to develop even the semblance of a concrete taxonomy of those processes should place such ephemera as consciousness and self-awareness outside of the scientific enterprise. If it does not do so, psychology will continue to face the prospect of locating, not actual cognitive processes, but what may well be "category errors" or nominal trivialities in the brain. This by itself should raise concerns about the entire enterprise.

However, this is not the only difficulty faced by those who would seek to localize hypothetical components in narrowly circumscribed regions of the brain. In this chapter, I consider a number of other impediments, both technical and conceptual, that make what may at first seem to be a straightforward task into one of great complexity and subtlety, far greater than is usually assumed.

I must make it absolutely clear from the outset that my argument against the strategies used to localize cognitive components and modules is not an argument for any kind of equipotentiality in the brain. As I have noted earlier, there is no question that the brain itself is divided into regions exhibiting functional and structural differences, both at the macroscopic and the microscopic level. Rather, I am asserting only that the question of the how these regions may be related to various mental processes may not, for profound theoretical reasons, be answerable either at the present time or in the future, despite the superficial directness that seems to be offered by the exciting new imagery techniques.

This chapter will point out the technical limitations of both traditional and current procedures, on the one hand, and the conceptual, procedural, and logical barriers that stand between the goals of the localization enterprise and their ultimate fulfillment, on the other. However compelling our desire to answer questions such as those proposed by localization researchers, must of the current quest is based on frail assumptions, technical artifacts, and even ill-posed questions.[1] My purpose here is to raise a flag of caution about the slippery slide toward what may be totally incorrect theories and explanations engendered by the ill-conceived quest for an answer to a highly problematic question—Where is a mental process located in the brain?

There are three general categories of difficulties (in addition to the premier difficulty of defining the psychological components to be localized) facing those who seek to correlate brain areas and psychological functions:

1. Neurophysiological and neuroanatomical difficulties;
2. Technological and instrumentation difficulties;
3. Conceptual and logical difficulties.

Each of these three clusters of difficulties should raise concern that all may not be well in a field of such rapidly increasing popularity.

The distinction between *linear* and *nonlinear* is well appreciated in mathematical and engineering circles, but ignored by many neuroscientists and psychologists, who all too often assume that the brain and the behavioral and mental responses it generates constitute a linear system that may be decomposed at will into modules and components. This, however, is an erroneous assumption, one that perhaps more than any other in our science has led to nonsensical theories. To help us clarify the nature of this problem, let us carefully define what we mean by linear and nonlinear systems.

A linear system is one in which the various contributing factors can simply be added together: these factors do not interact. For example, assume that a company is buying reams of three types of paper, X_1, X_2, and X_3, which cost Y_1, Y_2, and Y_3 dollars, respectively, and these costs are independent of each other. Then the total cost of the reams of paper would simply be the sum of the products of the number of reams of each type times its respective unit costs:

1. I am using "ill-posed" here in the formal mathematical sense. That is, a question is ill posed if there is inadequate information available in the relevant database to answer it, and additional constraints must be added to do so.

Total cost $= X_1Y_1 + X_2Y_2 + X_3Y_3$ $\hspace{3em}$ (4.1)

In other words, the system can be completely described as the sum of its individual parts.

If, however, the cost of any one of the types of paper depends on how many of some other type are purchased (for example, the cost of the X_3 paper depends on the number of X_1 reams purchased and vice versa), then the system is algebraically represented as follows:

Total cost $= X_1(Y_1/jX_3) + X_2Y_2 + X_3(Y_3/kX_1),$ $\hspace{2em}$ (4.2)

where j and k indicate the magnitude of the discount. In this case, we can completely describe the system as the sum of its parts only when we know precisely how those parts interact. This interaction indicates that the system of purchasing paper is nonlinear.

In a simple nonlinear case like this, the mathematics are generally tractable provided equations are available to determine all of the unknown interactions. In other nonlinear systems, the interactions may be much more complex and the mathematics can quickly become totally intractable. This is the essence of one of the most serious conceptual problems encountered in the study of both the brain and behavior—the components of these systems are highly interdependent and interact intricately. They are, by definition, therefore, nonlinear and often formally intractable. No matter how clever an experimenter may be, it is not possible to solve this class of "problems" by a simple linear addition of the function of the individual parts.

There is a natural tension between nonlinear intractability and our desire to answer some of the fundamental questions of human nature. Unfortunately, the desire sometimes prevents us from realizing and accepting the intractability.

4.1 Neuroanatomical and Neurophysiological Problems

4.1.1 Classic Difficulties with Ablation Experiments

In chapter 2, I examined some of the techniques popular in previous generations of physiological psychologies—lesioning, freezing, poisoning, stimulating, and recording. Although these older methods have largely been replaced by the newer imaging techniques in the quest to localize particular psychological functions in regions of the brain, a review of some of the problems faced by practitioners of the older methods can help us evaluate the rigor of assumptions underlying both traditional and modern techniques.

As we shall see later in this chapter, and as discussed in Uttal (1978, pp. 255–266), even the traditional methods of surgical extirpation and neuropsychological observation of the effects of accidental brain injuries suffered from anatomic, logical, and procedural difficulties, including

- inadequate definition of the boundaries of brain regions;
- system complexity arising from high interconnectivity, feedback, feedforward, redundant coding, massive parallelism, interplay of excitatory and inhibitory modules, and multiple roles of individual brain regions;
- variable and idiosyncratic data from human brain injuries;
- almost exclusive concentration on behavioral deficits;
- misinterpretation of the effects of inadvertently cut fiber tracts passing near or under the lesioned nuclei as functions of the lesioned region.
- recovery of function (see page 166 for a tabulation of the possible explanations for recovery of function).

Thus one can argue that the localization enterprise has from its beginnings been shadowed by serious and complex conceptual troubles, most of which have been seldom discussed. The proponents of the new imaging techniques have, at least to some degree, overlooked or disregarded similar problems with their approach. It is to this task that the rest of this chapter is dedicated. In considering the problems faced by the imaging approach, some of which are novel and some of which are associated with the older techniques, I shall focus on empirical and formal arguments that lift the discussion well above speculative arm waving.

Regions Are Not Sharply Demarcated in the Brain   Although there is almost universal agreement that the brain is not homogeneous, there is also abundant evidence that the identified areas of the brain are not precisely demarcated from one another. This holds true regardless of what technique is used to determine the boundaries of the various regions. Cytoarchitectonic, electrical recording, stimulation, and extirpation techniques yield equivocal and generally differing results with regard to the exact extent of any region. The problem is further compounded in the human brain by the nature of the cerebral fissures: where one region may at first glance seem to be sharply discontinuous with another, in actual anatomic fact it gradually fades into that other region deep within a fissure.

That cortical regions substantially overlap has been known for some time. Brazier (1961, p. 95) reminds us that the issue was even of importance to Polish brain physiologists in the late nineteenth and early twentieth century. Among the first to record the spatial course of a response elicited on the human cortex by an external stimulus, both N. N. Cybulski (1854–1919) and A. Beck (1863–1939) appreciated that the various somatic regions overlapped to a considerable degree.

Although at the time of their original studies, Broca (1861) and Wernicke (1874) considered the "speech" regions of the brain to be sharply demarcated, by the latter half of the twentieth century, it was generally acknowledged that this was not the case. Penfield and Roberts (1959, p. 78) observed: "No discrete localization of lesions producing various types of agnosia and apraxia [has] been found. It seems as Jackson (1931) stated that any acute lesion to any gross part of the left hemisphere will produce some disturbance in speech." And Lennenberg (1974, p. 524) pointed out that

there do not seem to be sharply delimited or structurally well defined areas that are alone responsible for the appearance of critical specific clinical language deficits. . . . In other words, there are gradients of probability for the occurrence of a symptom complex that may appear in connection with a lesion in a given area.

Unfortunately, the traditional view that brain regions are sharply demarcated is nowadays accepted (and, perhaps even worse, taught) with little attention given to the actual degree of overlap or the precision of boundaries between regions. For example, Kandel, Schwartz, and Jessel (1995) assert: "Different parts of the brain are *specialized* for different functions" (p. 8) and "Language and other cognitive functions are *localized* within the cerebral cortex" (p. 9; emphasis added). They give no consideration either to the concept of overlap or to statistical probabilities and associations.

In dogmatically presenting these statements, Kandel et al. (1995) set the stage for continued acceptance of mistaken premises about the precision of boundaries between functional areas. Far more illuminating, however, is their figure 1-9 (p. 17), in which the progression from purely sensory to complex cognitive functions recruits ever larger regions of the cerebral cortex in a PET scan. To use such frequently observed PET scan results without addressing the technological problem of statistical significance (dealt with later in this chapter) is to ignore that the results are based on arbitrary and variable criteria.

Furthermore, current research indicates that the uncertainty about the extent of a brain region is not just a matter of arbitrary criteria, but also of the dynamic modulation of the putative region by task and by psychological factors such as attention. Friston, Buechel, et al. (1997) and Buechel and Friston (1997) showed that attending and not attending to a moving stimulus could produce drastically different fMRI brain responses.

Although, to their credit, Kandel et al. (1995) go on to note that it is only the elementary components of mind that are localized, not "more elaborate faculties," this wisdom appears not to have percolated down to a large group of cognitive neuroscientists, who, as we saw in chapters 1 and 3, are willing to locate some very subtle psychological processes in what seem to be very sharply demarcated brain regions.

Cognitive Functions Activate Broadly Distributed Regions of the Brain

One of the basic guiding assumptions of any attempt to localize a cognitive function in the brain is that a circumscribed locale for that function actually exists. However, it is by no means certain that this is a valid assumption on which to build a theory of the relationship between brain and mind. Indeed, there is considerable evidence that the contrary is true—that any but the simplest (sensory or motor) cognitive function involves large and distributed regions of the brain.

There is a substantial history that many, if not all, of the regions of the brain may be involved even in such a fundamental type of learning as classical conditioning. In one of the most compelling arguments that this is so, Olds, Disterhoft, Segal, Kornblith, and Hirsch (1972) described their search to localize the neural correlates of simple classical conditioned learning in the rat brain. They discovered that the neurons involved were scattered throughout virtually the entire brain of the rat. Although not all nuclei at all levels contained activated neurons, there was no gross (macro) brain level, from the medulla to the neocortex, that did not contain at least some neurons that seemed to respond to the training.

At any given level, however, it did appear that the short-latency neurons were to be found within certain relatively well circumscribed nuclei. The neurons were most common in the posterior nucleus of the thalamus and a few other thalamic nuclei (a surprising location considering the generally accepted proposition that the thalamus mainly functions as a sensory relay station), the pontine reticular formation and the ventral tegmentum. They were also found in the CA3 but not in the CAI region of the hippocampus as well as in a number of parts of the cerebral cortical mantle. These regions are the ones to which Olds and his colleagues specifically attributed a role in learning. The general thrust of these experimental results, however, was that the learning process and the resulting "engram" are to be found in widely distributed regions throughout the entire brain.

Of course, the experimental animal of choice in this classic experiment was the rat, a creature well known to have an unusual brain in a number of ways.[2] Recent research using animals that are closer to us on the phylogenetic tree has, however, come to very much the same conclusion. Unfortunately, few of these newer reports are of the heroic proportions of Olds et al. 1972, and typically do not record from many different parts of the brain. The usual, but logically equivalent, result described in these recent reports is to demonstrate that an area long considered to have a single function can be activated in surprisingly different ways. All of which strongly suggests that, if many processes can activate a single region, it is only logical to assume that many different regions are involved in a single process.

In one very striking example of support for wide distribution of cognitive representations in the brain, Carpenter, Georgopoulos, and Pellizzer (1999) have demonstrated that what previously had been considered to be purely "motor" cortex is able to both recognize and remember something as subtle as the serial order of visually displayed, dotted stimulus

2. For example, the rat's cerebral visual receptive fields are typically simple monophasic functions, quite unlike the "Mexican hat" biphasic fields reported in cats and monkeys (Gourlay, Uttal, and Powers, 1974).

patterns. Carpenter and his colleagues recorded from neurons in the motor cortex and discovered that the observed neural responses were not just associated with particular muscular actions. Rather, many of the neurons in this "motor" region seemed to respond to the joint influence of the serial order and the position of the stimulus. This result was interpreted to mean that the neurons were able to recognize and remember aspects of the prolonged training protocol that the monkeys had undergone.

Thus, processes involved in complex scene interpretation, including recognition and learning of various types, are actually encoded in and represented by regions of the brain not usually considered to be involved in this kind of cognitive functioning. The traditional interpretation has been that these regions are exclusively motor output controllers. The assumption of extreme localization on which modern cognitive neurosciences bases so much of its current research program is severely challenged by such a result.

Similar evidence exists that the cerebellum, a region classically considered to be involved solely in the coordination of motor movements, may have substantial cognitive functions as well. Thompson (1990) and his group have been studying the conditioning of the response of a rabbit's eyelid to a conditioned stimulus (CS)—a tone—paired with an unconditioned stimulus (UCS)—a puff of air. If lesions are made in the cerebellum in particular regions (see page 21), the rabbits are unable to associate the CS with the UCS and do not learn to respond to the tone. This certainly would be considered by many in the localization business to be prima facie evidence that the learning is at least controlled by, and maybe mediated by and even encoded in, the cerebellum. This classic single dissociation experiment is of exactly the same logical genre as the typical lesion experiment of a few decades ago and leads to much the same conclusions reached by neuropsychologists with regard to fortuitous brain injuries. That conditioned learning occurs at all in the cerebellum, however, contradicts the usual localization of "learning" in the cerebrum.

Whether conditioned learning of this kind occurs because of neural changes localized solely in the cerebellum is only one part of a more widely distributed "learning" system, or involves the complex interaction of many regions of the brain, serious questions are raised about invoking a single specific locale for even such a well studied and superficially simple "cognitive" process as classical conditioning.

The expanded role for the cerebellum in the representation of other, more cognitive, functions than motor coordination has been summarized by Muller, Courchesne, and Allen (1998, p. 880), who cite a number of results that suggest that the cerebellum regulates, controls, or represents functions far beyond simple (or even complex) motor mechanisms including

1. the presence of neurons in the cerebellum sensitive to tactile stimuli;
2. neural activity in the cerebellum during language processing even when the motor aspects of speech are suppressed or controlled;
3. neural activity in the cerebellum during problem solving; and
4. neural activity in the cerebellum during memory tasks.

(For additional information on the role of the cerebellum in a diversity of cognitive tasks, see also Schmahmann, 1997.)

Just as traditional motor regions appear to play more extensive roles in higher cognitive processes than once supposed, so, too, even the traditional sensory regions appear to have functions far beyond those suggested by our current theories and models. Stein and Meredith (1993), in their comprehensive review of the literature on the overlap of the various sensory and motor regions of the brain in a number of different animals, describe the many different studies showing that these regions overlap substantially in most of the experimental animals. This overlap can be expressed in several different ways. First, the lines of demarcation between the several "sensory" regions are not sharp. Second, there is considerable overlap between these fuzzy boundaries. Third, many neurons, supposedly centrally located in a particular sensory region turn out to be multimodal—in that they can be activated by several different receptor modalities. The analysis produced by Stein and Meredith strongly supports the argument that the maps sharply defining sensory and motor function that have been a part of the physiological psychology culture for so many years may be seriously misleading.

How could neuroscientific thinking so pervasively fail to appreciate the fuzziness of the boundaries between the cortical regions? The answer may well lie in some methodological quirks. Whenever the cerebral cortex was examined for either motor or sensory functions, a decision about an acceptable threshold of activation had to be made. The very presence of such a cutoff limit on what would be accepted as "activation" inevitably came to mean that a sharp boundary was artificially created where none actually existed. That artificial boundary, however much the diagrams may have seemed to suggest it, was not the boundary between activity and no activity, but rather an arbitrary boundary between different levels of activity or sensitivity. The arbitrariness of the criterion used to determine that boundary was generally ignored. As the data were published and republished, however, the concept of sharply demarcated region for any of the sensory regions became instantiated in physiological psychology's theories and models. As we now see, the boundaries of the sensory and motor regions are not so clear-cut: there is considerable overlap among them, and, indeed, there is intrusion of one into the other at all levels of the brain.

The problems with the "intrinsic" or "association areas," in which the intermediate cognitive processes linking the input sensory pathways to the output motor responses are purported to reside, are even more complicated. As noted earlier, these transforming regions lack the anchor to the physical world enjoyed by the input and output stages of behavior. They also suffer particularly from the primary difficulty in the localization enterprise—the lack of clear definitions of the mental processes that are purported to be carried out in these regions.

That cognitive processes involve widely dispersed regions of the cerebral cortex has been appreciated for over a hundred years. Farah (1994, p. 43) calls our attention to a comment by Ferrier (1886):

The fact that the various parts of the encephalon, though anatomically distinct, are yet so intimately combined and related as to form a complex whole, makes it natural to suppose that lesions of a greater or lesser extent in any one part should produce such general perturbation of the functions of the organ as a whole as to render it at least highly difficult to trace any uncomplicated connection between the symptoms produced and the lesion as such.

Nowhere has the same point been more eloquently expressed than by Luria (1966, p. 691):

The clinical evidence shows that any complex behavioral function (perception, action, speech, writing, reading, calculation) is never lost in a patient with a lesion of only one circumscribed area of the cortex, but it may be impaired in lesions of widely different areas of the brain, sometimes far distant from each other. At the same time, a lesion of one circumscribed area of the brain never leads to the isolated loss of any one complex behavioral function, but causes a group of disturbances which, although they always possess some common link, is reflected in the normal course of what are apparently diverse functions.

This same point of view is held by some of the most active and productive leaders of the scanning approach to brain localization. Thus, for example, Roland et al. (1995, p. 784) contend:

All types of brain work—learning, recall, recognition, motor planning, motor execution, perception, and thinking—are associated with activations of multiple fields in cortex . . . the cerebral cortex participates in brain work in awake human subjects by activating multiple cortical fields for each task.

These deep and persistent insights have seemingly not displaced the prevailing conviction among many cognitive neuroscientists that a radically specialized modularity exists in the brain. As this chapter illustrates, this conviction runs counter to simple logic as well as to a large body of evidence, to which we may add the following:

1. Kertesz (1979), using a radioisotope marker techniques, has produced some composite charts that show that the brains of clinically defined aphasic patients can exhibit extremely wide-ranging lesions. Damage, for example, can occur at virtually any location (with the curious exception of the prefrontal lobes) to produce what is called "global aphasia."

2. Kohler, Moscovitch, Winocur, Houle, and McIntosh (1998), using a PET scanning technique, have discovered that episodic memory elicits activities in many different areas widely distributed across the brain. These areas include the right middle occipital gyrus, the supramarginal gyrus, the superior temporal sulcus, the bilateral lingual and fusiform gyri, as well as in the prefrontal cortex. They conclude:

Together our data suggest that encoding and retrieval in episodic memory depend on the interplay between domain-specific structures, most of which are involved in memory as well as perception, and domain-general structures, some of which operate more at encoding and others more at retrieval. (p. 129)

3. Clark, Fannon, Lai, Benson, and Bauer (2000), using a new technique for recording event-related fMRI responses (see page 194), reported that target stimuli produced responses that not only were totally different from those produced by distractor stimuli in a "three-stimulus oddball" experiment, but, again, were widely distributed across the brain.

4. Jiang, Haxby, Martin, Ungerleider, and Parasuraman (2000), also using event-related fMRI procedures, have found that the brain responses

involved in recognizing target faces versus distracter faces exhibited different patterns of activation in widely distributed regions. Responses produced by the target faces included occipital, parietal, temporal, frontal, and supplementary motor areas.

5. Buechel and Friston (1997) have also shown that a moving pattern of dots can produce fMRI responses in three different regions—V1, V5, the posterior parietal region—and that this pattern varies with the degree to which the stimulus is attended.

Clearly, the basic assumption of sharply localized brain representations of mental activity, challenged over a period of a century, is now under a new kind of empirical attack using the very tools that were originally used to support it.

Brain Regions Are Complexly Interconnected   As can be seen throughout this chapter, there are some unexpressed and hidden assumptions involved in the quest to localize particular mental activities in particular parts of the brain. A hidden assumption very close to the surface of our discussion is that the nervous system is made up of modules organized in such a way that they can and ultimately will be isolated and independently assayed. For example, the argument is often made that we should be able to specify the hierarchy of interconnections among a cluster of interacting centers. This concept has, however, been challenged by findings from a surprising subsystem of the brain—the ensemble of regions involved in processing visual information.

For reasons that are well known (e.g., its stimulus anchor, the primarily afferent flow, relatively straightforward coding, and representation of information within it), a system of cerebral components has been identified that plays an important role in processing visually acquired information. Current knowledge of the organization of this system has been summarized by Felleman and Van Essen (1991) in the form of a hierarchical chart showing the brain regions and the interconnections among them. There is no question that this chart is very complicated, showing many feedback and feedforward links between the various areas and centers involved in vision. This well-accepted version of the organization of the visual brain, which at the very least serves to enhance our appreciation of the many regions shown to be anatomically interrelated, may nevertheless be quite incorrect.

Hilgetag et al. (1996) have pointed out that, owing to basic properties of interconnected networks, complex systems like this cannot be organized into a unique hierarchical organizational chart in the way that Felleman and Van Essen (1991) have suggested. There is thus an *in-principle* barrier to the specification of a network hierarchy from observations of the components and the interconnections of that network, *no matter how many experiments may be carried out.* Hilgetag et al.'s criticism cannot be put aside simply by alluding to the need for "additional research." Rather, their computational analysis has shown that the anatomical constraints (i.e., data) are insufficient to specify *any* unique hierarchical arrangement as the actual one. Indeed, because the number of possible computed hierarchies with a given set of data seems to be infinite, they argue that "The information in the anatomical constraints cannot be expressed satisfactorily by any single hierarchical ordering. Further, conclusions drawn from considering only a single hierarchy will be misleading" (p. 776); moreover, they note that the hierarchy proposed by Felleman and Van Essen contains "eight violations and three fewer levels of visual cortical areas than any of the computed optimal hierarchies" (p. 776).

It is important to point out, however, that Hilgetag et al. (1996) are not denying that the primate cortex is hierarchical. Rather, they are asserting that "it is not possible to determine the exact hierarchy" (p. 776). Thus Felleman and Van Essen's map (1991) and others like it, though useful perhaps as tutorial aids, are not unique statements of the true arrangement of the parts of the brain. If this situation obtains in systems as relatively well defined and well anchored as the visual system, then imagine how much more difficult it must be to achieve a corresponding goal for higher-level cognitive functions.

Another way to express this same principle of brain complexity has been offered by Shallice (1988, p. 29) in the context of amnesia studies:

. . . it is virtually impossible to rule out the possibility that any association observed between two different deficits arises not because the same function subsystem is responsible for both relevant processes, but because more than one functional subsystem has been damaged in some patients in the group.

That the brain is composed of a heavily interconnected set of centers is well established. Indeed, connections exist between the two cerebral hemispheres through the great commissures. The exact details of these interconnections are not yet completely known, but clearly the brain is not a simple conglomerate of functionally isolated processing sites.

The idea that brain regions are complexly interconnected and that the resulting interactions may be more characteristic of the brain as a whole than of any localized and specialized region has been percolating recently into the literature that compares cognitive processes and fMRI responses. For example, Friston (1997, 1998, 2000a, 2000b, 2000c) has added a strong note of clarification to the notion that a cognitive process is localized in a particular region of the brain. Emphasizing that imaged brain responses are extremely context dependent, he argues persuasively that efforts directed at making maps of functional responses would be better directed at determining the interactions that occur between brain regions. The sources of the interactions are many: both the anatomy and the distributed nature of the brain regions involved in such processes as attention can drastically alter the pattern of observed fMRI responses.

Although, according to Friston, the proper goal of neuroscience should be to search for these interactions, given the nonlinear nature of the brain-mind, it is not at all clear that we could attain that goal. Nevertheless, if we followed Friston's lead, the mind-brain problem would, at the very least, become framed in the proper context—interactive integration of multiple components and regions. If this conceptual reframing—from localized specialization to interactive integration—were to occur, many of the peculiar logical and conceptual deficiencies introduced by the imaging approach might disappear.

Lesion Experiments Can Confirm Necessity but Not Sufficiency   Because the brain's regions are so heavily interconnected and because cognitive processes appear to interact so strongly, the results of classic brain lesion experiments should also be interpreted with caution. Any decline in performance on a specific cognitive task may be affected by an experimental lesion in many different ways. If the nervous system was truly made up of a number of independent modules, each solely responsible for a single cognitive task, then an experimental lesion in any one might well produce a diminution in the ability to perform a specific task. Any of the regions being lesioned in this case would a priori be both *necessary* and *sufficient* for carrying out the processes associated with the performance of that task.

Suppose however, that what the neuroscientist is actually examining is a distributed system of heavily interconnected and interacting regions rather than a collection of functionally isolated modules. In this case, the extirpation of any one of a number of these interacting cortical regions could also produce exactly the same performance decrement observed in the simpler case of independent modules. The difficulty is that, although the behavioral change might be exactly the same, the deficit might very likely be the result of an entirely different organizational aspect of the system. If truly modular brain units existed, the region that had been removed could be deemed both necessary and sufficient for the cognitive process underlying the execution of the task. In a heavily interconnected system, on the other hand, the removed region could play a secondary or even tertiary role in that process. Or removing the region could actually release some other region from being inhibited and the activation of that other region might then inhibit still another region. In other words, although *necessary* for the successful functioning of the complex system, the surgical removal might have destroyed a region that was not by itself *sufficient* to produce the behavior being observed. Clearly, any region of the brain that is dependent on the function of another region may be strongly affected by a lesion in that other region, even if the other region actually played no direct role in the process. There is even a neologism for such an interaction—*diaschisis*. In the case of a system of regions that collectively encoded or represented a given cognitive process, the confusion could be even greater.[3]

In light of these plausible (and, given the complexity of interactions between cerebral centers, likely) alternatives, it is dismaying to see how often researchers working with equivocal data that demonstrate, at best, necessity, leap to the conclusion that the lesioned region was, in fact, sufficient to encode, represent, or serve as the psychoneural equivalent of the cognitive process under investigation. Make no mistake, the association of a cognitive function with a particular region of the brain from such equivocal data is based on the still unsupported presumption of sufficiency.

---

3. It would be impossible to distinguish between a system in which the functions were distributed and one in which an irrelevant interaction occurred: either type of system could produce the same kind of results.

The salient point here—all too often overlooked by those using brain lesion procedures—is that the behavioral changes observed in classic lesion experiments are, in point of fact and logic, neutral with regard to the actual organization of the neural mechanisms underlying those behaviors. Indeed, a subtle realization of this point may have contributed to diminishing interest in neuroscience research based on such procedures in recent years. That the newest approaches to localization—the imaging techniques—also presume sufficiency where necessity alone has been demonstrated should raise some warning flags.

Human Neuropsychological and Experimental Data Are Idiosyncratic

Many conclusions about the localization of psychological processes in the brain have been drawn from the results of accidents or therapeutically necessary brain lesioning procedures on humans. Indeed, the earliest studies of the effect of brain lesions were largely based on injuries sustained in wars or in bizarre industrial accidents such as that of Phineas Gage.[4] In recent years, considerable attention has been directed at lesions produced by diseases of one kind or another. Unfortunately, results of such uncontrolled natural experiments vary substantially from one condition to another. Although some generalities have emerged from the data (e.g., contralateral motor control, lateralization of the left and right hemiretinas in each eye), a survey of the literature reveals serious doubts that such experiments can yield replicable findings on the precise localization of high-level cognitive processes.

The problem, as Shallice (1988) among others points out, is that by averaging together the data obtained from a number of different subjects, one creates a pseudo-localization, a false model of the brain that ignores the very wide discrepancies that can occur between individuals. In some cases, such a pooling of the data of individuals could even lead to the false appearance of localization when in fact there is none. The problem is exaggerated when cortical variability is heaped on the ill-defined nature of some of the deficits for which a specific brain locale is sought.

4. The Phineas Gage tale has become such a mainstay of pop psychology that it true significance is often lost in the telling. For a more balanced account, see Macmillan, 2000, a book in which the fantastic aspects are separated from the scientifically interesting ones.

This is not an unfamiliar problem. It is commonly faced in other scientific fields whenever statistical analyses of variable data are used to estimate central tendencies. The process of pooling data in psychophysical experiments by invoking simple power or logarithmic laws can result in response functions that are totally unlike those of any of the individual subjects. Similarly, in studies of brain localization, the pooling of a number of broad regions of activity from individuals can produce a fortuitous overlap that suggests a narrowly localized region where none exists.

The variability in the spatial dimensions of the proposed cerebral locales we have considered is matched by dynamic changes in localization occurring after an injury or after new experiences. *Recovery of function* poses profound problems for any study that purports to determine the effect of brain lesions on psychological functions. Not having a stable "platform" introduces not only confounds but also uncertainty as to which of several different, if not all equally plausible, explanations in fact accounts for the functional recovery. I have previously (Uttal, 1978, p. 285) tabulated some of these alternative and occasionally contradictory explanations:

1. The original behavioral deficit was not caused by the specific lesion but by a general "shock" from which the subject subsequently recovered.
2. A redundant system took over the function that was originally lost.
3. The ablated tissue recovered by regeneration.
4. The new behavior is not the same as the one originally lost, but a new function of a previously undisturbed region that has taken over the role played by the lesioned area.
5. The original lesion did not remove all of the brain tissue necessary to produce the temporarily lost behavior.

Recovery of function after intentional or fortuitous damage to the brain is not the only potential source of a dynamic temporal reorganization of the brain system. Zheng and Knudsen (1999) have recently reported that even well-established sensory maps can reorganize themselves: after lesioning, new functional pathways and new loci of activity appear to be created in the barn owl's brain. Such reorganization actually occurs even in the peripheral portions of the nervous system. Given that the central parts of the brain are generally considered to be the most flexible and adaptive, what extraordinary plasticity might be seen there?

The inference one can draw from the idiosyncrasies in both time (brain systems dynamically change) and space (brain systems are not arranged in the same way in every individual) is that individual data from either "definitive" neuropsychological observations or best-controlled animal experiments represent a treacherous base on which to build a theory of brain localization. The averaging of neuropsychological results is likely to produce a model of precise localization where none may actually exist.

In summary, there are many technical problems with any kind of lesion data. As noted earlier, lesions may interrupt tracts of passage from one region to another and thus produce behavioral results that can all too easily be misassociated with the region of the lesion. Other regions of the brain may participate in (i.e., be necessary), but not be the unique (i.e., sufficient) locus of, the mechanism underlying a behavioral deficit. Other centers may actually be responsible for multiple behaviors but, because of the behavioral assay method used, appear to have only singular functions. Collectively, all these problems and difficulties continue to raise concerns about basing theories of a modular brain chiefly on data from fortuitous or laboratory-induced lesions. All such data must be deemed substantially equivocal.

Can we ever hope to collect convincing data with the new imaging techniques to resolve these uncertainties? Given the mathematical conclusions of such investigators as Hilgetag et al. (1996), a likely working answer to this question is no. Obviously, many of these concerns also carry over into the new world of PET and fMRI systems.

4.2 Technological and Instrumentation Problems

4.2.1 The Threshold Effect in Functional Magnetic Resonance Imaging

In section 4.1, we consider methodological artifacts rooted in the neuroanatomy and neurophysiology of the brain that should raise cautions about whether cognitive processes can be precisely localized there. In particular, I considered the use of arbitrary criterion thresholds below or above which regional "activation" was deemed "significant" and thus present. Evidence of sharply defined and highly localized artificial boundaries arising from a poor choice of a threshold could easily lead to an erroneous conclusion about the cerebral localization or nonlocalization of a psychological process.

It turns out that there is a comparable, but much more explicit and mechanical, criterion-level artifact at work in when imaging techniques are used to localize psychological functions. This artifact takes the form of the choice of a particular setting on the computer displaying the images obtained with an fMRI machine. Specifically, it has to do with the arbitrariness in selecting the false colors used to indicate the amplitude of absolute or differential responses obtained at various stages in the analytic process. The difference image is presumed to reflect the extent of a brain region associated with the cognitive process under study.

The problem is that the assignment of colors to various levels of activity is completely arbitrary. It is up to the experimenter to decide whether any of the various levels should be colored and what colors should be used and thus what significance should be attached to the difference scores produced by subtraction of the control and experimental images. A conservative assignment could hide localized activity and a reckless one suggest unique localizations that are entirely artifactual.

Clearly, the problem of criterion level arises whenever signals are hidden in noise or tests of statistical significance must be used to evaluate and interpret observations. Because the two fMRI images fed into the subtraction process are going to be noisy and to consist of widely distributed activity, there is a problem of choosing a criterion level such that the "false alarm" rate and the "hit" rate are kept in optimum balance. Because these two measures are functions of each other whenever the underlying distributions of signal and signal plus noise, respectively, overlap, it is impossible to zero either rate without creating compensatory difficulties in the other. If one reduces the false alarm rate, one must increase the incorrect rejections. If one increases the hit rate, one necessarily increases the false alarm rate. Completely eliminating the two kinds of errors is impossible. Derived directly from the impeccable logic of signal detection theory (SDT) as described by Tanner and Swets (1954), this line of thought can be applied to any situation where decisions must be made about signals hidden in noise—the exact situation faced by those interpreting imaging data.

Wise et al. (1991, p. 1815) have discussed the problem of setting criterion-level thresholds in the context of PET activation studies:

There is a final, general caveat . . . and that is the presentation of data in terms of significantly activated regions. [I]nsignificant trends are lost in such a presentation, and such trends may ultimately increase our knowledge of cognitive processing when we are in a position to analyze the data in a more hypothesis-led way at which time the level of significance can be justifiably reduced.

The problem in following this advice is that, with lower criterion levels, more and more regions are likely to be shown to be activated. The end result would thus support the view I believe to be correct, namely, that broad distribution rather than narrow localization characterizes the activity of the brain. Nevertheless, the point is well made by Wise and his colleagues—varying the threshold is going to have a major effect on what regions are shown to have been activated.

4.2.2 Other Technical Problems

As elegant and powerful as they may seem, the scanning techniques are not simple tools that one can manipulate with the ease of, say, driving a car. Subtle interpretations and multidimensional judgments are demanded of the scientist who moves into the imaging laboratory. The evaluation of the results forthcoming from an fMRI system, for example, involve a number of complex steps in the processing that are not always obvious to the scientist using the devices. As described in chapter 2, there is a chain of assumptions and technical processes that make the interpretation of these wonderful images less than immediately direct. Initially, there is an assumption that a heightened metabolism in a given region of the brain is tantamount to that region's participation in the cognitive process being investigated. As we have also seen, this is counterindicated by a number of observations ranging from the earliest observations of alpha blockade in EEG measurements to the idea that an increase in activity in a inhibitory system can lead to a decrease in cognitive activity. This kind of negative correlation has to be weighed carefully in evaluating the validity of the "metabolic activity = cognitive activity" association that lies at the base of the entire localization enterprise, including its modern manifestation in the imaging laboratory.

Similarly, although the link between chiefly synaptic activity and neural metabolism, on the one hand, and glucose and oxygen consumption, on the other, seems to be well established, these activities are not what is usually measured. Rather, it is the amount of blood flowing to a region that is the main measure used by cognitive neuroscientists in their search for the locale of some mental activity. Given the complexity of blood flow control at the fine level of regional capillaries, the correlation between the exact correspondence of blood flow and metabolism may not be exact. Roland (1993) and Greenberg, Hand, Sylvestro, and Reivich (1979), though generally supporting the blood flow–metabolism link, cautiously call for continual evaluation of this essential assumption in using fMRI or PET data to localize psychological functions.

Others have not been quite so optimistic about some of the potential difficulties encountered if one uncritically accepts this assumption. Some technical problems concerning the direct linkage of blood flow and oxygen metabolism have been raised by Vanzetta and Grimvald (1999) among others. They note that in many experiments there have been discrepancies between the fMRI and PET estimates of blood flow and direct measurements of oxygen usage. The problem arises because an increase in blood flow does not occur simultaneously with an increase in oxygen consumption—the former lags behind the latter. The delay between the two measures and the fact that most current fMRI procedures are mainly sensitive to the later components of blood flow often give rise to results that differ in their respective definitions of the regions that appear to be activated during cognitive processes. Although Vanzetta and Grimvald suggest that tuning the fMRI device to concentrate on early components of the blood flow can help to alleviate this problem, this result lends further support to the position that one of the key steps in the chain of assumptions from neuronal activity to measured blood flow may not be as sound as is often assumed by contemporary workers.

Roland et al. (1995) have also pointed out that, for accurate imaging, the tracer substances used in PET scans must readily diffuse to the regions of high metabolism. Nevertheless, because the most often used tracer—radioactive water (H_2O^{15})—does not readily diffuse, several further assumptions must be incorporated into any analyses to make sense of ever more complex data.

The complexity of the chain of assumptions from metabolism to cognition is further compounded by the elusive temporal and spatial properties of the imaging techniques and the natural randomness of human brain sizes and shapes. To overcome this problem, many averaging and normalizing procedures are used (to be discussed later in this chapter) that add further distance between the actual measurements and their interpretation by the investigating neuroscientist. Finally, efforts to reduce image noise by various filtering algorithms introduce further uncertainties that remain to be explored.

Other, purely technical (i.e., physical and electronic) artifacts can distort or even misplace portions of the image. Although some of these artifacts have little to do with the topic at hand, others have the potential to make the images as equivocal as some of the conceptual and psychological problems we have discussed. For example, Hornak (1999) lists the following potential artifacts and their most likely causes in his web text on the basics of fMRI imaging:

Artifact	Cause
RF quadrature	Failure of RF detection circuitry
B_0 inhomogeneity	Metal object distorting B_0 field
Gradient	Failure in magnetic field gradient
RF inhomogeneity	Failure of RF coil
Motion	Movement of imaged object during sequence
Flow	Movement of body fluids during sequence
Chemical shift	Large B_0 and chemical shift difference between tissues
Partial volume	Large voxel size
Wrap around	Improperly chosen field of view

Reiman et al. (2000) also discuss some of the artifacts that can occur when the fMRI procedure is used without careful attention to the complexities of the recording process, the psychological uncertainties, and the mathematical tools used for analysis. In addition to some of those mentioned by Hornak (1999), they also note the possibility of emotional effects on the blood flow in the carotid artery that may mimic or distort cognitive influences. They even note that muscular responses such as "teeth clenching" can produce spurious results and false localizations of cognitive processes.

More serious artifacts, however, emerge as a result of the tasks that subjects are asked to perform in the scanning experiments. According to Reiman and his colleagues (2000), there is no independent assurance that the cognitive effects desired when the experimenter sets us up the experiments are actually extant during the course of the measurements:

> Differing instructional sets fail to influence the cognitive activity of interest, yielding no observable difference in brain regions which are indeed substrates for that cognitive process. . . . This outcome is likely to arise not because the "active" task fails to engage the targeted process, but because the "baseline" process does so as well.

In sum, because all imaging methods are based on a complex series of technical assumptions and processes that are potential sources of uncertainty and artifacts, using them to localize cognitive processes may result in misassociating those processes with particular regions of the brain. Of the technical difficulties the psuedocoloring difficulty (i.e., the arbitrariness of the criterion threshold) is potentially the most serious. However, the conceptual difficulties to be discussed next pose far more profound challenges to the validity of imaging methods as a locator of brain modules, highlighting problems in the fundamental logic and assumptions of the entire localization enterprise that may be even more subtle and disconcerting than the technical problems.

4.3 Conceptual and Logical Problems

Even though the number of technical problems involved in correlating brain locations and mental processes discussed thus far are important and often overlooked, there is a far more serious group of problems that arise out of the concepts, logic, and assumptions underlying the entire localization enterprise. There is, surprisingly, a substantial literature that speaks to these issues, but in the rush to achieve what may not be achievable, it has been largely ignored.

Most of the problems we shall consider here deal with the logic of experimental design. Before proceeding to the assumptions underlying the new imaging techniques, however, I first review in roughly chronological order several challenges raised to using those techniques for localizing cognitive processes in specific regions of the brain.

Criticisms directed against the theory that specific functions were localized in particular regions of the brain have been around for quite a while. The argument against phrenology discussed in chapter 3 represents one prong of these criticisms; the holistic argument made by Freud (1891), who presciently challenged radical and specific localization on the logical grounds that even a good correlation between a lesioned brain region and a given behavior was not proof that the region was the site of the behavior, represents another.

However, one does not have to go back to the nineteenth century to find arguments against brain or behavior modularity, or against both. As recently as 1950, Lashley was still arguing, with the support of many of his contemporaries, that the brain was equipotential and that no cognitive process could be specifically localized. His argument, in what is now considered to be one of the great classics of psychological science (Lashley, 1950), was succinct and to the point, if not sustained by subsequent research: "All of the cells of the brain are constantly active and are participating, by a sort of algebraic summation, in every activity. There are no special cells for special memories" (p. 477). Even though we know that the particular animal (the rat) Lashley used and the kind of experiments he performed are no longer adequate to provide support for such a radical stance on the equipotentiality of brain tissue, the repudiation of this "mass action" point of view was more evolutionary than revolutionary. However, it was not so much the repudiation of equipotentiality as it was the reemergence of earlier localization ideas that led to the equally radical stance on localization in brain regions so prevalent these days among cognitive psychologists, neuroscientists, and neuropsychologists. At Lashley's time, of course, the main localization method was the lesion procedure—cut out a piece of brain and observe the resulting behavioral deficits.

Some countercriticisms of the use of lesion experiments as the basis for conclusions about localization of function, however, arose fairly quickly and still ring true. Gregory (1961) questioned the logic of both the stimulation and the ablation (lesion) procedures as they were conventionally used around the middle of the twentieth century to search for localized regions responsible for particular psychological functions in the brain. His argument was based on a simple but clear-cut analogy between the evolved brain and hardware engineered by humans:

Suppose we ablated or stimulated various parts of a complex man-made device, say a television receiving set. And suppose we had no prior knowledge of the manner of function of the type of device or machine involved. Could we by these means discover its manner of working? (p. 320)

Gregory (1961) argued that, in general, such a procedure could not work, that we must know at least something about how such a device operates to pursue the functional analysis. Although there are some things that can be learned from this procedure—he suggested that we might be able to "map projection areas and delimit pathways" (p. 322)—Gregory asserted that it is all but impossible to define the causal relations of such a heavily interconnected system: there are so many different arrangements of the parts that could produce similar results. "Suppose," he went on to say, we ablate or stimulate some part of the brain, and lose or evoke something in behavior, then it is not clear—even quite apart for previous considerations—that this region is the seat of the behavior in question" (p. 324).

Gregory is alluding to two of the themes that pervade all subsequent criticisms of the localization approach—the necessity for some prior theoretical knowledge and the very high probability of mistaking what seems to be a simple dissociation for a key and essential functional representation. Unfortunately, these remarkably anticipatory insights were thoroughly ignored by his contemporaries and the experimental lesion procedures Gregory chastised simply faded away, only when it became more or less obvious to its practitioners that little progress was being made in answering the questions being asked.

Criticisms of lesion techniques became more sophisticated in subsequent years. Nevertheless, their essential point remained the same—analyzing a complex nonlinear, heavily interconnected system may simply not be doable. As time went on, the language and conceptual arguments against radical localization arguments evolved into something far more complex. Wood (1978), for example, renewed the attack on localization theory by *stimulating* a lesion experiment on a mathematical model of learning developed by Anderson, Silverstein, Ritz, and Jones (1977), a model based on a network of equipotential neurons similar in concept to Lashley's original mass action theory of equal roles for all participating neurons. Wood's method tested the Anderson et al. model by systematically removing neurons in specific places and in varying amounts. To the degree that the model simulated the mass action or equipotentiality idea, this was intended to be a direct analog of the original experiments carried out by Lashley. But Wood (1978) had a second, broader goal in using the Anderson et al. (1977) model: "to assess the degree to which principles of neural organization such as equipotentiality and localization of function can be inferred from lesion experiments" (p. 583). In other words, he wanted to use this type of model to resolve the contentious issue of modularity versus equipotentiality.

Wood's experiments (1978) were statistical and mathematically formal. He did no surgery and observed no organic behavior. Nevertheless, his conclusion was profoundly relevant to the argument made here. What he found was that the model was perfectly capable of producing results that supported *both* the radical equipotentiality and the radical specificity conclusions:

> The present results provide additional evidence of the profound logical difficulties in attempting to infer principles of neural organization from the results of lesion experiments. A persistent behavioral deficit following removal of a given brain region is often regarded as demonstrating that the region plays a specific functional role. Although this conclusion may be correct, similar lesion effects can also be obtained in nervous systems in which each neural element participates in a wide range of functions, depending upon task requirements. As the present results demonstrate, discriminating between these alternatives on the basis of the results of lesion experiments is a difficult if not impossible task. (p. 590)

After prominently featuring and discussing Wood, 1978, Shallice (1988) proposed a counterargument. Whereas Wood had argued that the Anderson et al. (1977) model could support either an equipotential or a modular type of organization, Shallice argued that this conclusion was spurious because it depended on the specific network that Anderson and colleagues had modeled and because Wood had ignored single dissociation data. Specifically, Shallice suggested that Wood's conclusion was built on a special case that involved only the careful selection of a single input neuron from among many possible candidates.

Shallice's critique can be countered in two ways. First, mathematical models are *in general* neutral with regard to the underlying mathematics (Uttal 1998). Second (as presented later in this chapter), "dissociation" experiments, even those carried out on organisms, are invalid supports for modular theories of mental activity.

Nevertheless, and however much disagreement any one has with his particular strategies, it must be accepted that Shallice, 1988, is one of the most remarkable works dealing with the problem of brain modularity and functional localization. I doubt if there is anyone in the literature of mental representation that presents as evenhanded and lucid a discussion of the arguments against specificity of function. All of us interested in this problem have at one time or another turned to his intelligent and comprehensive treatise for insight and wisdom about this problem area. Not only is the history of the problem laid out in much greater detail than I do here, but the alternative theories are tabulated in a way that suggests a significant level of appreciation on his part of the kinds of conceptual difficulties for the modular approach raised in this chapter.

Take, for example, Shallice's discussion of reductive uncertainty produced by system complexity. After tabulating and defining a variety of neural (or other) system organizations that can produce dissections into identical and indistinguishable sets of insoluble modules, he points out that it is impossible to choose between the different systems on the basis of the produced modules. However fundamental to many scientific and engineering enterprises, this conclusion is of course quite unpopular among those who hold to the specific representation or localization side of the argument and who assume, to the contrary, that the dissociation results determine a unique system organization. And here at least, unpopularity seems to have trumped logic.

By listing six different types of system organizations that could produce identical behavioral results even though they differ enormously in their internal structure, Shallice very effectively demonstrates the frailty of any conclusions that might be drawn about internal structure from behavioral findings. What he gives us is the physical instantiation of the argument that behavior is neutral with regard to internal structure. Although, it was apparently not his intent, Shallice's demonstration is also a powerful argument for a kind of psychological behaviorism based on the contention that the observed function of a system is indeterminate of its internal organization.

To be more specific, let us consider the six functionally equivalent types of systems listed by Shallice (1988, pp. 249–253):

1. *Modular systems.* The brain is organized into a cluster of semi-independent, functionally specific modules that, when damaged, produce well-defined behavioral deficits.

2. *Coupled systems.* The brain is composed of individual modules that strongly interact, but that each have their own specific functions.

3. *Systems having a continuous processing space.* The brain appears to be representing specific functions which turn out to be simply different points on a continuum.

4. *Systems of overlapping processing regions.* The brain is made up of overlapping pairs of modules, with both modules in each pair partially representing the particular function under investigation.

5. *Systems of semimodules.* The brain is made up of strongly interacting modular regions, whose respective functions are really only statistical averages of the many inputs that impinge on them.

6. *Distributed and multilevel systems.* The brain is organized such that its functions are widely distributed at different vertical and horizontal levels.

Shallice (1988) presents a particularly cogent and compelling argument that dissociation experiments purporting to distinguish between these alternative system types are deeply flawed:

Precise measurements that directly reflect significant aspects of the functional organization of the cognitive system do not exist. Hence any empirical procedure that stands a reasonable chance of helping to uncover the functional characteristics of the system is likely to involve as many assumptions as does the use of neuropsychological findings. (p. 265)

And, speaking of a fallacious syllogistic argument in favor of the modular hypothesis, he says: "'If modules exist, then . . . double dissociations are a relatively reliable way of uncovering them. Double dissociations do exist. Therefore modules exist.' Presented in this form the logical fallacy is obvious" (p. 248). Therefore, he continues: "So the idea that the existence of a double dissociation necessarily implies that the overall system has separable sub-components can no longer be taken for granted. (p. 249)

Shallice goes on to quite correctly point out that the only way this argument can be made valid is to assume further that none of the other systems he has proposed would produce dissociations. As he says, "This additional assumption was never, to my knowledge, explicitly stated but it was easy to hold implicitly" (p. 248). Later, he provides what should be the conceptual nail in the coffin of a radical localization approach by characterizing this chain of logic as a chain of "lazy assumptions" (p. 248).

Then comes a complete surprise! After so eloquently arguing that the techniques and methodology we have for establishing the existence of mental modules are so deeply flawed that the quest may be an impossible one, Shallice (1988) pulls one of the most extraordinary intellectual flip-flops since Watson's allusion to thinking as "implicit behavior": Stunningly, he states: "From this stage on, *these methodological cautions will be abandoned.* In general, it will be assumed that a (double) dissociation signifies the existence of an isolable subsystem" (p. 266; emphasis added).

How can this have happened? How could our hero suddenly have "abandoned" us? With characteristic lucidity, Shallice (1988) describes the nature of the thought process that made this defection possible for him: "Avoiding being deceived by a tempting shadow will be less important than dimly making out the existence of some possible path" (p. 266).

Shallice's hopeful, chimerical retreat from scientific rigor is probably all too typical of the localization enterprise, in which so many search for plausible relations between brain and mind ignoring serious warnings on the conceptual, technical, and methodological front that they may be on a fruitless quest. Their very likely wasted efforts are not the worst of it, however. Misdirection away from a valid understanding of the true nature of brain organization may be a much more severe penalty for not heeding what scientific rigor and logic have to tell us. Given the brilliance of his analysis of the localization problem, Shallice's defection is, however, particularly disappointing.

Others have also pointed out the dangers inherent in trying to analyze complex systems with what are essentially behavioral, or input-output, tools. Shallice's discussion (1988) was essentially paralleled by Wimsatt (1974), a philosopher who also appreciated that complex systems were capable of being segmented into many "different non-isomorphic decompositions" (p. 69). Citing Kauffman (1971) and Levins (1966) on biological systems, Wimsatt agrees that "in complex systems, there are a number of possible decompositions and often no way of choosing between them" (p. 74). Clearly, Shallice's argument that many different types of system organizations can be decomposed into the same set of modules and Wimsatt's that any given complex system can be decomposed into many indistinguishable sets are simply variants of Moore's second theorem (1956).

4.3.1 Dissociation Experiments Do Not Provide Proof of the Necessity or Sufficiency of Localized Function

The basic conceptual tool of those seeking to correlate the activity patterns in scanned brain images with particular psychological functions, the dissociation procedure, is relatively simple and seems convincing enough at first blush. Over the years, however, considerable criticism has been directed against even this apparently simple idea. We now consider that criticism in detail.

Although the assumptions underlying the dissociation procedure are few, when we examine them closely, we can see they are surprisingly fragile. Chief among these assumptions are two: first, that the behavioral observations resulting from localization experiments are pure, that is, they represent "true" subdivisions of the cognitive ensemble; and second, that the subdivisions can be assayed and identified by the dissociation procedure. Several authors (e.g., Van Orden, Jan op de Haar, & Bosman, 1997; Vishton, 1998) have argued that neither of these assumptions can be supported in a way sufficient to justify today's enormous research enterprise.

Vishton (1998) performs a useful service by clearly identifying the three principal types of dissociation experiments applied to the problem of brain localization in the past:

Single dissociation. Damage to a particular region of the brain produces an identifiable behavioral deficit.

Double dissociation. Damage to two different regions of the brain produces distinctly different behavioral deficits.

Multiple dissociation. Damage to three or more regions of the brain produces distinctly different behavioral deficits.

The fundamental logic of the dissociation argument thus goes something like this: if damage to a particular part or parts of the brain can be shown to produce a particular psychological deficit (or deficits, then that or those part or parts can be assumed to be the locus of representation of that or those psychological process or processes. The double and multiple association procedures simply expand the logic of this basic paradigm.

The problem with this seductively self-evident dissociation approach is that its subtleties are often ignored or overlooked. These subtleties come in many flavors. First, in the single dissociation experiment, although damage to one area can be shown to produce some kind of a measurable deficit, it is not so easy to show that the particular lesion is sufficient by itself to instantiate the missing cognitive process. That is, it is entirely possible that the effect of an injury or even a well-positioned surgical intervention might disrupt some behavior without being the "locus" of the cognitive process underlying that behavior—where the process resides or is represented. In a complex system, interaction of one region with a second intervening region that controls a third, and truly critical region may release that third region from some excitatory or even inhibitory influence. The end effect would be to lead an investigator to completely misidentify the regions responsible for the resulting behavioral deficit.

The problems, once again, are system complexity and the high degree of interconnectivity. Even the most committed "localizer" acknowledges that the brain, to whatever degree it may or may not be modular, is not organized a simple, serial chain of units. Thus, even though a correlation between a lesioned brain region and the diminution of some cognitive skill may be quite high, it is extremely difficult, if not impossible, to make the next inferential step, namely, to conclude that that area is *the* locus of the mental process underlying the behavior. All that we can really say is that the lesioned region is involved in some way in the cognitive behavior under study.

Vishton (1998, p. 8) raises this point eloquently:

If the human brain consists of a collection of anatomically distinct modules, then isolated deficits should result from isolated patterns of brain injury. While the logic of this statement is beyond dispute, cognitive neuropsychologists must reason in the opposite direction, from patterns of deficits to the architecture of brain organization. While damaging a modular system in a particular way will result in a single dissociation, damaging a non-modular system may produce single dissociations as well.

This statement, of course, conveys the same meaning as did many earlier arguments against modularity including those of Freud (1891) and Wood (1978), and Shallice (1988)—in particular, the second assumption Shallice asserts is required to make the dissociation argument work (see page 177).

Vishton then goes on to point out that the same counterargument holds for the double and higher-order dissociation designs as well. Nomatter how many dissociations may be concatenated to prove a point, the direction of the logical chain through which the investigator must move (i.e., from the behavioral data to the neural organization) makes it logically, conceptually, mathematically, and computationally impossible to prove the desired point—that a particular place in the brain is the critical and sufficient locus of a particular psychological process.

Others have made the same point—namely that double dissociations do not lead logically to modularity. Plaut (1995) and Farah (1994) have both argued, as did Wood (1978), from the point of view of computational modelers that disrupted connectionist systems (characterized by parallel distributed organization) are capable of producing exactly the same kind of results as lesioned localized systems. "The conclusion that the locality assumption may be false," writes Farah (1994, p. 60), "is a disheartening one. It undercuts much of the special appeal of neuropsychological dissociations as evidence about the functional architecture."

Plaut (1995, p. 316) raises virtually the same caveat in discussing the results of the typical double dissociation procedure:

[Because] random variations in quantitatively equivalent lesions would be expected to produce a distribution of effects . . . the effects of individual lesions may not be representative of the distribution.

This possibility raises concerns about the reliance in cognitive neuropsychology on single case studies. [E]ffects that appear to provide insight into the functional organization of the cognitive system may simply be statistical flukes.

Although all of these studies are based on the results of computational modeling, and thus do not provide "killer" proof that the brain and cognition are nonmodular, they do provide convincing arguments that the observations obtained using the double dissociation procedure are, in principle, neutral and should not be interpreted as definitive evidence of either modularity or nonmodularity.

We have thus discovered yet another way to express the broad generality that the observed behavior of a mental system may be neutral with regard to its internal structure. Conclusions drawn from ignoring this caveat can be enormously misleading theoretically and can have serious practical consequences as well, particularly in the field of neuropsychology, which is so closely related to the treatment of human beings.

4.3.2 You can Find Anything You Name

Other authors have joined the dispute about the data-processing methods and experimental procedures used to localize cognitive functions in the brain. Among the most concerned with the issue of what behavior can tell us about either cognitive or neural components is Guy Van Orden, my colleague at Arizona State University, and a group of his co-workers. Van Orden et al. (1997), for example, present another cogent and compelling argument that it is not possible to go from effects (i.e., behavior) to structure (i.e., either cognitive components or neural structures). Indeed, the prevalent assumption throughout psychology that "effect = structure" leads to a fatal kind of illogic:

> The conclusion that the observed pattern of dissociations demonstrates autonomous or independent representations (single causes) simply affirms the inevitable consequent of assuming that there were autonomous representations in the first place. . . . Thus we face an inescapable problem of circularity. Our goal is to induce general cognitive components entailed in a specific task from observed behavior, but the method by which we induce these components requires reliable a priori knowledge of the self-same cognitive components.
> No theoretical approach escapes this problem. (p. 135)

Vishton (1998, p. 17) makes the same point from a slightly different point of view:

> If the brain is organized around location-specific, specialized functions, then localized, relative changes in activation will occur. To reason from localized relative changes in activation to localized specialized function, however, is to commit the logical error of affirmation of the consequent.

When we recall the uncertain origins and transitory status of hypothetical cognitive or mental components discussed in chapter 3, it becomes clear that much of the foundation underlying the search for both cognitive components and their respective neural modules is very fragile indeed. Logic and data alike suggest that these proposed "modules" more often than not are merely artifices emerging from our methods, our hypotheses, and our hopes about the way the mind-brain system might be constructed.

Van Orden and his colleagues (1997) join Shallice, Wimsatt, and many others in noting that there are many different system organizations that can produce the same kind of behavior a strictly modular system does and that they may not be distinguishable from it by any conceivable experimental strategy. On the basis of logic and what we know about the brain-mind, would it not then be more accurate to describe it as a dynamic, self-organizing, recurrent, nonlinear, distributed system? Such a system would be composed of many heavily interconnected and interacting subsystems (of various complexities) with feedback and feedforward signals passing among them in complex manners that are mathematically and empirically intractable. Nonlinear, interconnected, dynamic systems are fully capable of producing the kind of behavior expected from modular systems. Among the pieces of evidence that Van Orden and his colleagues (1997, pp. 155–160) (whose research vehicle is perception and language) cite to support this argument:

1. Ziegler and Jacobs (1995) and Stone, Vanhoy, and Van Orden (1997) found counterintuitive feedforward and feedback effects in letter search and lexical decision tasks, respectively. Such consistent feedforward and feedback effects were only predicted by an explanation based on bidirectional—nonlinear—flow of information between the visual stimulus and the pronunciation.

2. Tuller, Case, Ding, and Kelso (1994) and Kelso et al. (1995) showed that, depending on the previous stimulus, there were two stable responses in some speech perception experiments in which a word was orally pronounced to a subject. This multistable type of response is also characteristic of nonlinear systems.

3. Gilden, (in press) observed that 1/f noise affected the recognition of words, contrary to the usual statistical notion of independence between trials. Because trials presented in sequence interacted in a demonstrably nonlinear way, the processing system involved could not be made up of causally independent modules.

Van Orden et al. (1997, p. 160) go on to conclude, on the basis of the complexity of dynamic cognitive systems displayed in these results, that they cannot be accessed in a way that would allow us to specify the nature of any cognitive components even if they did actually exist:

Dissociations cannot be trusted to isolate independent representations. The existence of plausible alternatives undermines their ability for reducing performance phenomena to single causes. . . . Induction of single causes required a priori the truth of single causes.

In a subsequent paper, Van Orden, Pennington, and Stone (in press, p. 5) have vigorously supported this point of view and summed up some of the problems faced by the double dissociation technique. One of the most important contributions of this article was their expanded explication of the assumptions that are built into the double dissociation procedure. Mainly concerned with brain lesion associations, Van Orden and his colleagues point out some of the logical features of the double dissociation strategy. They challenge the implicit assumption that the effects of a lesion are really simple and "pure." That is, are the behavioral deficits that arise from either an accidental or experimental brain injury independent of all of the other behaviors that might have been measured? Like Vishton (1998), Van Orden, Pennington, and Stone (in press) argue that they may not be—the problem is that independent validation does not exist. They say: "Whether dissociations are truly pure cases, and whether combinations of dissociations are truly opposite pure cases, cannot be determined outside of one's theories of mind and task."

They also support the argument made by both Shallice (1988) and Vishton (1998) that there is an a priori requirement to assume the existence of modules before they can be sought in an experiment. Having made this assumption, then you can and always will find something to confirm it. The modules found are likely to be the modules hypothesized by whatever model or theory was initially invoked—even if it had been based on nothing more than ad hoc or unscientific origins. Thus, once again, the circularity of the double dissociation argument becomes clear. As is so often the case, the researcher ends up seeing what he expected and ignoring the data and arguments that do not fit into a preexisting theoretical structure.

After extensively reviewing the literature on lexical processing, Van Orden et al. (in press) showed that, when examined from a point of view free of the usual assumptions underlying double dissociation theory, there were many experimental counterexamples to a purely modular hypothesis. Conflating the a priori assumptions of the approach with a modicum of self-justifying data, they noted, simply leads to "fantasy components" (p. 31). The key problem is that the original theory, whatever its origins, arbitrates the acceptability of data and often dictates the conclusions—valid or not. Arguments then arise concerning exlusionary criteria and, given some leeway in accepting or rejecting particular findings, theories can become self-perpetuating.

Because there is no way to exclude any but the most implausible hypothetical components, there is an unending succession of ever more finely defined mental components: "Dissociation methods have no empirical failure point. Any new dissociations contrary to an extant modular theory can always be accommodated by additional exclusionary criteria, by adding modules, or by replacing existing modules with more refined modules" (Van Orden et al., in press, p. 24).

The open-ended property of the dissociation technique that is emphasized by all of these commentators—Van Orden and his colleagues, Shallice, and Vishton—is a strong argument against applying this procedure to both the search either for cognitive modules or for the localized brain sites representing cognitive functions derived from brain lesion studies.

There is perhaps no more compelling argument that you can find whatever you seek by means of the brain imaging techniques than the strange story of the "God Spot." Speaking at a recent scientific meeting, one distinguished neuroscientist described the discovery of a region of the brain associated with accentuated religious experience in epileptics and deeply religious subjects. Although this report naturally produced a large number of comments in the popular literature, I have been unable to find a serious scientific report that spells out the details of the brain-religiosity association. Nevertheless, the speed with which the idea that religious experience is built into our nervous system in a particular place slipped into the popular culture (e.g., see the websites authored by Connor, 1998; Trull, 1998; and Anonymous, 1998) suggests how easy it can be for even usually critical scientists to slide down the slippery slope toward a chimerical modularity.

4.3.3 There Is Always a Peak of Response in a Scanned Image
Van Orden and Paap (1997, p. S87) make another important point: "One cannot disconfirm false models, however, because subtractions always highlight some brain region." The reason for this is obvious when one thinks about it a bit. The subtraction process always produces a peak someplace at some level of the threshold control. If a peak is not visible at one criterion level, the threshold can be lowered until some difference value is accepted as a response. The subtraction process is never going to be perfect, no two real practical images are going to be

so perfectly matched that they produce exactly a zero difference. Therefore, the difference map is never going to be perfectly flat. Rather, it is a difference between two uneven (for all practical purposes, quasi-random) surfaces that must display some peaks that must be discernible at any reasonable level of threshold acceptance. Further, given the irregularity of the typical scanned and bounded image, it is very likely, indeed it is almost certain, that one of these peaks will be larger than the others.

The point is that a localized peak or maximum of activity in a brain scan almost always occurs even if the underlying forces producing the original maps were random or even partially random. The likelihood of not seeing some kind of a peak, especially in a system with widespread activation, is probably very small. Indeed, by depressing the threshold value at which a difference is accepted, an experimenter should be able to raise many more peaks from the background. What credibility can then be given to the largest one as a locus of some cognitive process given the arbitrariness of the decision criterion and the presence of other, previously hidden, peaks?

If this informal argument is not adequate, my readers should also be reminded that mathematicians make the same point when they say that any bounded surface must have at least one maximum value. All images are bounded surfaces; ergo, all images must have a maximum or peak value. Given that a peak value is what is being sought when one attempts to localize some cognitive function, such a search is always rewarded.

4.3.4 The Subtractive Method Also Does Not Provide Proof of the Necessity or Sufficiency of Localized Function

Derived from the dissociation procedures used in neuropsychology and cognitive psychology, the subtractive method has some special attributes as a result of the specific technology involved in brain scanning. The method is based on two fundamental assumptions, the first of which is that brain activity should differ when two different cognitive processes are carried out. This is an incontestable truism at the micro neural level. It is necessary for any materialist monist to assume that two different thoughts are somewhere instantiated by different neural states, although the critical neural states may not be the ones we are observing or can observe. As Albert Einstein is reputed to have said, "Not everything that can be counted counts, and not everything that counts can be counted."

However, there is a second, more complicated assumption, one that transcends such ontological certainties, that also deserves our attention. In its simplest form, it can be expressed as follows. Assume that an experimenter wishes to compare the brain effects produced by two cognitive conditions. If one of the cognitive conditions involves some action that the other does not, then any difference in the brain responses observed in the PET or fMRI image for those two cognitive conditions should indicate the region in which the action is localized. Therefore, for example, if in condition A a subject is performing a mental activity and in condition B the subject is not, then if one subtracts the image obtained in condition B from the one obtained in condition A, the common elements subtract out and the residual trace indicates where the mental activity particular to condition A is localized.

Stated in terms of these two assumptions, the method seems relatively straightforward. For example, consider the following gedanken-experiment in which two fMRI images are reconstructed and then the first subtracted from the second. The first comes from a subject whose eyes are closed during the time the data necessary to reconstruct image were collected. The second comes from the same subject (ideally), with all conditions as close to the same as possible, except that the subject is visually active—looking at a picture of some object. Each of the fMRI images shows substantial amounts of brain activity—the subject is, after all, alive and mentally active in both instances. Nevertheless, the subtractive method makes the strong assumption that the two conditions differ only with regard to the presence or absence of the visual stimulus.

The mathematics of the subtractive method here are trivially simple. The images are arrays of numerical values. Each pixel or voxel (in the case of a three-dimensional image) in each of the images has a certain numerical value. Therefore, the two images can be numerically subtracted from each other in a very simple way—the value of a particular voxel in the first image is subtracted from the value of the corresponding voxel in the second image. When this is carried out over the entire image, a new *difference* image is generated. Regions whose activity does not change should show a zero (or near-zero) value in the difference image; regions that are more active when the subject is actively doing something should show positive values; and regions that are less active should show negative values. Regions showing strong positive values in the difference image are here assumed to be those responsible for the process of "seeing." These "positive difference" scores are thus considered by the localization practitioner to designate the neuroanatomical site of "seeing."

Logically, the process is much less straightforward than the verbal description suggested. Even the strongest proponents of the imaging–cognitive function correlation approach agree that the method is based on a string of assumptions that transcend the seeming simplicity of the arithmetic details just presented. Van Orden and Paap (1997, p. S86) highlight four critical assumptions that stand between the raw image data and the inferences and conclusions drawn from them:

1. One must begin with a "true" theory of cognition's components. . . .
2. [One must] assume that corresponding functional and anatomical modules exist in the brain.
3. [T]he brain must be composed of feed forward modules to insure that the component of interest makes no qualitative changes "upstream" on the shared components of the experimental and control tasks.
4. Finally, each contrasted task must invoke the minimum set of components for successful task performance.

"If any one of these assumptions is false," they go to say, "the entire enterprise fails" (p. S86).

Given the unarguably critical nature of these assumptions, we need to examine each one carefully. First, do we have a "'true' theory of cognitive components?" Proceeding from the classificatory uncertainty about mental modules or faculties established in chapter 3, it would be premature, if not foolhardy, to assume that any "'true' theory" or logical taxonomy of mental processes exists. There is no consensus even on the existence and nature of the individual psychological components, faculties, abilities, or modules, much less on how they may be organized or interact. It should thus be extremely difficult to arrive at an integrated theory of how these hypothetical mental components are organized into functioning systems once one passes beyond the well-anchored sensory and motor subsystems. (I say "should" because unsubstantiated theories of this kind abound in the literature.)

Second, are there direct correspondences between the proposed components and their proposed locations in the brain? At first glance, this seems like a purely empirical question. One can simply go into the laboratory and determine whether particular regions of the brain reliably "light up" in a image when a particular mental activity is present. However, the very act of asking this second question is based on an affirmative answer to our first question. If we cannot validly and reliably identify a particular psychological component, we should see a wide variance in the active regions as different experimenters carry out what appear to be similar experiments. Indeed, this is the usual result (as we shall see in section 4.4, where the problem of "fragile data" is discussed).

Although this second critical assumption of a correspondence between functional and anatomic modules is a sine qua non of the whole approach, it also cannot be uncritically accepted. This assumption in turn assumes a particular nature of the nervous system, one that is contraindicated by the widespread activity observed in brain tissue whenever even the least significant cognitive process is carried out. The substantial overlap of the proposed cerebral regions also argues against it. Furthermore, it must not be overlooked that, before one image is subtracted from another, the typical fMRI or PET scan shows near-universal activation of the cerebral cortex. It is only when the subtraction is carried out that a more or less sharply demarcated response is observed. The assumption that only this difference is significant and that all of the subtracted activity is irrelevant is another weak link in a highly questionable chain of logic.

Third, is the brain a linear, feedforward only system, one that can be analyzed with the tools of linear mathematics and psychophysical assay procedures? Apart from localization studies, virtually every body of data on the brain and behavior suggests it is not, that there are strong feedback loops and that the nervous system, whether measured in terms of behavioral interactions or in terms of the interactions among the various centers and nuclei of the brain, is a highly complex and nonlinear system. Mental and neural processes, from the most basic chromatic experiences to the highest levels of cognitive penetration, clearly interact with each other. Furthermore, the behavior observed in virtually every cognitive experiment is unstable; slight differences in experimental design often produce qualitatively and catastrophically different results (Thom, 1975) in what are incorrectly assumed to be identical protocols. Even the most peripheral coding mechanisms produce coded signals that are typically nonlinear functions of the input stimulus. Reversible images produce catastrophic reversals of perceptual experiences that would be hard to explain in linear terms. The course of learning is filled with sudden discontinuities such as insightful discovery, a phenomenon that suggests nonlinear interactions are the norm rather than the exception.

How could this false hyperlinearization and oversimplification of the underlying model of brain localization have come about? Throughout the history of cognitive psychology, this new mentalism has been based on the idea of a simple, linear, mental system made up of isolable components, which can be added and subtracted from each other without disrupting their function. Simple "block diagram" models have been the conceptual mainstay of contemporary cognitive psychology. However, as Pachella (1974) has so eloquently pointed out, this particular model of the mind is based on premises and assumptions that require that the mind-brain be inherently linear and decomposable. If one starts off by accepting the premises that it is possible to isolate mental processes and that they act according to simple arithmetic rules, it is an easy step to searching for locales in the fabric of the brain in which these components could be localized.

There have been many challenges to this linear, modular conceptualization of the mind, but despite what appear to be strong counterarguments, these ill-founded assumptions have uncritically become the basis of a major movement in contemporary cognitive neuroscience.

Fourth and finally, is each experimental task for which a brain locale is sought simple enough that its components are really isolated from other equally simple tasks? In other words, is the psychological process under study pure, neither interacting with nor influencing other processes? Clearly, the assumption that *any* human cognitive component is uninfluenced by and independent of all others is hardly justifiable, given the evidence we have of the influence of set and expectations on even simple visual perceptual experience.

The assumption of "functional isolability" is also counterindicated by the difficulty of identifying the base, neutral, or inactive condition that is being subtracted from the active condition in a dissociation or image subtraction procedure. For example, how can one isolate attention from a task in which the subject is supposed to be actively paying attention? How can one be assured that "attention is not being paid" to something? It seems unlikely that any conscious mental task would not involve attention to some degree. Can a subject, following the experimenter's instructions, truly *not* think about something?

The issue of the baseline has been raised anew by Reiman et al. (2000). Given the rich variety of cognitive processes such as rehearsal, daydreaming, imaging, and other conscious and unconscious activities that may fleetingly be present in the brain, they ask, how can we be sure that two different experimental conditions do not activate common brain mechanisms (which would then be spuriously subtracted to "null" the relevance of some area)? Simple instructions to a subject—"Do not think about it"—represent a particularly fallible link in the chain of assumptions justifying the image subtraction approach to localizing mental functions in the brain.

Roland et al. (1995) also call our attention to a very general methodological constraint concerning the subtractive method. Even if a subtraction shows that there is no difference in the blood flow and arguably, therefore, in the metabolism of a region, this is an integrated result and

does not imply that the processing in the field was identical in the two conditions. Since every cortical field is probably anatomically connected to between 10 and 20 other cortical areas (Felleman & Van Essen, 1991) one cannot from the mere localization and intensity of an activated field [in the brain] deduce what type of information transformation underlies that activation. . . . (p. 783). Conversely a field presumably may also participate in identical information transformation but show a different intensity of activation depending on effects of attention [or some other variable]. (p. 783)[5]

Here again, the confusion between what must be so at some level of psychoneural identity and what can be measured is clearly highlighted.

5. It should be noted that even though Roland and his colleagues (1995) are critical of some of the limitations of the averaging, standardization, and subtractive methods, they have been among the leaders in the localization field. Most of their work, however, is directed at sensory and learning topics for which the subtractive method is best adapted and for which there is the greatest degree of consistency with what has previously been discovered using other methods.

Thus it is not necessarily the case that the chain of logic from (1) changing information state to (2) increased neurophysiological activity to (3) accelerated metabolism to (4) increased oxygen uptake to (5) increased blood flow to (6) image "hot spot" to (7) the presence or absence of a representation of the cognitive activity is unbroken and, therefore, sound. In addition to the logical distance between the primary representation and the distal measurement in this chain of logic, the meaning of each of the steps remains controversial. Thus there is no way to tell exactly what even the most precisely defined "hot spot" means in the functioning of a complex system of interacting brain modules and centers. Indeed, *increased* activity in an inhibitory area could as well be associated with a reduced level of the very cognitive activity under study. The hot spot could equally well indicate a region that actually diminishes that activity, which is being encoded in an increased *negative* score someplace else in the brain. As we have seen already, this impenetrability is characteristic of nonlinear systems of many different kinds, any one of which can produce identical functional measures.

Throughout virtually the entire localization enterprise, inadequate attention is paid to the areas that show negative scores in the subtractive method (reflecting significantly decreased blood flow), whereas attention is heaped on regions that show high positive scores (reflecting significantly increased blood flow). The interaction of inhibitory and excitatory processes in the brain inevitably, therefore, can produce serious mislocalizations and mislead rather than enlighten us concerning any possible localization of mental processes.

Inadequate attention is also paid to the regions that are "zeroed out" by the subtraction process. It is incorrect to assume, if region's function did not change drastically between the neutral and experimental conditions, that its action has remained constant. It must not be forgotten that the true neural correlate of mental activity is not to be found at the molar level at which the PET and fMRI scans work. What is the correct level? Although no one yet has a convincing empirical answer to this question, it does seem most likely, given the overabundance of cellular neurophysiological data already available, that the true equivalent of what we behaviorally observe at the molar level as a result of conscious self-awareness or mental activity is the information state of intricate networks of neurons. The localization issue—Where is that informational process occurring?—in fact, does not speak to this essential level. The point here is that the apparent cumulative activity of a brain locus may not change even though the state of the network in that region has been profoundly altered.

Moreover, even if we could find precise modular locations in the brain associated with well-defined psychological constructs, we still would not have solved the problem of how brain activity becomes mental activity. That question has to be answered in terms of the informational state of the network of neurons, something that cannot be done for reasons of numerousness, complexity, chaotic loss of information, and thermodynamic irreversibility (Uttal, 1998).

Despite the cogency of this argument, practitioners of the imaging approach to functional localization in the brain continue to assume that the regions that are zeroed out by the subtraction process or that produce negative differences play little or no role in the psychological events being studied. It must be remembered, however, that substantial amounts of activity are present in these regions during both the control and experimental data collection periods. A difference between the two experimental conditions need not signify that the small region illuminated in the subtraction image is the sole locus of the mental activity of interest. To assign even "simple" mental activities to a small localized portion of the brain runs counter to a substantial database suggesting that cognitive activity of virtually *any* complexity produces widespread cerebral activity.

There have been many other criticisms of the subtractive method as it is used in imaging experiments. In a particularly cogent argument, Pulvermüller (1999) details additional reasons that the subtractive method so used is logically flawed. According to him, it is the method's unproven simplifying assumptions that are fundamentally at fault.

The single difference often assumed to exist between the experimental and control conditions in a fMRI experiment, Pulvermüller (1999) explains, may actually be a complex set of several differences. Paying attention to a visual stimulus presentation and observing a blank screen are tasks not likely to differ in only a single way. Clearly, this difficulty is compounded by our not having a clear sense of what different processes may be involved even in tasks as superficially simple as "looking" and "not looking" at something. Thus there is no assurance that a "hot spot" in an fMRI image is actually the locus of what we think we are manipulating.

It is sometimes argued that the subtractive method is but the first of a long line of new procedures that, with time, will overcome some of their attendant difficulties. For example, one of the most recently developed procedures, the event-related fMRI, requires much faster MRI systems than were previously available in order to measure the temporal course of the effect of a single event. Typically, two stimuli are repeatedly presented in random order and the resulting responses are averaged separately for each of the two stimuli or conditions. For example, Friston et al. (1998) studied the different fMRI responses to familiar and unfamiliar visually presented words. The data were processed by various smoothing and normalization procedures and then the responses from each type of stimulus statistically combined and tested for significant differences. The analysis is comparable to that used for visually evoked cortical electrophysiological signals but has the advantage of specifying the spatial pattern of a brain response much more precisely.

Although the event-related fMRI is a step forward from the much lower temporal discriminability of early fMRI procedures, it is subject to many of the same problems, particularly with regard to the averaging process, that plague evoked brain potential (EVBP) and other forms of MRI imaging. The advance in technology does not overcome the logical and conceptual problems all brain imaging techniques most ultimately confront.

There is another point that is important in evaluating the results obtained with either the subtractive method or event-related fMRI. Cumulative neurophysiological activity, in this case measured by the metabolic activity of regions of the brain, is assumed to be associated with activation of a region that represents some psychological process. However, the link between the informational state of the neural network—the essential correlate of any cognitive activity—and cumulative metabolic activity remains uncertain. This raises, once again, a profoundly disconcerting problem for the users of imaging procedures: the cumulative measure of brain metabolism is neither theoretically not empirically linked to the momentary details of the neural network at the micro level—the essential level of the information processing system that is really the psychoneural equivalent of mentation. From this point of view, the "signs" of brain activity obtained from the scanning systems are no more "codes" of what is going on than any other physiological correlate, such as the electrodermal response or an electromyogram. (For a discussion of the distinction between signs and codes, see Uttal, 1967.) Although localization studies may provide insights into and heuristics about how the brain is organized in a macroscopic fashion, it is the microscopic details of the ebb and flow of synaptic activity that are the psychoneural equivalent of mentation.

4.3.5 Statistical Measures Sometimes Hide Individual Differences and Create False Localizations

The data obtained from imaging procedures are usually very noisy. Although there are many sources of this noise or uncontrolled variability, the main source is that individual brains differ significantly in the details of their functional organization and anatomy. Even some of the gross anatomical structures of the brain differ noticeably from one person to the next. With the exception of the major fissures, it is now thought that the complex sulcus and fissure pattern on the brain may be a random development of the need during fetal development to squeeze a potentially large cerebral surface into the confines of the developing skull (see page 30). On a more detailed level, neurosurgeons know that they must be very careful during their operations to individually map out the exact location of cortical regions that may influence motor or speech; there is sufficient variability from one brain to the next that no "standard" map of a prototypical brain could be precise enough to avoid a surgically induced disaster. Brain centers vary from place to place, sometimes by relatively small amounts, but sometimes by amounts so large as to make the difference images produced by a fMRI or PET scan look very different from subject to subject. Superimposed on this anatomical intersubject variability are the many technical source of noise, metabolic, neurological, electronic, and so on.

Other sources of variability are less well appreciated. The extraordinary adaptiveness of human thought processes is prima facie evidence that there are many ways in which the brain may arrive at a solution to a cognitive problem. Thus the brain mechanisms operating at one instant may not be exactly like those at work the next.

One strategy to handle the noisy data of imaging studies is to simply average several difference images pixel by pixel, that is, to add the numerical value of each pixel in the images from one subject to the values of all of the corresponding pixels in all of the other images obtained from other subjects or from that same subject in other trials and then to divide the sums by the number of images processed. When these new values are plotted out in proper order they represent a kind of "average image" suggesting a more or less precise localization of the cognitive function that was under study. To reduce the variability produced by individual differences between subjects even further, the several difference images are sometimes standardized in size and shape before the averaging is carried out, although this standardization can also degrade the very information being sought.

As Roland et al. (1995) point out, the elaborate and extensive standardizing and averaging process often results in images still so noisy that contemporary researchers find it necessary to use even more sophisticated processing tools. Some of these tools are comparable to the spatial frequency filters used to sharpen the original scans. Just how elaborate and extensive this manipulation of data can become is evident in the following account by Wise et al. (1991, p. 1806) of their procedure in a typical experiment:

The data from each subject were first standardized for brain size and shape and reconstructed parallel to the intercommissural line. . . . To increase the ratio of signal to noise and to account for the normal variability of the anatomy of the cerebral gyri and sulci between individuals, the reconstructed images were smoothed using a low pass filter of length 9 pixels on a side in the transaxial plane. As the study was designed to examine regional changes in blood flow across activation conditions, the data were first normalized for global flow differences by analysis of covariance, with measured global flow as the confounding covariate . . . and the averaged for each condition across the six subjects. . . . Subsequent statistical analysis of the data to detect significant areas of change between task and rest were performed by a planned comparison of means with a Bonferroni correction at a P level of 0.05 accounting for the effective number of independent pixel measurements by analysis of the autocorrelation function of the images.

Discussing the complex nature of these averages, transformations, and corrections performed in almost all currently active imaging laboratories, Roland et al. (1995, p. 783) noted: "As a consequence, neither the extent of individual activations nor the extent of mean activations can be determined. However, it is possible to determine a center of each activation or a point where the change is maximal."

The result of all of this correcting, noise reducing, standardizing, and averaging is that the final image obtained tends to obscure the sometimes very wide differences between different subjects. More seriously, it can produce the illusion of a localized process by emphasizing fortuitous regions of overlap to the exclusion of the more widely distributed active regions in the individual subject.

There is considerable discussion in the statistical literature about how much "validity" is lost when averaging processes such as those discussed are carried out. As Pulvermüller (1999, p. 265) explains:

> If many comparisons are being made (when data from tens of channels or thousands of voxels are contrasted) the likelihood of a difference occurring by chance is high. On the other hand, if critical significance levels are adjusted to reduce the likelihood of significant results . . . an actual difference between brain responses may be masked because the too rigid statistical criterion is almost impossible to reach.

An analogous issue concerns the criterion value that should be used. Although it is typical and traditional to use 0.05 as the cutoff point for psychological experiments, some investigators (e.g., E. Reiman of the Good Samaritan PET center in Phoenix, Arizona) prefer to use 0.005 to further minimize the possibility of a "false alarm" in their imaging studies, although this also means that some active areas will be "missed" that might well have shown up otherwise.

Obviously, statistical considerations add to the uncertainty of the conclusions drawn from the data. Moreover, because of the limited availability of the scanning devices and the cost of this kind of research, the amount of data collected on specific problems is limited. Complete data sets sufficient to establish statistical significance are thus likely to be rare.

4.3.6 Conceptual Contradictions Abound in the Imaging Literature

One of the most disconcerting characteristics of the localization literature is how often conceptual and logical inconsistencies between the theories and analyses coexist with a steadfast commitment to an empirical approach suffering from those very inconsistencies. I have already spoken of the startling non sequitur between the data and concepts contraindicating a radical localization theory and Shallice's determination (1988) to forge ahead.

The opposite kind of logical contradiction also occurs—collecting data based on an extreme view of localization and then drawing conclusions that run counter to it. For example, Posner and Raichle's enormously influential semipopular book (1994/1997) presents many examples of brain images purported to represent the localization of such complex cognitive processes as language, attention, imagery, and even mental disorders. Nevertheless, in their concluding remarks they propose several general principles that run entirely counter to the "localized function" philosophy that permeates their book. Two of their ten general principles are particularly surprising:

2. Cognitive tasks are performed by networks of widely distributed neural systems.

3. Computations in a network interact by means of "reentrant" processes. (p. 242)

Indeed, given their championing of the idea that cognitive functions are highly localized, principle 2, arguing that wide distribution rather than localization is the true state of affairs, is more than just surprising. It contradicts at the most fundamental level the message they are seeking to send as well as the central assumption of the entire localization enterprise.

Similarly, principle 3 also runs strongly counter both to their conclusions and to the assumptions on which the interpretations of their empirical work are based. Essentially an affirmation of the nonlinearity of the brain system, principle 3 implicitly makes two important arguments against the use of the subtractive method:

1. It contradicts the validity of the method's central assumption, that linear superimposition gives an accurate depiction of brain activity, thus asserting that the brain system is actually nonlinear and thus superimposition does not hold.

2. It contradicts a corollary assumption of the subtractive method, namely, that cognitive functions are constant and unalterable.[6] Reentry

6. This corollary assumption, referred to as "pure insertion" by Sternberg (1969a), has in fact been contradicted by a large amount of psychophysical evi-

or feedback implies that the functions of the various regions involved in complex cognitive processes are not constant when these regions are involved in different tasks or organized in different arrangements.

Perhaps one of the most egregious conceptual errors of the localization enterprise is the assumption that the brain modules are able to encode only a single cognitive process. Throughout the fMRI literature there is an implicit acceptance of the assumption that, once associated with a particular cognitive process, a cortical module is irrevocably assigned to that process. Coupled with the continuing difficulty of defining cognitive processes, this assumption inevitably leads to false conclusions, theories, and explanations.

To see how badly wrong things can go when this assumption is accepted let us return to a mainstay of current localization theory—"face recognition." We have already seen that electrophysiological (see page 21) and imaging (see page 134) data have zeroed in on the fusiform cortex as the locus of "face recognition." Upon further investigation, however, it turns out that, though this region may be deeply involved in some kind of visual image processing, there is nothing special about the face as a stimulus. Indeed, as Gauthier, Skudlarski, Gore, and Anderson (2000) are quick to point out, familiarity with cars and birds also tends to produce responses in this same area: "These results suggest that the level of categorization and expertise, rather than superficial properties of objects, determine the specialization of the [fusiform gyrus] (p. 191).

The misidentification of fusiform gyrus as a "face recognition" region can, in retrospect, be attributed to two different, but intertwined, factors. The first is the inadequate definition of the cognitive process under investigation. Where once "face recognition" was sought, now something more generic—"familiarity"—seems to better characterize the process in which this area participates. The second is the profoundly incorrect assumption that activity in this area of the brain accounts for an isolatable mental component that we could designate either as "face recognition" or as "familiarity." Indeed, when "expertise" can be substituted for a

---

dence showing strong interactions between the attributes of cognitive activity (see, for example, Stoner and Albright, 1993). I have discussed the problems engendered by assuming "pure insertion" and the arguments for assuming that interattribute interaction is the norm in Uttal, 1998.

particular kind of object recognition, it becomes clear that we must be far from the true organization of the brain-mind system.

In summary, there appears to be a logical disconnect between the arguments proposed by localization theorists and some of their conclusions. Likewise, there is a clash between their analyses and their empirical strategies. Obviously, the seductive simplicity of the approach has won the day, pushing aside logic and even data, with many of the resulting theories driven more by hopeful expectations than by the findings and observations.

4.4 Fragile and Contradictory Data

Another problem faced by those seeking to localize cognitive processes in the brain is the fragility and transitoriness of the actual empirical data. We have already discussed some examples of this problem, but there are many others. In Uttal, 1988, I considered the matter of data fragility in considerable detail in the context of high-level visual cognition. From the plethora of studies of the cognitive processing of visual stimuli, it was very difficult to identify any kind of conclusion that lasted for more than a few years. Almost any replication came up with different results that differed either somewhat or completely from those of the original study. The slightest difference in experimental design, intended or unintended, could produce dramatic differences in the experimental outcome. Indeed, I posed this as a practical "law" asserting that "Slight changes in the procedure, stimulus materials, or methodology often produce dramatic changes in the rules of perception." (Uttal, 1988, p. 289)

There are other indications in the localization literature that speak even more directly to the fragility of the raw database. Nothing makes this point more clearly than a figure prepared by Pulvermüller (1999). Superimposed on a diagram of the human brain (figure 4.1) are the several areas that have been designated by a number of investigators as *the key region for the processing word meanings*. The startling impression projected by this figure is that most of the major regions of the brain have been so designated by one or another of these investigators. Pulvermüller helped to make this breadth of representation clear by labeling this figure with the names of the investigators who made these as-

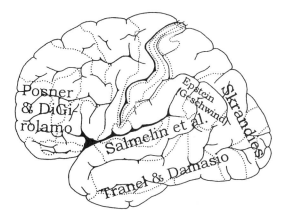

Figure 4.1
Areas identified by different laboratories using different methods to localize the processing of word meaning in the brain. Note that virtually all areas of the brain has been associated with word meaning. From Pulvermüller 1999, used with the permission of Cambridge University Press.

sociations (Epstein, 1999; Geschwind, 1970; Posner & DiGirolamo, 1999; Salmelin, Helenius, & Kuukka, 1999; Skrandies, 1999; and Tranel & Damasio, 1999).

Poepple (1996) has also surveyed a group of studies on phonological processing and found essentially the same result. He reported, to the contrary, that there was little or no overlap in the activated brain regions even though all of the five studies he surveyed involved very similar cognitive tasks.

Harpaz (1999) reviewed over a hundred reports of PET and fMRI correlations with cognitive functions published in 1997. He was particular interested in three aspects of replicability: (1) interexperimental replications—the frequency of one report being replicated by another; (2) intrasubject replications—going back to see if the same subject produced the same results when the experiment was repeated; and (3) intersubject replicability in the same study. With regard to (1), Harpaz states:

In [116 of] the 125 studies I surveyed, there wasn't any report of a robust replication of the results of another study. [Other than nine studies] the rest of the 116 studies either ignore completely the data of other studies, or compare it in qualitative terms, or compare the interpretation of the data (rather than the data itself). (p. 4)

And:

The data about replication of cognitive imaging between different studies and different research groups is extremely sparse, and the sparse data is virtually all negative. (p. 7)

Harpaz was equally critical of the individual experimental protocols that did not adequately check for intersubject or intrasubject variability. He states: 'The data about replicability between individual subjects in the same study is also very sparse. It contains a single case of what looks like robust replicability . . . but the rest is mostly negative" (p. 7). Given how few metastudies of this kind have been carried out, Harpaz is to be given a great deal of credit. (Readers interested in reasons for this paucity of metareviews should consult appendix B.)

Another convincing and dramatic demonstration of one of the main sources of "fragile data" can be found in the previously cited work of Grafman et al. (1995), whose list of cognitive processes associated with the frontal cortex spans over seven pages. Obviously, either investigators have discovered a region of the brain that is involved in everything (a real possibility) or their idiosyncratic definition of psychological processes is much too varied. If the latter, this is prima facie evidence of a breakdown in a systematic definition of psychological processes. If the former, what better argument could be made against even a limited form of localization?

Another way in which the data may be "fragile" can be observed in the inconsistencies among the conclusions drawn from the application of different tools. For example, PET studies of memory formation indicate that both the anterior and posterior portions of the parahippocampal gyrus are involved in memory encoding and storage. Quite to the contrary, however, fMRI studies of the same tasks by Schachter and Wagner (1999) indicate that only the posterior region is activated. Such conflicting results, the authors speculate, "could reflect differences in experimental protocols between the studies, or could be attributable to loss of fMRI signal (susceptibility artifact) in the anterior MTL" (p. 1504). The possibility of some even more deeply flawed conceptual artifact cannot be excluded. A simple admonition that "further experiments" are needed is inadequate in the absence of a thoughtful consideration of the fundamental premises on which this type of research is based.

The important point made by all of these demonstrations of widespread activity in imaging studies is not that there has been any error on the part of most of these investigators, but rather that they all are likely to be correct. The slight differences that are inevitable in the experimental paradigm used by each laboratory probably led their measuring techniques to emphasize different parts of what are actually complex and widely distributed brain processes. The inescapable conclusion, notwithstanding the variability and fragility of all these data, is that broad distribution and interaction among multiple regions of the brain are the true attributes of the representation of mental activity.

4.5 Conclusion

In this chapter, I have examined some of the anatomical, physiological, technical, logical, and data difficulties that should caution against any premature acceptance of a simple theory linking hypothetical components of mental activity with precisely circumscribed brain locations. The desire to find neat answers to some of the most profound questions of human existence may have primed us to accept what is actually a highly flawed theory of the way in which the human mind is instantiated in neural tissue. The problem is that correlative studies of imaging and cognition are based on a set of tenuous and possibly (perhaps probably) incorrect assumptions of the relationships between behavior, mental activity, and brain activity. Setting aside for the moment the problem of the accessibility of mental activity by means of behavioral analyses, supporters of localization hold it as axiomatic that both the brain and the mind consist of analyzable, isolable, independent units interacting within the confines of a linear system. There are many corollaries of this central axiom including the notion that brain images can be superimposed in a linear fashion, that the hypothetical cognitive and brain modules are "purely insertable," and that the mental components can be assigned, at least to some degree, to specific brain locales. Although supporters of localization implicitly accept these and related fundamental assumptions, each of assumptions is fraught with uncertainty and most have been challenged at one time or another on both theoretical and empirical grounds. Collectively, the corpus of studies challenging much of the recent work on brain localization suggests that its "conclusions" are untenable and, even worse, misleading.

Why should this be? Pointing out that both the strategies and the objects of science evolve, Ashby (1960, p. 5) said:

Science stands today on something of a divide. For two centuries it has been exploring systems that are either intrinsically simple or that are capable of being analyzed into simple components. The fact that such a dogma as "vary the factors one at a time" could be accepted for a century shows that scientists were largely concerned in investigating such systems as *allowed* this method. [However,] this method is often fundamentally impossible in complex systems.

Perhaps, today the classic approach of science to segment and isolate is not appropriate for the kinds of brain-mind systems we are studying. Rest assured, this is not a unique problem for the cognitive neurosciences. Even in physics, there are analogous constraints at work. No one has been able to deterministically solve the three-body problem. Yet cognitive neuroscientists relentlessly pursue a task of even greater complexity and intractability.

An alternative, and perhaps more realistic, point of view to the notion of isolatable cognitive-neural modules postulates a complex mind-brain system instantiated as a unified entity in which the various parts interact too strongly to be isolated. That they cannot be isolated from each other has to do with their fundamental nonlinear nature and heavy interconnectedness and not with inadequate research tools or incomplete data. In the final chapter of this book, the nature of this alternative point of view is considered in detail.

5

Summary and Conclusions

This book has identified and discussed some of the fundamental assumptions that underlie both historical and current efforts to localize psychological processes in particular regions of the brain. It is offered as a critique of an increasingly popular strategy to bridge the databases of cognitive psychology and the neurosciences. The thesis presented here is that much of the "localization" research effort, now and in the past, has been based on assumptions that are demonstrably incorrect or that cannot be validated either in principle or in practice. This book is presented with the understanding that the problems, issues, and questions it has dealt with are some of the most important and most challenging conundrums facing science.

We have seen that the controlling assumption of the cognitive localization enterprise is that mental processes are analyzable into distinct and separable modules, components, or faculties and that localized brain regions instantiate these processes. It is this unproven and often-contradicted assumption, taken as an axiom, that seems to be the central weakness in this enterprise. My goal has been to add one more voice to those arguing for reconsideration and reexamination of the conceptual and technical assumptions underlying localization research, particularly current efforts that use the powerful new imaging techniques.

This book has also been a study of the epistemological constraints on our efforts to determine the relationship between the brain and the mind. There exist, it has argued, certain well-defined limits on our ability to bridge the gap between psychological and neurophysiological findings. It is my conviction that the attractiveness of the new imaging technologies and the unremitting urge to answer some of the most profound questions of human existence have led many of my colleagues to make serious misestimates concerning the nature of these limits.

One other general goal of this book has been to champion the resurrection of an underappreciated, yet scientifically sounder, approach to the study of psychological processes—behaviorism. My critique of localization, along with my arguments against reductionism (Uttal, 1998) and accessibility (Uttal, 2000a), if well founded, support an argument for a major change in the prevailing zeitgeist of experimental psychology. Whereas the cognitive school has been predominant in recent years, it seems to me that a new look at some kind of a modernized and revised behaviorism is in order. Even though the older classical versions of behaviorism were disappointing and inadequate to many of us, I believe that some of the fundamental premises of the behaviorist approach to the study of psychological activity merit review and, perhaps, readoption.

Behaviorism was accused of everything from "inhumanness" to "hyperempiricism" to "irrelevance" to being "antireligious." My review of behaviorism (Uttal, 2000a) unequivocally demonstrated that criticisms of the behaviorist approach to psychological science went far beyond its actual tenets and assumptions. My frank expectation, therefore, is that many of the changes that I would like to see for experimental psychology are unlikely to ever be achieved. There is too much vested interest and too little consideration of the truly essential and fundamental assumptions to make revolutionary changes in the current consensus likely. Nevertheless, before proceeding further with my final chapter, I feel it necessary to identify and repudiate, as clearly as I can, some of the false issues that may be imputed to this book.

First, my analysis of the effort to bridge psychological and neurophysiological or neuroanatomic data is not intended in any way to challenge the most basic principle of psychobiology or the cognitive neurosciences, namely, that any human mental process is solely a reflection of or equivalent to some aspect of brain activity.

Whatever the actual relation is between the brain and mental activity, and however difficult it may be to unravel that relationship, this book is in no way intended to support the notion that some kind of a dualist (or pluralist) ontology underlies organic thought. Nothing I have said here should be taken to imply anything other than the common reality of both brain and mind—one as mechanism and the other as function of that mechanism. Without this principle, all else in neuroscience and psychology is nonsense.

There is no goal motivating my work other than to energize the scientific search for understanding the true nature of the mind-brain relationship. I share the goal of an objective search for this understanding with many others, regardless of our points of view. I certainly do not hold that any identified epistemological limits constraining research in this field can or should be used as grounds for revising or "reconstructing" the scientific method. All of us, behaviorists and cognitivists alike, stand together or this issue.

Second, the analysis presented in this book is aimed at a better understanding of the localization issue, per se, and no other. The macroscopic question of where a process may be occurring in the brain is only one of several neuroreductionist issues that confront psychobiologists. However much we may learn (or not learn) about how the brain activity underlying mental activity is localized, this information is incapable of providing any fundamental insight into the primary question of psychoneural equivalence, that is, how mental activity is represented or encoded in the brain. An analysis of the quest to answer this primary question, the effort to determine the microscopic details of the brain, which represents a different kind of neuroreductionism, was the target of my earlier work (Uttal, 1998), where I argued that it, too, is probably unachievable.

Third, although studies of the dynamics of learning and memory may help us understand something about the localization problem, the actual transformations involved in learning and memory are also manifestations at a more microscopic level of analysis than the one addressed by the localization enterprise—and the one with which this book has been concerned. One important contribution that physiological studies of learning and memory do make, however, is to support the idea of the distributed involvement of many brain centers and nuclei in these two aspects of cognitive information processing.

Fourth, this critique of localization research is not intended to put a stop to additional research and to whatever understanding can be achieved by that research. I am not suggesting that the tools of the neurophysiologist, the neuroanatomist, or the psychologist be laid aside and no further research be done in each of these exciting, fruitful, and even elegant fields of inquiry. Each approach to understanding offers much in its own right and can be expected to provide both practical and theoretical concepts and procedures that may better the human condition or deepen our understanding of who and what we are. The difficulty is that, all too often, what is offered as "progress" may actually be misleading—misdirecting our attention and energies away from whatever it is that we will ultimately consider to be the "truth" about ourselves. This may be especially true for studies that attempt to build illogical bridges between the findings of different sciences. It is the attempt to build such bridges that I challenge. Imaginative, but erroneous, neuroreductive bridges between the different domains may cause more damage than a realistic appreciation of the barriers to building those bridges.

Nor am I suggesting that the wonderful scanning devices I have described are not extraordinarily useful in many other kinds of application. The power brought by the scanning systems to study the anatomy and physiology of the brain is profound. Whole new areas of medical treatment are now available that were unimaginable only a few years ago. The relief from pain and suffering that these devices have already provided makes them one of the most important scientific developments of all time. As a colleague once said to me, "Would you deny the use of fMRI to the brain surgeon who was about to perform surgery on you?" The answer, of course, is—of course not!

These wonderful machines are not omnipotent, however, and one of the places where their application has run ahead of a thoughtful and rigorous analysis is in localizing notoriously ill-defined mental activities in what may be nonexistent modules of the brain.

Fifth, this book is not intended to reject all aspects of the localization of mental processes. The domains in which these ideas work are well enough established and almost universally accepted: they are the sensory input channels and their respective receiving areas and the motor regions and output pathways of the brain. A considerable amount of PET and fMRI localization research has simply confirmed some things that we have long known. Muller's law on the specific energy of nerves remains as valid today as when it was first enunciated in 1840. The regions sub-serving the great sensory modalities and the motor output portions of the brain are highly structured and localized even in light of newer informa-tion that suggests that these regions may also have other functions. Cur-rently, we are discovering new information that takes Muller's law from the level of the great modalities and applies it to the action of single neu-rons—but, again, only in the sensory transmission pathways and pri-mary receiving areas for each modality. Even within a modality such as vision, some spatial encoding (not inconsistent with localization of func-tion) is known for different dimensions or attributes of the visual stimu-lus. In some cases, we have even been successful in decoding the exact nature of the language used by the afferent or efferent pathways to con-duct patterns of stimuli or responses into and out of the central nervous system. However, because more complex functions recruit ever larger portions of the cerebral cortex during their activation, an equivalently narrow localization or "decoding" of cognitive functions seems to be far less likely.

Therefore, even though I have argued here against the radical localiza-tion ideas that permeate this field of science, I am not arguing for any kind of Lashley-like mass action or equipotentiality. There is ample evi-dence that the central nervous system is not homogeneous and does have specialized regions and functions. The case for the existence of spe-cifically tuned motor and sensory regions (notwithstanding their other overlapping functions) is unassailable. The physical anchors available for defining stimuli and responses in these regions simply do not exist for the vaguely defined cognitive processes that researchers, so often inappropriately, seek to localize in the brain. Clearly, it is the complexity and nonlinearity of the interactions among the regions of the brain that is the source of the difficulty in this broader field of research. Unfortu-nately, successes that have been enjoyed in the periphery have sometimes misled us to think that more complex, central processes are equally ame-nable to analysis. My argument is with the extrapolation from the ac-ceptable concept of well demonstrated input-output functions to the unacceptable idea that much less well defined "higher-order" cognitive constructs (vaguely defined and lacking physical anchors) are equally well localized.

Sixth, because of the multidimensional complexity of the brain and its processes, I believe that the localization effort is fraught with difficulties that do not obtain in other reductionist efforts. This book is thus not an attack on reductionism in general.[1] Indeed, reductionism has worked well enough in some spheres of science. One cannot help but admire the progress made on the essentially one-dimensional problem encountered when studying the genome of various organisms or on the two-dimensional problem encountered in the simulation of a human chess player. However, when science confronts three-dimensional, nonlinear systems with very large numbers of components and much more complex rules of interaction, even those much simpler than the brain (e.g., gravitational interaction of three bodies or the solar system), the situation is qualitatively different. Simply put, some of the concepts and strategies that work in lower-dimensional worlds may not be applied to the more complex ones. Koch and Laurent (1999, p. 98) put it very well:

Any realistic notion of brain complexity must incorporate, first, the highly nonlinear, nonstationary, and adaptive nature of the neuronal elements themselves and, second, their nonhomogeneous and massive parallel patterns of interconnection whose "weights" can wax and wane across multiple time scales in behaviorally significant ways. For now, perhaps the most obvious thing to say about brain function from a "complex system" perspective is that continued reductionism and atomization will probably not, on its own, lead to fundamental understanding.

Seventh, the caveats raised here about the future of psychological science are not intended as grounds for pessimism, but as necessary cautions, to be evaluated on their scientific merits. Many other sciences confront their limits and boundaries and not only live with them but are stimulated to deeper understanding by them. Psychology must do the same. A mature understanding of its limits may well lead to a more fruitful and psychobiologically valid future—far sooner than any understand-

1. It should be noted, however, that some other simpler sciences are not immune to some of the criticisms made here of neuroreductionism. The increasing appreciation of complexity and the limits it may place on reductionism has become a hot topic for scientists in many fields of endeavor. Gallagher and Appenzellar (1999) have collected a number of articles dealing with the implications of system complexity on potential efforts to "reduce" such systems to the language of more basic units.

ing based on a chimerical search for a neuroreductionist never-never land. Eighth, this book is not intended to suggest either that the current situation in experimental psychology is unremittingly dismal or that research efforts there are totally misdirected. Notwithstanding any suggestions to the contrary, changes are occurring in experimental psychology that suggest that "barefoot" neuroreductionism is not as prevalent as it was even quite recently. Many journals, particularly in the field of perception, in which allusions to any available kind of neurophysiological data, however remote their connection to the work at hand might actually be, were rampant only a few years ago, have now assumed a much less reductive tone. Many of the problems faced in this field are not due to the laboratory scientists who often carefully qualify the implications of their scientific discoveries, but rather to "bridging" psychobiologists, who are prone to read too much into the difficult imaging and physiological data and to practitioners, even more remote from the laboratory, who are sometimes guilty of far wilder extrapolations. No better example of this is the nonsensical "left brain–right brain" tutoring mythology that has crept into our public education.

Ninth and finally, this book makes no attempt to unravel the logical and linguistic difficulties of defining mental terms. Indeed, failure to clearly define such terms is the most glaring weakness of the entire localization enterprise. If anything, chapter 3 makes it clear that there is little agreement and an abundant opportunity for controversy concerning the nature of the mental processes for which brain localizations are sought. Any time anyone has made an effort to define mental activities, it has produced only circularity and vagueness. This is probably also true for any subsequent effort to develop a taxonomic organization of mental processes. I use the mentalist vocabulary as it is, but with the understanding that each "mental" term may have some different connotation or denotation to others or seem to have some consensual meaning where, in fact, there is none. The disturbing aspect of the situation is that in even in the glaringly bright light of the circularity and uncertainty associated with cognitive terminology, our science has such a strong proclivity to make such heroic efforts to localize these phantoms!

This final chapter is intended to summarize many of the points brought out in the previous chapters, to set forth the explicit and to tease out the hidden assumptions of the localization theorists' approach, and to compare and contrast these assumptions with a set of counterassumptions intended to convey what I consider to be the salient and fundamental principles of the brain-mind relationship.

5.1 The Implicit and Explicit Assumptions of Localization Research

Contemporary efforts to localize psychological functions in specific regions of the brain, particularly when applying the imaging tools, are based on a string of assumptions, many of which are controversial and some of which are demonstrably wrong. Nevertheless, if we are to understand both the strengths and weaknesses of this enterprise, it is necessary to define these fundamental assumptions as specifically as possible. The following assumptions[2] collectively make up the chain of logic underlying virtually all variants of the localization hypothesis:

1. Cognitive processes can be defined and exclusively denoted in precise terms.

2. Cognitive processes are accessible to experimental assay and examination.

3. Cognition is actually made up of a collection of quasi-independent modules or faculties.

4. Cognition can be analyzed by appropriate techniques; that is, it can be decomposed into components that can be examined independently.

5. These components can be used to guide empirical studies.

6. The cognitive modules, components, or faculties including high-level cognitive processes such as speech, reading, "executive decision making," and perception can be localized in the particular places in the brain.

7. The double dissociation procedure is an effective means of identifying and localizing individual cognitive components.

8. The brain is a nonhomogeneous organ with many regions specialized for different cognitive functions.

2. Inclusion on this list does not necessarily mean that the assumption is "wrong." Indeed, some of the assumptions in this list may also appear in the "antilocalization" list in section 5.2. It is the entire logical chain that is being considered in this summary.

9. These brain regions are discrete and stable and relatively constant in location from person to person and from time to time.

10. Although these brain regions may interact with other areas, their respective functions can be determined.

11. The brain regions purported to represent or control the cognitive functions can be identified by surgical, electrophysiological, and tomographic techniques.

12. The intrinsic or association (i.e., nonsensory and nonmotor) areas of the cortex are where cognitive processes are represented or encoded.

13. The localized regions representing cognitive functions can be specifically identified by the changes in their metabolism—either oxygen use or glucose consumption—that are assumed to occur when these regions carry out different cognitive processes.

14. Increased cognitive activity is associated with increased neural activity.

15. Active neurons have higher metabolic rates than inactive ones.

16. Localized metabolic rate changes are highly correlated with blood flow during activation of one of the cognitive modules.

17. Brain processes interact in simple ways and can be, to a valid first approximation, described collectively as a linear system by superposition and other arithmetic procedures, as well as by statistical analyses.

18. The location of brain regions associated with particular cognitive processes is sufficiently stable in time and space so that experiments can be replicated.

19. The location of brain regions associated with a particular cognitive processes is sufficiently constant from person to person that the data from individuals may be pooled to produce precise estimates of localization.

20. Dissociation experiments are a powerful and effective tool for associating a brain region with a cognitive process.

21. The subtractive method is a powerful and effective procedure for observing the differences in brain response between experimental and control conditions. If an image obtained from a condition in which a cognitive process was not activated is subtracted from one in which it is activated, the difference image will be an indication of just the regions that are associated with the activation of the process—other irrelevant, noisy, or common information is arithmetically cancelled out.

22. Regions that show positive differences in subtracted images (activations) indicate real peaks of brain metabolism.

23. Regions that show increased activation in experimental (as opposed to control) conditions are associated with he corresponding activation of particular cognitive processes.

24. Regions of decreased activation are unimportant or irrelevant.

25. Selective behavioral deficits produced by brain lesions and studied by neuropsychologists are sufficiently stable, specific, and replicable to support hypotheses of highly localized mental functions.

26. The various averaging, smoothing, and normalizing transformations applied to scanning images do not distort the final outcome of an experiment or the conclusions to be drawn from it.

27. The localization of a cognitive process utilizes existing theories and hypothetical cognitive components. This is required to guide our search for the brain region in which the proposed cognitive components may be localized.

28. The findings obtained at the gross level of cerebral organization by localization studies "explain" some aspects of cognitive activity. This is the level of psychoneural equivalence and a valid statement of cognitive neuroreduction.

29. The main conclusion to be drawn from this chain of logic and the findings it produces is that there exists a high degree of specific and localized representation of cognitive processes.

5.2 Some Counterassumptions: A Behaviorist View

The opposing, behaviorist point of view, collectively represented by the following, often antagonistic, counterassumptions argues that, in the main, the localization of high-level cognitive functions in specific regions of the brain is not achievable. It argues further that efforts to achieve such cognitive localization, however seductive and straightforward it may seem to be, are seriously misleading our quest to understand how cognitive processes are represented by the brain.

1. Even the simplest cognitive process is of enormous informational complexity, involving perception, memory, decision making, emotion, set, and virtually any other mental activity invoked by mentalist psychologists.

2. There is a vast amount of "cognitive penetration" in which the state of the organism alters the nature of a response. This cognitive penetration suggests widespread involvement of parts of the brain of which we know very little in even the simplest kind of cognitive activity.

3. Cognitive processes, particularly the more complex ones, are in large part indivisible and unitary. They cannot be analyzed into components, modules, or faculties because of the very strong interactions between what may only be apparently different aspects of cognition.

4. It is extremely difficulty to define cognitive components in a way that is commensurate with any kind of psychobiological reality.

5. Cognitive processes are inferences (i.e., post hoc explanations or hypothetical constructs) intended to provide explanations of the underlying mechanisms that account for the complexities of observed behavior.

6. Cognitive activity cannot be examined directly; it is largely inaccessible.

7. Observed behavior and verbal reports are neutral concerning the actual nature of the underlying cognitive processes or cognitive activity.

8. Computational and mathematical models are neutral concerning the actual nature of the underlying cognitive processes.

9. Neurophysiological findings, because of their complexity at the essential neural net level, cannot be analyzed in a way that permits a reconstruction of cognitive processes.

10. The reality of cognitive faculties, modules, or components of all kinds depends on a set of assumptions that is impossible to confirm. No widely accepted taxonomy or lexicon of cognitive processes exists or is on the intellectual horizon.

11. There are strong practical, social, human, humane, and conceptual forces that drive us, incorrectly, into accepting the reality of reducible and accessible components of mental activity.

12. The brain is not homogeneous and can be divided into sensory, motor, and association regions with different functions by many different methods and procedures.

13. Identifiable brain regions overlap, are redundant, and may also be multifunctional in a way that adds to their complexity. Thus the brain is spatially uncertain.

14. The brain is also a dynamic system, its activity changing as a result of experience, recovery of function, the passage of time, and perhaps also as a result of alternative tasks or strategies. Because of its continuous ongoing activity, it is likely that it constantly reorganizes itself in a normal course of events. Thus the brain is temporally uncertain.

15. It is very difficult to determine narrowly defined and independent functions of the so-called intrinsic or association areas of the brain.

16. The main reason for this difficulty is the high degree of interconnection of different functional regions. Thus, however profoundly stimula-

tion or lesioning of a particular area may affect some process (e.g., speech), the mechanism of the alteration or deficit is never exactly clear.

17. Neuropsychological studies in human beings are idiosyncratic, anecdotal, and of only marginal value in unraveling the organization of the brain-mind.

18. Although necessity is easy to demonstrate, sufficiency is extremely difficult to define in a system as complex as is the brain. Furthermore, a determination of necessity is inadequate as an argument for localized function.

19. The brain is a nonlinear system, to which the tools of linear mathematics do not apply.

20. Extensive parts of the so-called association area, and, increasingly, of the sensory and motor regions and even of the cerebellum are now thought to be involved in cognitive activity.

21. The greater the complexity of information processing, the broader the distribution of cerebral centers recruited to take part in the processing.

22. The double dissociation procedure is deeply flawed, potentially misleading, and based on unjustified a priori assumptions.

23. The subtractive method is a deeply flawed and potentially misleading procedure that can potentially distort our knowledge of brain organization.

24. Some brain activation images produced by the subtractive method may produce false and misleading associations of brain regions with cognitive activity.

25. Some brain activation images produced by the subtractive method may hide salient cognitive activity.

26. The averaging, normalizing, and standardizing transformations used to process brain images can potentially distort our knowledge of brain organization.

27. The observed spatial and temporal instability of both intrasubject and intersubject brain responses and their extreme variability suggests that mathematical and statistical methods may be subject to severe artifacts.

28. Arbitrary criterion threshold levels can potentially distort our knowledge of brain organization.

29. All brain scanning procedures are constrained in serious ways. They may, in some special circumstances, tell you where something that is a part of a complex system is happening, but not what is happening there or what its role is in the system.

30. The localization of activity associated with a certain cognitive process in one part of the brain does not exclude the participation of other regions in the process.

31. Any cognitive process involves broadly distributed regions of the cerebral mantle and probably many brain stem centers and nuclei.

32. There are several potentially misleading technical artifacts involved in the use of a scanning device that can affect the accuracy of the data analysis. These artifacts result specifically from hardware limitations and both internal and external interferences.

33. The chain of logic from the data obtained in a brain scanning procedure to the assumption that such data are identifiable with cognitive functions is long and treacherous.

34. Given the complexities of the scanning methods and the lack of constraints on hypothesizing cognitive components, any cognitive process that can be named, no matter how outlandish, can be localized in a brain region—if sought.

35. Because the localization of a cognitive process requires an existing theory and hypothetical cognitive components, any results obtained will largely be determined by that theory and by those hypotheses or by the experimental design, and not by the true psychobiology of the system.

36. The main conclusion to be drawn from this chain of logic and the findings it produces is that the brain represents cognitive processes in a highly distributed and interactive manner. The idea that these processes can be precisely localized, though it has persisted, is fundamentally incorrect.

Perhaps it is even more important to appreciate a more damaging aspect of the precise localization hypothesis. Even if we could associate precisely defined cognitive functions in particular areas of the brain (and this seems highly unlikely), it would tell us very little if anything about how the brain computes, represents, encodes, or instantiates psychological processes. The answer to that neuroreductionist goal must be found at another level of analysis in the details of the interactions among the neurons of the great networks of the brain, not where these networks may be located. For reasons discussed here and elsewhere, this is even less likely to be achieved. This is not to argue that localization research is useless. Clearly it has very definite contributions to make in helping us to understand which structures (among others) may be involved in certain behaviors. However, on the theoretical level at which brain activity becomes mind activity, the entire localization issue may be an ill-posed question that is being asked at the wrong level.

5.3 Final Comments

The difficulties that emerge in the search for narrowly circumscribed brain regions in which cognitive processes are supposed to be localized are typical of virtually any attempt to reduce cognitive activity to neural or process components. All are beset by some of the same problems and difficulties. Perhaps the most serious difficulty and one common to all such enterprises is the inadequate (and possibly impossible) definitions of the mental terms that are supposed to be localized or reduced. Noncircular definitions in this arena of science are virtually impossible to produce. Although there may be some shared connotations, precise denotations are nonexistent, primarily because the definitions are rarely operationally anchored. Psychology, often characterized as the study of these cognitive mechanisms, is thus faced with an initial handicap—How does one measure that which is indefinable?

Other problems of complexity, numerousness, and chaotic or thermodynamic irreversibility also bedevil our goals to achieve neuro- or cognitive reductionist explanations. There are also important questions of the accessibility of mental processes and their analyzability into components that perhaps should take precedence over the search for neural correlates of mental activity. All of these problems are far more severe than any arising from the technical details of the methods used. Nevertheless, potential technical artifacts also complicate the search for localized representations.

It seems that the only way to overcome these fundamental epistemological difficulties is to acknowledge the limits of any mentalist approach to scientific psychology and to return to some revitalized and improved form of behaviorism—an approach to solving psychological problems that is deaf to the siren song of reductive explanation and that makes rigorous use of descriptive terms and methods. When one peers deeply into psychological science, it is not too difficult to discern that a far larger portion of what we do is actually description rather than reductive explanation. Hence this suggestion is not so far-fetched as many current cognitive mentalists would argue.

What form should this new behaviorism take? Over the years I have described one vision of it in Uttal (1981, 1988, 1998, 2000a). In the briefest of summaries, the new behaviorism can be characterized as follows:

Psychophysical. It must utilize the well-controlled methods of psychophysical research.

Anchored. Stimuli must be anchored to independent physical measures.

Simple. Responses must be limited to simple (class A) discriminations such as "same" or "different" to minimize the cognitive penetration effects that distort functional relationships.

Operational. Its concepts must be defined in terms of procedures, not in terms of unverifiable, ad hoc hypothetical constructs.

Behaviorally descriptive. Its formal theories must be acknowledged to be only behaviorally descriptive and to be neutral with regard to underlying mechanisms.

Neuronally nonreductive. It must abandon any hope of reducing psychological phenomena to the details of neural nets because of their computational intractability.

Experimental. It must continue to engage in the empirical tussle with nature that has characterized the best psychology in the past.

Molar. It must look at behavior in terms of the overall, unitary, integrated activity it is and avoid invoking a false modularity.

Empiricist$_1$ and nativist. It must accept the compromise that both experience and evolved mechanisms motivate and drive behavior.

Empiricist$_2$ and rationalist. It must accept that compromise that behavior accrues from both stimulus determined (automatic) and logical (inferential) causal sequences.

Antipragmatic. It must accept psychology's primary role as a theoretical science and base its goals on the quest for knowledge of the nature of our nature rather than on the immediate needs of society or the utility that some of its findings may seem to have.

The pendulum, I believe, is about to swing back from a falsely reductive cognitive mentalism to a more positivist, operational, behaviorist perspective. If this book, along with its predecessors, has helped in some small way to renew the dialogue about the nature of the differences between the two perspectives, it will have realized its goals.

Appendix A
The Great Questions of Scientific Psychology

Questions about Theories

1. Is a unified theory of mind possible, or will it always be a system of microtheories?
2. What are the conditions of necessity and sufficiency that make a theory or law acceptable?
3. What is an acceptable theory in psychology?
4. Are the methods of a science evolved from the needs of physical sciences appropriate for the study of psychological processes?
5. Why is description not the same as explanation?
6. Is there a psychological "uncertainty principle" that says we cannot examine mental processes without altering them?
7. Which is the best approach to psychology—dualism, monism, or something else?
8. What relation do mathematics and computer models have to the processes they describe?
9. Are the data of psychology sufficiently objective so that the great questions can be resolved?
10. How can analogies mislead us into assuming that some processes are homologous?
11. How can functional isomorphisms mislead us into assuming that some processes are identical?
12. Can a semantic engine be simulated by a syntactic one?
13. What are the arguments against identity theory or other monisms?
14. What are the arguments against dualisms?
15. How do the various schools of psychology really differ?
16. Is functionalism synonymous with cognitive mentalism?

17. Is there some kind of a physical reality that is the ultimate target of our psychological theories?

18. Should pragmatic concerns or current ignorance or fundamental barriers specify what is a good or complete theory rather than the true natural reality?

Questions about Mentalism and Behaviorism

19. What is the relation between behavior and mind?

20. What is behavior?

21. Are descriptions of inner processes possible even though the inner processes cannot be dissected or reduced?

22. Can behavior permit us to infer mental events?

23. Are psychological states always associated with overt behavior?

24. Of what value are verbal and introspective reports?

Questions about Brain-Mind Relationships

26. What are the epistemological limits of physiological psychology? What can we know about the mind-brain?

27. What possible neural mechanisms could account for mental activity? Is it possible to say? Is it possible to know?

28. Is reductionism possible?

29. What is the proper level of inquiry for a neurophysiological analysis of mental processes?

30. How does mind (macro properties) emerge from the concatenated action of neurons (micro properties)?

31. Could the same psychological state be encoded by vastly different neural states, even in the same individual at different times? Can brain states be variable and flexible?

32. What is the relation between brain and behavior—or between brain and mind? How does the brain represent and encode mind?

33. Is it possible to explain mind in neural terms?

34. Can mental or psychological processes be localized in particular portions of the brain?

35. If so, where are psychological processes located in the brain? What is the site of psychoneural equivalence?

36. How are actions of the different regions of the brain coordinated?

37. How do chemicals affect thought and behavior?
38. Is mind or consciousness separable from brain events?
39. What is the difference between psychoneural equivalence and transmission codes?
40. Can the mind affect the brain or other bodily activity?

Questions about Mind

41. Is mind accessible?
42. Is mind measurable?
43. What is the ontological nature of mind?
44. What is self-awareness or consciousness?
45. Do animals have self-awareness or consciousness?
46. Does mind or consciousness persist after brain death?
47. Is mind or consciousness accessible?
48. Are cognitive processes independent entities, or do we have a single unified mental existence?
49. If there are anything like cognitive faculties, are they localizable in different parts of the brain?
50. What do fMRI and PET scans mean?
51. Is mind or consciousness analyzable into components?
52. Are we limited to molar behaviorism or some kind of modified operationalism?
53. Is an analytic mentalistic science possible?
54. What regulates behavior—environment, heredity, or both?
55. Are some behaviors (e.g., speech) innate or must everything be learned?
56. What is emotion?
57. What, in general, is the nature of the terms we use to describe cognitive entities, faculties, and processes such as learning, perceiving, thinking, or emotion?
58. Are these terms the result of our experimental designs or do they refer to true psychobiological realities?
59. Are cognitive entities hypothetical constructs, intervening variables, or post hoc theories?
60. Are our thoughts represented by isomorphic or symbolic representations?
61. Is it possible to answer the question of inner representation?

Questions about Sensation and Perception

62. What are the codes for sensory communication?
63. How do we sense the outside world?
64. What are the implications of the nonveridicalities between the perceived world and the independently measured world?
65. How do we create three dimensions from two?
66. Must we learn to perceive?
67. How do we recognize patterns? Why are some patterns equivalent to others, even though they may be greatly distorted or abstracted?
68. Are visual illusions determined by simple networks interactions or cognitive symbolic processing?
69. Do we see by features or wholes?
70. What is the role of high-level vision (cognitive penetration) in perception?
71. What is the role of low-level (peripheral) vision in perception?
72. Is there any difference between sensation and perception?
73. What can infants sense?
74. Is there any difference between early and late vision? Do both exist?

Questions about Learning

75. Do we learn by associating micro components or by encoding configurations?
76. What kinds of memory are there?
77. How do we recover information from these memories?
78. Where is the engram? Is there an engram?
79. Do we learn by reason or by experience?
80. What is the nature and role of reinforcement in learning.
81. Do early childhood experiences regulate later mental life?

Questions about "Cognition"

82. How do we solve problems and make decisions?
83. Can you think of two things or do two things at once?
84. Are subjects aware of the logic of their decision processes?

85. What are the laws that govern mental processes?
86. What is attention?
87. What do we mean by "attentive" as opposed to "preattentive"?

Other Questions

88. What are the source and causes of mental health problems?
89. How do we cure mental health problems?
90. Can mind be measured in the same way as length and mass?
91. Is the human governed by deterministic laws or does "free will" exist?
92. Does mind have any influence on our body or brains?
93. Is mind epiphenomenal?
94. What are good psychological research questions?
95. Do parapsychological processes, repressed memories, hypnosis, polygraphs, and the like have any validity?
96. Are we "responsible" for our actions?
97. Why do we sleep?
98. How does our integrated awareness of the external world emerge from the coded components of sensory processing?

Appendix B
A Comment on the Zeitgeist

To a surprising, but very disappointing degree, many of the articles encountered as I was doing the research for this book had to be acknowledged only as "submitted" or "personal communication"—or underwent unusually long and troublesome review and publication lags. There appears to be a quite strong resistance to publishing arguments against the localization hypothesis among the editors and reviewers of the relevant journals. On the other hand, if one examines the pages of America's preeminent and perhaps most prestigious scientific journal—*Science*—in recent years, virtually the only type of psychological article accepted for publication have been those involving some kind of correlation study between an imaging technique and a cognitive task. Obviously the zeitgeist is powerful and tends to reject that which is not in tune with the prevailing set of scientific assumptions. Often such papers are subject to nitpicking in ways that those with more conventional approaches are not.

This conservatism is not the result of any conscious conspiracy. Indeed, within reason, such a selectivity is an important stabilizing feature of any science, preventing the clearly erroneous and idiosyncratic from diverting attention and resources from more consensually acceptable topics. However, a hyperconservative barrier to the publication of novel or unpopular ideas as such can be extremely damaging to our search for understanding. In lieu of some startling paradigm-changing discovery, when attempting to come to grips with a phantom such as a modular mental activity, it especially important that the logic, assumptions, and fundamental conceptualizations of research in that direction be scrutinized to determine their validity.

The point I make here is that many of the authors that I have turned to for support and leadership often report having a very difficult time making their antilocalization messages public. Some have used the scientific underground such as the Internet; some have dropped out of the fray; others (e.g., Shallice, 1988) have simply walked away from the very arguments they themselves have made so compellingly and decided that presumed "progress" at any cost is better than an acceptance of the constraints and limits that they themselves have identified. I find this a very disappointing solution to what is obviously a very important problem.

An interesting case history of this difficulty in making its way past the guardians of the zeitgeist can be found in a Internet-posted, but unpublished, article written by Harpaz (1999). The argument offered by the author was that the few PET and fMRI results on cognitive localization that had been replicated produced data that were best characterized as "irreplicable." This web site article then went on to list the history of the submission of the article to a series of journals and to publish verbatim accounts of the reviews (and rejection letters and E-mails) that were received.

It is not possible, of course, to determine from such a presentation if Harpaz, 1999, was actually inadequate in some way or if it was being subjected to a higher set of acceptability standards because of its antilocalization views. There is a certain "breathlessness" about the author's writing style and incompleteness in his presentation suggesting that his position was not the only source of difficulty. On the other hand, the tone of some of the reviews indicates that the criteria used in evaluating this paper were far more severe than might have been used for a paper more in concert with current opinion. Whether Harpaz's complaints are justified or not, his harsh and uniformly negative treatment at the hands of reviewers is consistent with reports I have received from some of the other antilocalization authors mentioned in this book.

In the past, during the heyday of experimental brain lesion research, there was rarely any criticism of the logic and assumptions that lay behind the technical procedure. On the other hand, the journals were filled with articles demonstrating proposed relationships between damaged brain sites and hypothetical cognitive components. Eventually, the once popular lesion procedures were replaced or simply fell out of favor. Today, we are confronted with a new approach to the localization problem and, once again, there is at least the possibility that we are moving down the track to the same kind of conceptual dead end. I believe this is occurring because of an inadequate examination of the most fundamental assumptions of the new imaging approaches to the localization of psychological processes.

As much as I find the refusal to consider minority counterviews repugnant, it must be pointed out that such a reaction is not unusual in psychology. As Leahey (1997, p. 327) points out, Watson's seminal work (1913) on behaviorism was met with "published responses [that] were both few and remarkably restrained."

Similarly, Dawes's comprehensive review (1994) of the myths lying behind so much of the psychotherapy enterprise has encountered a huge silence in the psychological literature and the halls of academe—a silence reminiscent of the absence in the scientific literature of other views that run counter to the zeitgeist.

For this reason—the widespread tacit agreement to bury unpopular ideas—some of the papers that I feel are important may not be generally available. Although one could always argue that these authors are so patently wrongheaded that a serious reviewer would be well advised to recommend rejection, I do not believe this is always the case. Because the ideas advanced by these critics converge to a considerable degree, I believe attention should be paid to their arguments. The refusal to consider what they have to say should be replaced by vigorous controversy.

Philosophers have dealt with the problematic power of the zeitgeist for years. Hanson (1958)—a philosopher of the physical sciences—wrote a deeply insightful essay on the relationships between observation, evidence, facts, causality, hypotheses, laws, principles and our theories of the world. Although, his main interest was directed at the new "microphysics" of the twentieth century, much of what he had to say is directly relevant to the problems of neuroreductionism of which the localization problem is a major part. Among the many points he made is that what we "see" when confronted with some stimulus depends very much on our past experience and theoretical orientation. In Hanson's

words, "there is more to seeing than meets the eyeball. . . . Disparities in
. . . accounts arise in ex post factor interpretations . . . not in the fundamental visual data." (pp. 7, 8).

Just as the layperson's experience dictates what it is that is "seen",[1] so
the scientist's a priori theory or point of view dictates how experimental
observations are interpreted. For example, one of the major theoretical
points of view, widely held among classic as well as contemporary scientists, is that causality is due to a linear string of events. Hanson (1958)
points out that the beautiful bit of poetry beginning "For want of a nail a
shoe was lost" and ending with "all for the want of a nail" represents a
dominant, but highly incorrect approach to the study of complex systems. In such systems, the real sources of behavior are multiple and interacting causes, and it is impossible to trace backward to some single cause
or initial condition. Such arguments have a very familiar ring. The arguments in support of specific localization of mental functions in particular
parts of the brain and even of the existence of isolable cognitive components often are implicitly based on assumptions of a nonexistent linearity
or simplicity using a fallacious logic of exactly this same genre. Shallice's
discussion (1988) of alternative, equally probable models of system organization, Wimsatt's comments (1974) on multiple decompositions, and
more recent ideas about the multiple causation involved in chaotic systems should alert us once again to how relevant Hanson's admonition is
to the context of localization theory. Indeed, many of the systems in
which we are currently interested may be more chaotic internally than
their superficial behavior may suggest. However well ordered observed
behavior may be, it may be based on the concatenation of a multitude of
inaccessible nonlinear mechanisms.

Not only is publication sometimes more difficult for those who run
counter to the zeitgeist, but even after an article has been published, the
minority view does not receive the same attention as the majority per-

---

1. Would my readers be more comfortable if "perceived" was used here rather
than "seen"? Both these words seem to me to convey the same meaning. I have
always had a deep conviction that there was little to be gained by distinguishing
between sensation and perception in psychology. Even the simplest "sensations"
usually turned out to be much more complicated than they seemed at first, and to
be heavily affected by what psychologists call "cognitive penetration."

spective. For example, Wise et al. (1991) carried out a PET study seeking to determine if any differences in the images occurred between words and nonwords. Their data indicated that this was not the case:

> We demonstrated that categorical judgments on heard pairs of real words activate neural networks along both superior temporal gyri, but with an anatomical distribution no different from that seen when the subjects listened to non-words. (p. 1803)

This finding contradicts the pioneering studies of nearly the same problem carried out by Petersen et al. (1988, 1989), which observed that real words and nonwords activated different regions. Wise et al. (1991) went on to discuss what might be critical differences between the two experiments, but given the discrepancy between the two studies, it is hard to understand how their impact could have been so different. The Citation Index lists 321 citations for Wise et al., 1991, and 746 citations for Petersen et al., 1989. Thus, an article with a result that runs counter to a popular point of view is cited less than half as many times as the one consistent with the zeitgeist.

Collectively, the points of view and the experience of a scientific community, as well as its corpus of current formal theories, may act to select, often incorrectly, which observations and data are to be transmitted within that community. Therefore, what the antilocalization gadflies are experiencing these days is neither unusual nor entirely unexpected. At the present time, the mentalist zeitgeist, dominated by cognitive neuroscience, has reified separate mental modules and their distinct cerebral localization. It implicitly assumes that systems are linearly causal and that dissociative and subtractive strategies do indeed peer directly into the organization of the brain-mind. This point of view is so ingrained that even some of those who see its confusions, circularities, and logical inconsistencies especially clearly are able to abandon logic for romantic fantasies of a totally unconstrained and limitless science. However appealing the prospect of attaining such a chimerical goal may be, many sciences confront and live happily with their limits and constraints. Cognitive neuroscience should also.

References

Altarelli, M., Schlacter, F., & Cross, J. (1998). Making ultrabright X rays. *Scientific American, 279* 66–73.

Anderson, J. R., & Lebiere, C. (1998). *The Atomic Components of Thought.* Mahwah, NJ: Erlbaum.

Anderson, J. A., Silverstein, J. W., Ritz, S. A., & Jones, R. S. (1977). Distinctive features, categorical perception, and probability learning: Some applications of a neural model. *Psychological Review, 84,* 413–451.

Anonymous. (1998). *God in the Brain? Maybe, Say Researchers* [On-line]. Available Internet: http://users.universe.com/?tfrisen/brain.htm

Ashby, W. R. (1960). *An Introduction to Cybernetics.* New York: Wiley.

Bain, A. (1859). *The Emotions and the Will.* London: Parker.

Barch, D. M., Braver, T. S., Nystrom, L. E., Forman, S. D., Noll, D. C., & Cohen, J. D. (1997). Dissociating working memory from task difficulty in human prefrontal cortex. *Neuropsychologia, 35,* 1373–1380.

Bartholow. (1874). Experimental investigations into the functions of the human brain. *American Journal of Medical Sciences.*

Beatty, J., & Uttal, W. R. (1968). The effect of grouping visual stimuli on the cortical evoked potential. *Perception and Psychophysics, 4,* 214–217.

Bell, C. (1811). *Idea of a New Anatomy of the Brain Submitted for the Observation of His Friends.* London: Strahan and Preston.

Berger, H. (1929). Über das Elektrenkephalogramm des Menschen. *Archiv für Psychiatrie, 87,* 527–570.

Blakemore, S.-J., Rees, G., & Firth, C. D. (1998). How do we predict the consequences of our actions? A functional imaging study. *Neuropsychologia, 36,* 521–529.

Bloch, F., Hansen, W. W., & Packard, M. (1946). The nuclear induction experiment. *Physical Review, 70,* 474–485.

Boring, E. G. (1929/1950). *A History of Experimental Psychology.* New York: Appleton-Century-Crofts.

Braak, H. (1992). The human entorhinal cortex: Normal morphology and lamina-specific pathology in various diseases. *Neuroscience Research, 15,* 6–31.

Brazier, M. A. B. (1961). *A History of the Electrical Activity of the Brain.* London: Pitman Medical.

Broca, P. (1861). Remarques sur la siège de la faculté du langage articulé, suivés d'une observation d'aphémie (perte de la parole). *Billions de la Société Anatomique de Paris, 36,* 330–357.

Brodmann, K. (1909). *Vergleichende Lokalisationlehre der Grosshirnrinde in ihren Prinzipen dargestellt auf Grund des Zellenbaues.* Leipzig: Barth.

Bruneau, N., Roux, S., Guirin, P., Barthilimy, C., & Lelord, G. (1997). Temporal prominence of auditory evoked potentials (N1 wave) in 4–8-year-old children. *Psychophysiology, 34,* 32–38.

Buechel, C, Coull, J. T., & Friston, J. K. (1999). The predictive value of changes in effective connectivity for human learning. *Science, 283,* 1538–1541.

Buechel, C., & Friston, K. J. (1997). Modulation of connectivity in visual pathways by attention: Cortical interactions evaluated with structural equation modeling and fMRI. *Cerebral Cortex, 7,* 768–778.

Carpenter, A. F., Georgopoulos, A. P., & Pellizzer, G. (1999). Motor cortical encoding of serial order in a context-recall task. *Science, 283,* 1752–1757.

Carpenter, M. B., & Sutin, J. (1983). *Human Neuroanatomy.* Baltimore: Williams and Wilkins.

Carroll, J. B. (1993). *Human Cognitive Abilities: A Survey of Factor-Analytic Studies.* Cambridge: Cambridge University Press.

Caton, R. (1875). The electric currents of the brain. *British Medical Journal, 2,* 2.

Caton, R. (1877). Interim report on investigation of the electric currents of the brain. *British Medical Journal, suppl. vol. 1,* 62–65.

Caton, R. (1877). Interim report on investigation of the electric currents of the brain. *British Medical Journal, Supplement, 1,* 62–65.

Chomsky, N. (1980). Rules and representations. *The Behavioral and Brain Sciences, 3,* 1–15.

Clark, V. P., Fannon, S., Lai, S., Benson, R., & Bauer, L. (2000). Responses to rare visual target and distractor stimuli using event related fMRI. *Journal of Neurophysiology, 83,* 3133–3139.

Cohen, J. D., Perlstein, W. M., Braver, T. S., Nystrom, L. E., Noll, D. C., Jonides, J., & Smith, E. E. (1997). Temporal dynamics of brain activation during a working memory task. *Nature, 386,* 604–608.

Connor, S. (1998). *"God Spot" in Our Brain??* [On-line]. Available Internet: http://www.blazenet.com/thewatchman/godspot.html

Crosby, E. C., Humphrey, T., & Lauer, E. W. (1962). *Correlative Anatomy of the Nervous System.* New York: Macmillan.

Damadian, R. (1971). Tumor detection by nuclear magnetic resonance. *Science, 171,* 1151–1153.

Damasio, H. (1991). Neuroanatomical correlates of the aphasias. In M. T. Sarno (Ed.), *Acquired Aphasia.* New York: Academic Press.

Damasio, A. R., Damasio, H., & Christen, Y. (1996). *Neurobiology of Decision Making.* Berlin: Springer.

Davies, J. D. (1955). *Phrenology: Fad and Science. A 19th-Century American Crusade.* New Haven, CT: Yale University Press.

Dawes, R. M. (1994). *House of Cards: Psychology and Psychotherapy Built on Myth.* New York: Free Press.

Dawson, G. D. (1950). Cerebral responses to nerve stimulation in man. *British Medical Bulletin, 6,* 326–329.

Dawson, G. D. (1954). A summation technique for the detection of small evoked potentials. *EEG and Clinical Neurophysiology, 6,* 65–84.

Dehaene, S., Spelke, E., Pinel, R., Stanescu, R., & Tsivkin, S. (1999). Sources of mathematical thinking: behavior and brain Imaging evidence. *Science, 284,* 970–974.

Donders, F. C. (1868/1969). On the Speed of Mental Processes. W. G. Koster, (Trans.) *Acta Psychologica, 30,* 412–431.

Dowsett, D. J., Kenny, P. A., & Johnston, R. E. (1998). *The Physics of Diagnostic Imaging.* London: Chapman and Hall.

Dresp, B., & Bonnet, C. (1995). Subthreshold summation with illusory contours,. *Vision Research, 35,* 1071–1078.

DuBois-Reymond, E. (1848). *Untersuchungen über thierisch Elektrizität.* Berlin: Reimer.

Duncan, J. (1995). Attention, intelligence, and the frontal lobes. In M. I. Gazzaniga (Ed.), *The Cognitive Neurosciences.* Cambridge, MA: MIT Press.

Efron, R. (1990). *The Decline and Fall of Hemispheric Specialization.* Hillsdale, NJ: Erlbaum.

Elfgren, C. I., & Risberg, J. (1998). Lateralized frontal blood flow increases during fluency tasks: influence of cognitive strategy. *Neuropsychologia, 6,* 505–512.

Epstein, H. T. (1999). Other brain effects of words. *Behavioral and Brain Sciences, 22,* 287–288.

Farah, M. J. (1994). Neuropsychological inference with an interactive brain: A critique of the "locality" assumption. *Behavioral and Brain Sciences, 17,* 43–104.

Felleman, D. J., and Van Essen, D. C. (1991). Distributed hierarchical processing in primate visual cortex. *Cerebral Cortex, 1,* 1–47.

Ferrier, D. (1875). Experiments on the brains of monkeys. *Proceedings of the Royal Society* [161].

Ferrier, D. (1886). *Functions of the Brain*. New York: Putnam.

Fitzgerald, M. J. T. (1985). *Neuroanatomy: Basic and Applied*. London: Baillere Tindall.

Flourens, P. (1846). *Phrenology Examined*. Philadelphia: Hogan and Thompson.

Fodor, J. (1983). *The Modularity of Mind: An Essay on Faculty Psychology*. Cambridge MA: MIT Press.

Freud, S. (1891). *Zur Auffassung der Aphasien*. Vienna: Deuticke.

Friston, K. J. (1997). Imaging cognitive anatomy. *Trends in Cognitive Science, 1*, 21–27.

Friston, K. J. (1998). Imaging neuroscience: Principles or maps? *Proceedings of the National Academy of Sciences, U.S.A., 95*, 796–802.

Friston, K. J. (2000a). The labile brain: 1. Neuronal transients and nonlinear coupling. *Philosophical Transactions of the Royal Society of London B, 355*, 215–236.

Friston, K. J. (2000b). The labile brain: 2. Transients, complexity, and selection. *Philosophical Transactions of the Royal Society of London B, 355*, 237–252.

Friston, K. J. (2000c). The labile brain: 3. Transients and spatio-temporal receptive fields. *Philosophical Transactions of the Royal Society of London B, 355*, 253–265.

Friston, K. J., Buechel, C., Fink, G. R., Morris, J., Rolls, E., & Dolan, R. J. (1997). Psychophysiological and modulatory interactions in neuroimaging. *NeuroImage, 6*, 218–229.

Friston, K. J., Fletcher, P., Josephs, O., Holmes, A., Rugg, M. D., & Turner, R. (1998). Event-related fMRI: Characterizing differential responses. *NeuroImage, 7*, 30–40.

Fritsch, G., & Hitzig, E. (1870). Über die eletkrische Erregbarkeit des Grosshirns. *Archiv für Anatomie, Physiologie, und Wissenschaftliche Medizin, 37*, 300–332.

Fuster, J. M. (1989). *The Prefrontal Cortex: Anatomy, Physiology, and Neuropsychology of the Frontal Lobes*. New York: Raven.

Gall, F. J., & Spurzheim, J. C. (1808). Recherches sur le système nerveux en général, et sur celui du cerveau en particulier. *Academie de Sciences, Paris, Memoirs*.

Gallagher, R., & Appenzeller, T. (1999). Beyond reductionism. *Science, 284*, 79–109.

Galton, F. (1883). *Inquiries in Human Faculty and its Development*. London: Dent.

Gardner, H. (1983). *Frames of Mind: The Idea of Multiple Intelligences*. New York: Basic Books.

Gardner, H. (1999, February). Who owns intelligence? *Atlantic, 283*, 67–76.

Gautier, I., Skudlarski, P., Gore, J. C., & Anderson, A. W. (2000). Expertise for cars and birds recruits brain areas involved in face recognition. *Nature Neuroscience, 3,* 191–198.

Gazzaniga, M. S. (1983). Right hemisphere language following brain bisection. *American Psychologist, 38,* 525–537.

Geshwind, N. (1970). The organization of language and the brain. *Science, 170,* 940–944.

Gilden, D. L. (1997). Fluctuations in the time required for elementary decisions. *Psychological Science, 8,* 296–301.

Gourlay, K., Uttal, W. R., & Powers, M. (1974). VRS: A programming system for visual electrophysiological research. *Behavior Research Methods & Instrumentation, 6,* 281–287.

Grafman, J. (1994). Alternative frameworks for the conceptualization of prefrontal lobe functions. In F. Boller & J. Grafman (Eds.), *Handbook of Neuropsychology.* New York: Elsevier.

Grafman, J., Partiot, A., & Hollnagel, C. (1995). Fables in the prefrontal cortex. *Behavioral and Brain Sciences, 18,* 349–358.

Gratton, G., & Fabiani, M. (1998). Dynamic brain imaging: Event-related optical signal (EROS) measures of the time course and localization of cognitive-related activity. *Psychonomic Bulletin and Review, 5,* 535–563.

Greenberg, J., Hand, P., Sylvestro, A., & Reivich, M. (1979). Localized metabolic-flow couple during functional activity. *Acta Neurologica Scandinavica, 60,* 12–13.

Gregory, R. L. (1961). The brain as an engineering problem. In W. H. Thorpe & O. L. Zangwill (Eds.), *Current Problems in Animal Behavior.* Cambridge: Cambridge University Press

Grey Walter, W., Cooper, R., Aldridge, V. J., MaCallum, W. C., & Winter, A. L. (1964). Contingent negative variation: An electric sign of sensorimotor association and expectancy in the human brain. *Nature, 203,* 380–384.

Gross, C. G., Roche-Miranda, G. E., & Bender, D. B. (1972). Visual properties of neurons in the inferotemporal cortex of the macaque. *Journal of Neurophysiology, 35,* 96–111.

Gulyas, B., & Roland, P. E. (1994a). Cortical fields activated by form, color, and binocular disparity discrimination: Functional anatomy by positron emission tomography. *European Journal of Neuroscience, 6,* 1811–1827.

Gulyas, B., & Roland, P. E. (1994b). Binocular disparity detection in human visual cortex: Functional anatomy by positron emission tomography. *Proceedings of the National Academy of Sciences, U.S.A., 91,* 1239–1243.

Hammond, K. R., Hamm, R. M., & Grassia, J. (1986). Generalizing over conditions by combining the multitrait multimethod matrix and the representative design of experiments. *Psychological Bulletin, 100,* 257–269.

Hanson, N. R. (1958). *Patterns of Discovery: An Inquiry into the Conceptual Foundations of Science*. Cambridge: Cambridge University Press.

Harmon, L. D. (1959). Artificial neuron. *Science, 129*, 962–963.

Harpaz, Y. (1999). *Replicability of Cognitive Imaging of the Cerebral Cortex by PET and fMRI: A Survey of Recent Literature*. [On-line]. Available Internet: http://www.yehouda.com/replicability.html

Herbart, J. F. (1809/1891). *A Text-Book in Psychology: An Attempt to Found the Science of Psychology on Experience, Metaphysics, and Mathematics*. M. K. Smith, Trans.. New York: Appleton.

Herbart, J. F. (1902. *The Science of Education: Its General Principles Deduced from its Aim and The Aesthetic Revelation of the world*. Boston: Heath.

Hilgetag, C. C., O'Neill, M. A., & Young, M. P. (1996). Indeterminate organization of the visual system. *Science, 271*, 776–777.

Holzinger, K. J., & Harman, H. H. (1941). *Factor Analysis: A Synthesis of Factorial Methods*. Chicago: University of Chicago Press.

Hornak, J. P. (1999). *The Basics of MRI* [On-line]. Available Internet: http://www.cis.rit.edu/htbooks/mri

Ishai, A., & Sagi, D. (1995). Common mechanisms of visual imagery and perception. *Science, 268*, 1172–1174.

Iwai, E., & Mishkin, M. (1990). *Vision, memory, and the temporal lobe*. Paper presented at the Proceedings of the Tokyo Symposium, Tokyo.

Jacobsen, C. F. (1935). Functions of the frontal association areas in primates. *Archives of Neurology and Psychiatry, Chicago, 33*, 558–569.

James, W. (1892). *Psychology: Briefer Course*. New York: Holt.

Jardine, C. J., Jardine, N., & Sibson, R. (1967). The structure and construction of taxonomic hierarchies. *Mathematical Biosciences, 1*, 173–179.

Jiang, Y., Haxby, J. V., Martin, A., Ungerleider, L. G., & Parasuraman, R. (2000). Complementary neural mechanisms for tracking items in human working memory. *Science, 287*, 643–646.

Kandel, E. R., & Kupfermann, I. (1995). From nerve cells to cognition. In Kandel, E. R., Schwartz, J. H., & Jessell, T. M. (Eds). *Essentials of Neural Science and Behavior*. Norwalk, CT: Appleton and Lange.

Kandel, E. R., Schwartz, J. H., & Jessell, T. M. (1991). *Principles of Neural Science*. New York: Elsevier.

Kandel, E. R., & Kupfermann, I. (1995). From nerve cells to cognition. In E. R. Kandel, J. H. Schwartz, & T. M. Jessell (Eds.), *Essentials of Neural Science and Behavior*. Norwalk, CT: Appleton & Lange.

Kandel, E. R., Schwartz, J. H., & Jessell, T. M. (1995). *Essentials of Neural Science and Behavior*. Norwalk, CT: Appleton & Lange.

Kanwisher, N., McDermott, J., & Chun, M. M. (1997). The fusiform face area: A module in human extrastriate cortex specialized for face perception. *Journal of Neuroscience, 17*, 4302–4311.

Kapur, S., Tulving, E., Cabeza, R., McIntosh, A. R., Houle, S., & Craik, F. I. M. (1996). The neural correlates of intentional learning of verbal materials: A PET study in humans. *Cognitive Brain Research, 4,* 243–249.

Kastner, S., De Weerd, P., Desimone, R., & Ungerleider, L. G. (1998). Mechanisms of directed attention in the human extrastriate cortex as revealed by functional MRI. *Science, 282,* 108–111.

Kauffman, S. A. (1971). Articulation of parts explanations in biology. In R. C. Buck and R. S. Cohen (Eds.), *Boston Studies in the Philosophy of Science: Vol. 8* (pp. 257–272). Boston: Reidel.

Kelso, J. A. S., Case, P., Holroyd, T., Horvath, E., Raczaszek, Tuller, B., & Ding, M. (1995). Multistability and metastability in perceptual and brain dynamics. In M. Stadler & P. Kruse (Eds.), *Ambiguity in Mind and Nature.* Berlin: Springer.

Kennedy, J. L. (1959). A possible artifact in electroencephalography. *Psychological Review, 66,* 347–352.

Kertesz, A. (1979). *Aphasia and Associated Disorders: Taxonomy, Localization, and Recovery.* New York: Grune & Stratton.

Kelin, D. B. (1970). *A History of Scientific Psychology: Its Origins and Philosophical Backgrounds.* New York: Basic Books.

Kleist, K. (1934). *Gehirnpathologie.* Leipzig: Barth.

Koch, C., & Laurent, G. (1999). Complexity and the nervous system. *Science, 284,* 96–98.

Koch, S. (1959). Epilogue. In S. Koch (Ed.), *Psychology: A Study of a Science: Vol. 3.* New York: McGraw-Hall.

Kohler, S., Moscovitch, M., Winocur, G., Houle, S., & McIntosh, A. R. (1998). Networks of domain-specific and general regions involved in episodic memory for spatial location and object identity. *Neuropsychologia, 36,* 129–142.

Koizumi, H., Yamashita, Y., Maki, A., Ito, Y., & Watanabe, E. (1998). Optical topography: A new concept for human brain mapping. In T. Yuasa, J. W. Prichard, & S. Ogawa (Eds.), *Current Progress in Functional Brain Mapping: Science and Applications.* Niigata, Japan, and London: Nishimura and Smith Gordon.

Kopelman, M. D., Stanhope, N., & Kingsley, D. (1997). Temporal and spatial context memory in patients with focal frontal, temporal lobe, and diencephalic lesions. *Neuropsychologia, 35,* 1533–1545.

Kosslyn, S. M., Pascual-Leone, A., Felician, O., Camposano, S., Keenan, J. P., Thompson, J. P., Ganis, G., Sukel, K. E., & Alpert, N. M. (1999). The role of area 17 in visual imagery from PET and rTMS. *Science, 284,* 167–170.

Kuhn, T. S. (1962). *The Structure of Scientific Revolutions.* Chicago: University of Chicago Press.

Laberge, D. (1995). Computational and anatomical models of selective attention in object identification. In M. S. Gazzaniga (Ed.), *The Cognitive Neurosciences.* Cambridge MA: MIT Press.

Land, E. H. (1977). The Retinex theory of color vision. *Scientific American, 237,* 108–128.

Lane, R. D., Reiman, E. M., Bradley, M. M., Lang, P. J., Ahern, G. L., Davidson, R. J., & Schwartz, G. E. (1997). Neuroanatomical correlates of pleasant and unpleasant emotion. *Neuropsychologia, 35,* 1437–1444.

Langlois, J. H., & Roggman, L. A. (1990). Attractive faces are only average. *Psychological Science, 1,* 115–121.

Lashley, K. S. (1929). *Brain Mechanisms and Intelligence.* Chicago: University of Chicago Press.

Lashley, K. S. (1942). The problem of cerebral organization of vision. *Biological Symposium, 7,* 301–322.

Lashley, K. S. (1950). In search of the engram. *Symposium Society of Experimental Biology N.Y., 4,* 454–482.

Lauterbur, P. C. (1973). Image formation by induced local interactions. Examples employing nuclear magnetic resonance. *Nature, 242,* 190–191.

Leahey, T. H. (1997). *A History of Psychology: Main Currents in Psychological Thought.* Upper Saddle River, NJ: Prentice Hall.

LeDoux, J. E. (1996). *The Emotional Brain.* New York: Simon & Schuster.

Lennenberg, E. H. (1974). Language and brain: Developmental aspects. *Neurosciences Research Program Bulletin, 12,* 511–656.

Levins, R. (1966). The strategy of model building in population biology. *American Scientist, 54,* 421–431.

Lichteim, L. (1885). On aphasia. *Brain, 7,* 433–484.

Livingstone, M., & Hubel, D. (1988). Segregation of form, color, movement, and depth: Anatomy, physiology, and Perception. *Science, 240,* 740–749.

Lockhead. (1992). Psychological scaling: Judgments of attributes of objects. *Behavioral and Brain Sciences, 15,* 543–601.

Lumer, E. D., Friston, K. J., & Rees, G. (1998). Neural correlates of perceptual rivalry in the human brain. *Science, 280,* 1930–1933.

Luria, A. R. (1966). *Higher Cortical Functions in Man.* London: Tavistock.

Luria, A. R. (1966). *Human Brain and Psychological Processes.* New York: Harper & Row.

MacCorquodale, K., & Meehl, P. E. (1948). On a distinction between hypothetical constructs and intervening variables. *Psychological Review, 55,* 95–107.

MacLean, P. D. (1949). Psychosomatic disease and the "visceral bran": Recent developments bearing on the Papez theory of emotion. *Psychosomatic Medicine, 11,* 338–353.

Macmillan, M. (2000). *An Odd Kind of Fame: Stories of Phineas Gage.* Cambridge, MA: MIT Press.

Magendie, F. (1822). Expériences sur les fonctions des racines des nerfs rachidiens. *Journal de Physiologie Experimentale et Pathologique, 2,* 276–279.

Mattson, J., & Simon, M. (1996). *The Pioneers of NMR and Magnetic Resonance in Medicine: The Story of MRI.* Jericho, NY: Dean Books.

McCullough, C. (1965). Color adaptation of the edge detectors in the human visual system. *Science, 149,* 1115–1116.

McGinn, C. (1994). Can we solve the mind-body-problem? In R. Warner & T. Szubka (Eds.), *The Mind-Body Problem: A Guide to the Current Debate.* Oxford: Blackwell.

McIntosh, A. R., Rajah, M. N., & Lobaugh, N. J. (1999). Interactions of prefrontal cortex in relation to awareness in sensory learning. *Science, 284,* 1531–1533.

Merians, A. S., Clark, M., Poizner, H., Macauley, B., Rothi, L. J. G., & Heilman, K. M. (1997). Visual-imitative dissociation apraxia. *Neuropsychologia, 35,* 1483–1490.

Mettler, C. C, & Mettler, F. A. (1947). *History of Medicine.* Philadelphia: Blakiston.

Milner, B. (1963). Effects of different brain lesions on card sorting. *Archives of Neurology, 9,* 90–100.

Mishkin, M. (1966). Visual mechanisms beyond the striate cortex. In R. Russell (Ed.), *Frontiers in Physiological Psychology* (pp. 93–119). New York: Academic Press.

Moore, E. F. (1956). *Automata Studies.* Princeton, NJ: Princeton University Press.

Moruzzi, G., & Magoun, H. (1949). Brain stem reticular formation and activation of the EEG. *Electroencephalography and Clinical Neurophysiology, 1,* 455–473.

Muller, J. (1840). *Handbuch der Physiologie des Menschen, vol. 2.* Koblenz: Holscher.

Muller, R.-A., Courchesne, E., & Allen, G. (1998). The cerebellum: So much more. *Science, 282,* 879–880.

Munk, H. (1881). *Über die Funktionen der Grosshirnrinde.* Berlin: Hirschwald.

Nagel, T. (1994). Consciousness and objective reality. In R. Warner & T. Szubka (Eds.), *The Mind-Body Problem: A Guide to the Current Debate.* Oxford: Blackwell.

Neisser, U. (1967). *Cognitive Psychology.* New York: Appleton-Century-Crofts.

Newell, A. (1990). *Unified Theories of Cognition.* Cambridge, MA: Harvard University Press.

Ojemonn, J. G., Ojemonn, G. A., & Lettich, E. (1992). Neuronal activity related faces and matching in human right nondominant temporal cortex. *Brain, 115,* 1–13.

Olds, J., Disterhoft, J. F., Segal, M., Kornblith, C. L., & Hirsch, R. (1972). Learning centers of rat brain mapped by measuring latencies of conditioned unit responses. *Journal of Neurophysiology, 35,* 202–219.

Olds, J., & Milner, P. (1954). Positive reinforcement produced by electrical stimulation of septal area and other regions of rat brain. *Journal of Comparative and Physiological Psychology, 47,* 419–427.

Pachella, R. G. (1974). The interpretation of reaction time in information processing research, In B. H. Kantowitz (Ed.), *Human Information Processing: Tutorials in Performance and Cognition* (pp. 41–82). Hillsdale, NJ: Erlbaum.

Papez, J. (1937). A proposed mechanism of emotion. *Archives of Neurology and Psychiatry, Chicago, 38,* 725–743.

Pardo, J. V., Pardo, P., Janer, K., & Raichle, M. E. (1990). The anterior cingulate cortex mediates processing selection in the Stroop attention conflict paradigm. *Proceedings of the National Academy of Sciences, U.S.A., 87,* 256–259.

Penfield, W. (1958). *The Excitable Cortex in Man: The Fifth Sherrington Lecture.* Liverpool: Liverpool University Press.

Penfield, W., & Jasper, H. (1954). *Epilepsy and the Functional Anatomy of the Human Brain.* Boston: Little, Brown.

Penfield, W., & Rasmussen, T. (1950). *The Cerebral Cortex of Man.* New York: Macmillan.

Penfield, W., & Roberts, L. (1959). *Speech and Brain Mechanisms.* Princeton, NJ: Princeton University Press.

Petersen, S. E., Fox, P. T., Posner, M. I., Mintun, M., & Raichle, M. (1988). Positron emission tomographic studies of the cortical anatomy of single-word processing. *Nature, 331,* 585–589.

Petersen, S. E., Fox, P. T., Posner, M. I., Mintun, M., & Raichle, M. (1989). Positron emission tomographic studies of the processing of single words. *Journal of Cognitive Neuroscience, 1,* 153–170.

Pinker, S. (1997). *How the Mind Works.* New York: Norton.

Plaut, D. C. (1995). Double dissociation with out modularity. *Journal of Clinical and Experimental Neuropsychology, 17,* 291–321.

Plaut, D. C., & Farah, M. J. (1990). Visual object representation: Interpreting neurophysiological data within a computational framework. *Journal of Cognitive Neuroscience, 2,* 320–343.

Ploghaus, A., Tracey, I., Gati, J. S., Clare, S., Menon, R. S., Matthews, P. M., & Rawlins, J. N. P. (1999). Dissociating pain from its anticipation in the human brain. *Science, 284,* 1979–1981.

Poepple, D. (1996). A critical review of phonological processing. *Brain and Language, 55,* 317–371.

Posner, M. I., & DiGirolamo, G. J. (1999). Flexible neural circuitry in word processing. *Behavioral and Brain Sciences, 22,* 299–300.

Posner, M. I., & Petersen, S. E. (1990). The attention system of the human brain. *Annual Review of Neuroscience, 13,* 25–42.

Posner, M. I., & Raichle, M. E. (1994/1997). *Images of Mind.* New York: Scientific American Library.

Pravdich-Neminsky, V. V. (1913). Experiments on the registration of the electrical phenomena of the mammalian brain (Original in German). *Zentralblatt Physiologie, 27,* 951–960.

Pribram, K. H., Nuwer, M., & Baron, R. J. (1974). The holographic hypothesis of memory structure in brain function and perception. In D. H. Krantz (Ed.), *Contemporary Developments in Mathematical Psychology: Vol. 2.* San Francisco: Freeman.

Pulvermüller, F. (1999). Words in the brain's language. *Behavioral and Brain Science, 22,* 253–336.

Purcell, E. M., Torrey, H. C., & Pound, R. V. (1946). Resonance absorption by nuclear magnetic moments in a solid. *Physical Review, 69,* 37–38.

Rabi, I., I,, Zacharias, J. R., Millman, S., & Kusch, P. (1937). A new method for measuring nuclear magnetic moments. *Physical Review, 53,* 318.

Rabi, I. I., Zacharias, J. R., Millman, S., & Kusch, P. (1939). The molecular beam resonance method for measuring nuclear magnetic moment: The magnetic moments of 3Li6, 3Li7, and 9F19. *Physical Review, 55,* 526–535.

Radon, J. (1917). Über die Bestimung von Funktionen durch ihre Integralwerte längs gewisser Mannigfaltigkeiten. *Mathemtische Physiks, Berichte Saechsische Akademie der Wisenschaften, Lepzig, 69,* 262–277.

Rafal, R., & Robertson, L. (1995). The neurology of visual attention. In M. S. Gazzaniga (Ed.), *The Cognitive Neurosciences.* Cambridge MA: MIT Press.

Regan, D. (1989). *Human Brain Electrophysiology: Evoked Potentials and Evoked Magnetic Fields in Science and Medicine.* New York: Elsevier.

Reiman, E. M., Lane, R. D., Van Petten, C. K., & Bandettini, P. A. (2000). Positron emission tomography and functional magnetic resonance imaging. In Berntson, G., Cacioppo, J. T., Tassinary, L. G. (Eds.), *Handbook of Psychophysiology.* Cambridge: Cambridge University Press.

Richman, D. P., Stewart, R. M., Hutchinson, J. W., & Caviness, V. S. J. (1975). Mechanical model of brain convolutional development. *Science, 189,* 18–21.

Robin, N., & Holyoak, K. (1995). Relational complexity and the functions of prefrontal cortex. In M. Gazzaniga (Ed.), *The Cognitive Neurosciences.* Cambridge, MA: MIT Press.

Robinson, D. N., & Uttal, W. R. (1983). *Foundations of Psychobiology.* New York: Macmillan.

Roland, P. E. (1993). *Brain Activation:* Wiley.

Roland, P. E., & Gulyas, B. (1992). Anatomical studies in the human brain participating in discrimination of visual patterns and formation of visual memories. *Biomedical Research, 13,* 11–14.

Roland, P. E., Kawashima, R., Gulyas, B., & O'Sullivan, B. (1995). Positron emission tomography: Methodological constraints, strategies, and examples from learning and memory. In M. S. Gazzaniga (Ed.), *The Cognitive Neurosciences* (pp. 781–788). Cambridge, MA: MIT Press.

Romero-Sierra, C. (1986). *Neuroanatomy: A Conceptual Approach.* New York: Churchill: Livingstone.

Rushworth, M. F. S., Nixon, P. D., Renowden, S., Wade, D. T., & Passingham, R. E. (1997). The left parietal cortex and motor attention. *Neuropsychologia, 35,* 1261–1273.

Salmelin, R., Helenius, P., & Kuukka, K. (1999). Only time can tell: words in context. *Behavioral and Brain Sciences, 22,* 300.

Samelson, F. (1980). J. B. Watson's Little Albert, Cyril Burt's twins, and the need for a critical science. *American Psychologist, 35,* 619–625.

Savoy, R. L., & Gabrielli, J. D. E. (1991). Normal McCullough effect in Alzheimer's disease and global amnesia. *Perception and Psychophysics, 49,* 448–455.

Schacter, D. L., & Wagner, A. D. (1999). Remembrance of things past. *Science, 285,* 1503–1504.

Schmahmann, J. D., (1997). *The Cerebellum and Cognition.* San Diego, CA: Academic Press.

Sciamanna, E. (1882). Gli avversari delle localizzazioni cerebrali. *Psi chiatria, Scienze Penali ed Antropologia Criminale, 3,* 209–215.

Scoville, W. B., & Milner, B. (1957). Loss of recent memory after bilateral hippocampal regions. *Journal of Neurology, Neurosurgery, and Psychiatry, 20,* 11–21.

Sekuler, R. (1994). Perception and its interactive substrate: Psychophysical linking hypotheses and psychophysical methods. *Behavioral and Brain Science, 17,* 79.

Shallice, T. (1988). *From Neuropsychology to Mental Structure.* Cambridge: Cambridge University Press.

Simon, H. A. (1969). *The Science of the Artificial.* Cambridge, MA: MIT Press.

Skinner, B. F. (1963). Behaviorism at fifty. *Science, 140,* 951–958.

Skrandies, W. (1999). Early effects of semantic meaning on electrical brain activity. *Brain and Behavioral Sciences, 22,* 301–302.

Smith, A. T., Greenlee, M. W., Singh, K. D., Kraemer, F. M., & Hennig, J. (1998). The processing of first- and second-order motion in human visual cortex assessed by functional magnetic resonance imaging (fMRI). *Journal of Neuroscience, 18,* 3816–3830.

Smith, E. E., Jonides, J., Marshuetz, C., & Koeppe, R. A. (1998). Components of verbal working memory: Evidence from neuroimaging. *Proceedings of the National Academy of Sciences, U.S.A., 95,* 876–882.

Smith, E. E., & Jonides, J. (1999). Storage and executive processes in the frontal lobes. *Science, 283,* 1657–1661.

Spearman, C. (1904). "General Intelligence," objectively determined and measured. *American Journal of Psychology, 15,* 201–293.

Spearman, C. (1923). *The Nature of "Intelligence" and the Principles of Cognition.* London: Macmillan.

Sperry, R. W. (1968). Mental unity following surgical disconnection of the cerebral hemispheres. *The Harvey Lecture Series: Vol. 62* (pp. 293–323). New York: Academic Press.

Spitzer, M., Belleman, M. E., Kammer, T., Guckel, F., Kischka, U., Maier, S., Schwartz, A., & Brix, G. (1996). Functional MR imaging of semantic information processing and learning-related effects using psychometrically controlled stimulation paradigms. *Cognitive Brain Research, 4*, 149–161.

Spurzheim, G. (1832). *Outlines of Phrenology.* Boston: Marsh, Capen, & Lyon.

Squire, L. R. (1992). Memory and the hippocampus: A synthesis from findings with rats, monkeys, and humans. *Psychological Review, 99*, 195–231.

Stein, B. E., & Meredith, M. A. (1993). *The Merging of the Senses.* Cambridge, MA: MIT Press.

Sternberg, S. (1969a). The discovery of processing stages: extension of Donder's method. *Acta Psychologica, 30*, 276–315.

Sternberg, S. (1969b). Memory scanning: Mental processes revealed by reaction time experiments. *American Scientist, 57*, 451–457.

Sternberg, R. J. (1977). *Intelligence, Information Processing, and Analogical Reasoning.* Hillsdale, NJ: Erlbaum.

Sternberg, R. J. (1988). Intelligence. In R. J. Sternberg & E. E. Smith (Eds.), *The Psychology of Human Thought* (pp. 267–308). New York: Cambridge University Press.

Stone, G. O., Vanhoy, M., & Van Orden, G. C. (1997). Perception is a two way street: Feed forward and feed backward phonology in visual word recognition. *Journal of Memory and Language, 36*, 337–359.

Stoner, G. R., & Albright, T. D (1993). Image segmentation cues in motion processing: Implications for modularity. *Journal of Cognitive Neuroscience, 5*, 129–149.

Tanner, W. P. Jr., & Swets, J. A. (1954). A decision making theory of visual detection. *Psychological Review, 61*, 401–409.

Teder-Sälejärvi, W. A., & Hillyard, S. A. (1998). The gradient of spatial auditory attention in free field: An event-related potential study. *Perception and Psychophysics, 60*, 1228–1243.

Thom, R. (1975). *Structural Stability and Morphogenesis.* Reading, MA: Benjamin.

Thompson, R. E. (1990). Neural mechanisms of classical conditioning in mammals. *Philosophical Transactions of the Royal Society of London, 329*, 161–170.

Thorndike. (1923). *Educational Psychology. Vol. 3: Mental Work and Fatigue and Individual Differences and Their Causes.* New York: Teachers College, Columbia University.

Thurstone, L. L. (1931). Multiple factor analysis. *Psychological Review, 38*, 406–427.

Thurstone, L. L. (1947). *Multiple Factor Analysis: A Development and Expansion of the Vectors of the Mind.* Chicago: University of Chicago Press.

Tononi, G., & Edelman, G. M. (1998). Consciousness and complexity. *Science, 282,* 1846–1851.

Torgerson, W. S. (1958). *Theory and Methods of Scaling.* New York: Wiley.

Tranel, D., Damasio, H., & Damasio, A. R. (1997). A neural basis for the retrieval of conceptual knowledge. *Neuropsychologia, 35,* 1319–1327.

Trannel, D., & Damasio, A. (1999). The neurobiology of knowledge retrieval. *Behavioral and Brain Sciences, 22,* 303.

Trull, D. (1998). *The God spot.* [On-line]. Available Internet: http://www.sonic.net/~ric/otters/godspot2.htm

Tuller, B., Case, P., Ding, M., & Kelso, J. A. S. (1994). The nonlinear dynamics of speech categorization. *Journal of Experimental Psychology: Human Perception and Performance, 20,* 3–16.

Tulving, E. (1979). Memory research: What kind of progress? In L. G. Nilsson (Ed.), *Perspectives in Memory Research.* Hillsdale, NJ: Erlbaum.

Tunturi, A. R. (1952). A difference in the representation of auditory signals for the left and right ears in the isofrequency contours of right ectosylvian auditory cortex of the dog. *Journal of Comparative and Physiological Psychology, 168,* 712–727.

Uttal, W. R. (1967). Evoked brain potentials: Signs or codes? *Perspectives in Medicine and Biology, 10,* 627–639.

Uttal, W. R. (1978). *The Psychobiology of Mind.* Hillsdale, NJ: Erlbaum.

Uttal, W. R. (1988). *On Seeing Forms.* Hillsdale, NJ: Erlbaum.

Uttal, W. R. (1998). *Toward a New Behaviorism: The Case against Perceptual Reductionism.* Mahwah, NJ: Erlbaum.

Uttal, W. R. (2000a). *The War between Mentalism and Behaviorism: On the Accessibility of Mental Processes.* Mahwah, NJ: Erlbaum.

Uttal, W. R. (2000b). Summary: Let's pay attention to attention. *The Journal of General Psychology, 127,* 100–111.

Uttal, W. R., & Cook, L. (1964). Systematics of the evoked somatosensory cortical potential: A psychophysical-electrophysiological comparison. *Annals of the New York Academy of Sciences, 112,* 60–80.

Valenstein, E. S. (1996). *Great and Desperate Cures: The Rise and Decline of Psychosurgery and Other Radical Treatments for Mental Illness.* New York: Basic Books.

Valenstein, E. S. (1998). *Blaming the Brain.* New York: Free Press.

Valenstein, E. S., Ed. (1980). *The Psychosurgery Debate: Scientific, Legal, and Ethical Perspectives.* San Francisco: Freeman.

Van Essen, D. C. (1985). Functional organization of the primate visual cortex. *Cerebral Cortex, 3,* 259–329.

Van Essen, D. C., Anderson, C. H., & Felleman, D. J. (1992). Information processing in the primate visual system: An integrated systems perspective. *Science,* 225, 419–423.

Van Orden, G. C., Jansen op de Haar, M. A., & Bosman, A. M. T. (1997). Complex dynamic systems also predict dissociations, but they do not reduce to autonomous components. *Cognitive Neuropsychology, 14,* 131–165.

Van Orden, G. C., & Paap, K. R. (1997). Functional neuroimages fail to discover pieces of mind in the parts of the brain. *Philosophy of Science Proceedings, 64,* S85–S94.

Van Orden, G. C., Pennington, B. F., & Stone, G. O. (in press). What do double dissociations prove? Modularity yields a degenerating research program. *Cognitive Science.*

Vanzetta, I., & Grinvald, A. (1999). Increase cortical oxidative metabolism due to sensory stimulation: Implications for functional brain imaging. *Science, 286,* 1555–1558.

Vishton, P. M. (1998). Double dissociation can not indicate the presence of anatomical modules in human brains (or kitchen appliances): Reasons to distinguish information and anatomical complexity. Personal communication.

Von der Heydt, R., & Peterhans, E. (1989). Mechanisms of contour perception in the monkey visual cortex. I. Lines of pattern discontinuity. *The Journal of Neuroscience, 9,* 1731–1748.

Warner, R., & Szubka, T. (Eds.). (1994). *The Mind-Body Problem: A Guide to the Current Debate.* Oxford: Blackwell.

Watanabe, T. (1995). Orientation and color processing for partially occluded objects. *Vision Research, 35,* 647–656.

Watson, J. B. (1913). Psychology as the behaviorist views it. *Psychological Review, 20,* 158–177.

Wauschkuhn, B., Verleger, R., Wascher, E., Klosterman, W., Burk, M., Heide, W., & Kampf, D. (1998). Lateralized human cortical activity for shifting visuospatial attention and initiating saccades. *Journal of Neurophysiology, 80,* 2900–2910.

Welker, W. I. (1976). Brain evolution in mammals: A review of concepts, problems, and methods. In R. B. Masterson, M. E. Bitterman, B. Campbell, & N. Hotton (Eds.), *Evolution of Brain and Behavior in Vertebrates.* Potomac, MD: Erlbaum.

Wernicke, C. (1874). *Der aphasische Symptomenkomplex.* Brieslau, Germany: Cohn and Weigert.

Wimsatt, W. C. (1974). Complexity and organization. In K. F. Schaffner & R. S. Cohen (Eds.), *PSA 1972: Proceedings of the 1972 Biennial Meeting Philosophy of Science Association* (Vol. 20 of the Boston Studies in the Philosophy of Science). Boston: Dordrecht-Holland.

Wise, R., Chollet, F., Hadar, U., Friston, K., Hoffner, E., & Frackowiak, R. (1991). Distribution of cortical neural networks involved in word comprehension and word retrieval. *Brain, 114,* 1803–1817.

Wood, C. C. (1978). Variations on a theme by Lashley: Lesion experiments on the neural model of Anderson, Silverstein, Ritz and Jones. *Psychological Review, 85,* 582–591.

Woolsey, C. N. (1952). Pattern of localization in sensory and motor areas of the cerebral cortex. *The Biology of Mental Health and Disease.* New York: Hoeber.

Woolsey, C. N. (1961). Organization of the cortical auditory system. In W. A. Rosenblith (Ed.), *Sensory Communication.* Cambridge MA: MIT Press.

Wurtz, R. H., Goldberg, M. E., & Robinson, D. L. (1980). Behavioral modification of visual responses in the monkey: Stimulus selection for attention and movement. *Progress in Psychobiology and Physiological Psychology, 9,* 43–83.

Yuasa, T., Prichard, J. W., & Ogawa, S. (1998). *Current Progress in Functional Brain Mapping: Science and Applications.* Niigata, Japan, and London: Nishimura and Smith Gordon.

Zheng, W., & Knudsen, E. I. (1999). Functional selection of adaptive auditory space map by $GABA_A$-mediated inhibition. *Science, 284,* 962–965.

Ziegler, J. C., & Jacobs, A. M. (1995). Phonological information provides early sources of constraint in the processing of letter strings. *Journal of Memory and Language, 34,* 567–593.

Index